Author
Wing Shing Ma

Translator
Peter Vlach

Editor
Duncan Cameron
Jeffrey Macey

Production Artists
Li-Cheng Yu
Hung-Ya Lin

US Cover Design
Yuki Chung

Lettering Fonts
Comicraft
www.comicbookfonts.com

President
Robin Kuo

www.comicsworld.com

English translation by
ComicsOne Corporation 2002

Publisher
ComicsOne Corp.
48531 Warm Springs Blvd., Suite 408
Fremont, CA 94539
www.ComicsOne.com

First Edition: March 2002
ISBN 1-58899-143-1

The "chess form" head figure is mark of and used under
license from Magnum Consultants Limited.

S0-CFO-833

Preface to Storm Riders
About the Author

Wing Shing Ma, born in Hong Kong in 1961, showed a deep love for painting from a very young age. In 19 at the age of 14 he read in a newspaper about positions available as an apprentice in comic book art. Determined, he in his submission. This step marked his official entrance into the Manga profession.

After entering the comics world, he spent his time moving around between different Manga companies, suc Ru Xi Bao, Jin Manga (Gold Manga) and Xin Lang Chao. In the beginning, Wing Shing Ma worked only as an assis tant, but before long he had published some of his own work. His first creation was formally published in 1976 unde title, *Daydream* (Bai Ri Meng). However, it wasn't until the year of 1982, when Ma formally joined the Jade Group Publishing Company Ltd., that he began working on the famous Manga novel, *Chinese Hero*.

By the middle of 1983, he had already leaped into the highest levels of the Manga market. Apart from his m ket success, Wing Shing Ma had established a new and distinctive Manga style. This realistic style, painted with exq ite brush strokes and detail, allowed for a deeply expressive form of Manga. From that day forward, production of Manga comics would forever be changed due to the impact of Ma's original approach. In the beginning of 1989, Ma Jade Publishing, and in July of the same year established Jonesky Limited, which began publishing *Storm Riders, Black Panther,* and *Heaven Sword and the Dragon Saber,* a Manga trilogy, as well as a fourth book, *Punishment from the Heavens.* By August 2000, Ma had released what to this day still stands as Hong Kong's most important and cutting-edge Manga comic. At present, *Storm Riders* has already been in publica- tion for more than ten years. From the beginning, and through- out the entirety of those ten years, it has remained Hong Kong's foremost classic Manga novel. Apart from its success in Hong Kong, it is also a book that is in great demand throughout many countries of the world, such as Taiwan, Malaysia, Singapore, Korea, Thailand, Mainland China, America and Canada.

Besides the Storm Riders Manga, *Storm Riders* has also given birth to a wide array of peripheral products that bear likenesses from the Storm Riders Manga, such as a li of letter openers based on Storm Riders' weapons, T-shirts, wrist watches, action figures, pens, paper fans, etc. Also, 1998 a *Storm Riders* video game, as well as the *Storm Riders* movie was released. The *Storm Riders* movie achieved great box office success in Hong Kong, with box office sales exceeding 40 million Hong Kong dollars. Also in the works are a *Storm Riders* television series as well as a *Storm Riders* Net-based video game that will push the bounda of the genre.

Wing Shing Ma has not been restricted to creating Mangas. He has also published many other books and per odicals, such as Manga novels, hardcover Manga novels and collections of individual artwork, as well as Chinese wa color paintings. Also, in 1993 he began to import Japanese Mangas for translation into Chinese. His publication of a large number of high quality Japanese Mangas gave Hong Kong Manga readers the opportunity to come into contact with many different types of Manga genres, thus furthering diversification in the Manga market.

Apart from Hong Kong Manga, he has been invited many times to attend Manga exhibitions and conference Canada, Taiwan, Singapore and Macau, where he always receives an enthusiastic reception. Wing Shing Ma's succes has shown the Hong Kong Manga world that a local product can most certainly reach the foreign marketplace and indeed achieve unprecedented success.

STORM RIDERS 風雲

Relationship Chart

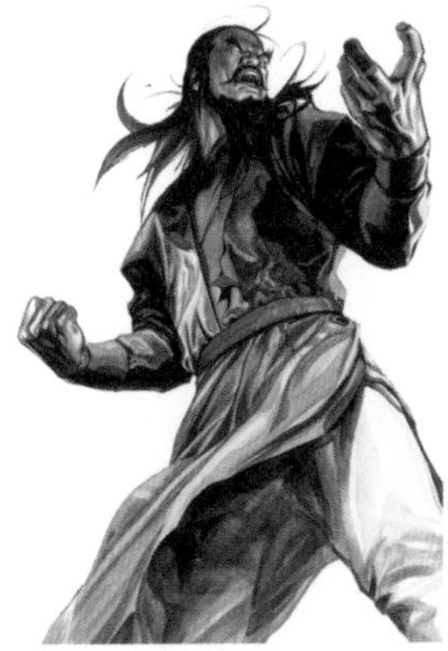

Conquer: Exceptionally powerful martial artist with plans of controlling the World Fighting Association. He takes on Wind and Cloud as his disciples in order to fulfill his destiny.
Technique: Chi of Triplication Returns to One , Triplication Fingers

Kong-Chi

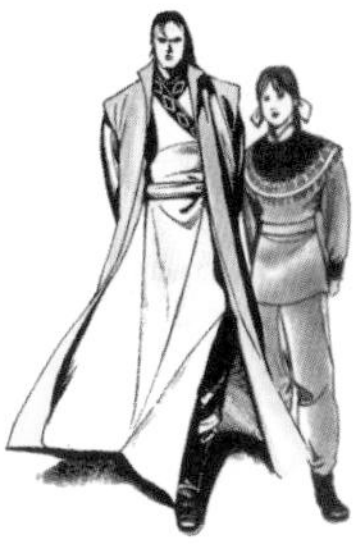

Kong-Chi: Adopted daughter of Conquer and wife of Frost, though her heart lies elsewhere.

Frost: Long-time disciple of Conquer. Married to Conquer's adopted daughter Kong-Chi. Leader of the Frost Corps: an elite fighting unit which is a part of the World Fighting Association. His Mission to find Mud Buddha.
Technique: Sky Frost Fist

Adopted Daughter of Conquer

Frost

Disciple of Conquer

Conquer

Disciple of Conquer

Mud Buddha: Prophet who is sought by many to predict their future. Gravely ill, his gift of prophecy brings him closer to death each time he uses it. Flaming Monkey holds the cure to his condition.

Disciple of Conquer

Wind: Disciple of Conquer and leader of the Wind Corps: an elite fighting unit which is part of the World Fighting Association. Son of Master Nie. His mission to find Mud Buddha.
Techniques: Ice Heart Knack, Deity of Wind Kick
Weapon: Inherits the Snowy Saber

Cloud: Son of Master Ho and disciple of Conquer. Leader of the Cloud Corps: an elite fighting unit which is part of the World Fighting Association.
Technique: Repelling Palm
Weapon: Ultimate Sword

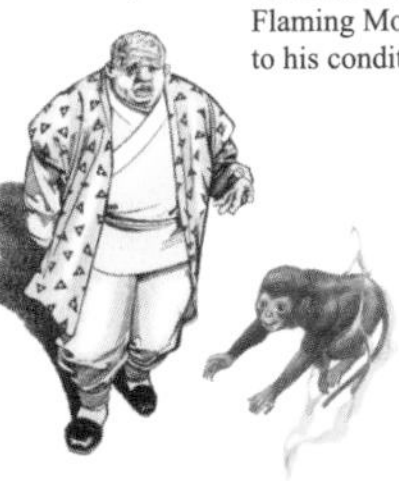

Flaming Monkey: He holds the cure to Mud Buddha's condition. The forces that seek Mud Buddha's wisdom battle to control Flaming Monkey.

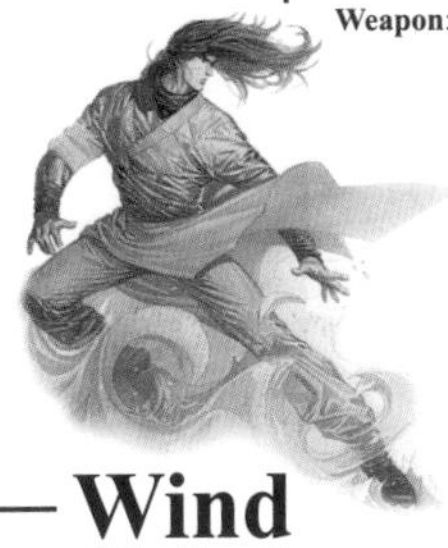

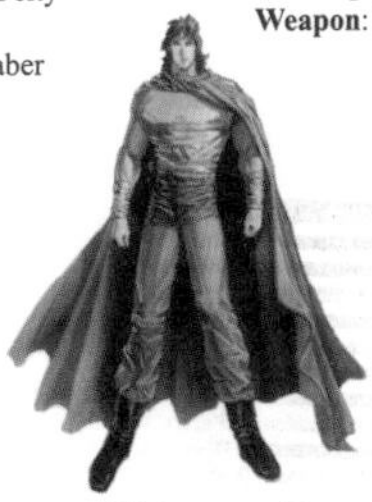

Mud Buddha & Flaming Monkey

Wind
(Nie-Fong)

Cloud
(Bu-Jing-Yun)

Good Friends

Servant of Cloud

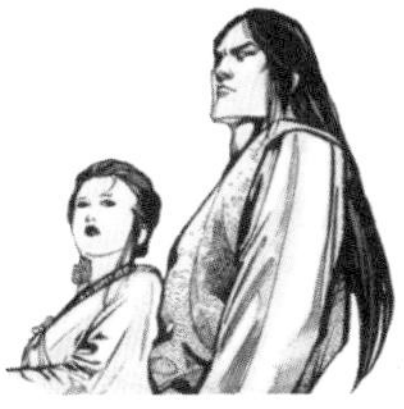

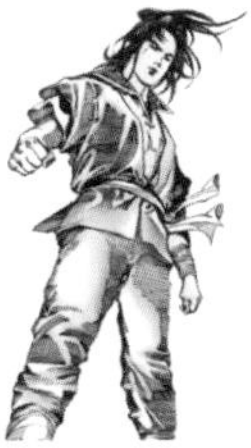

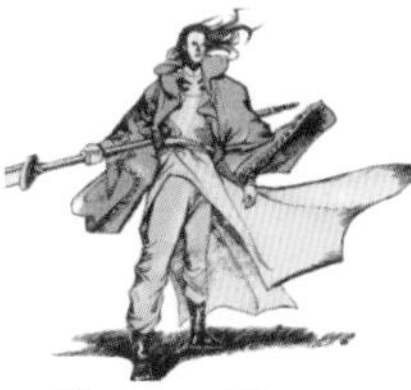

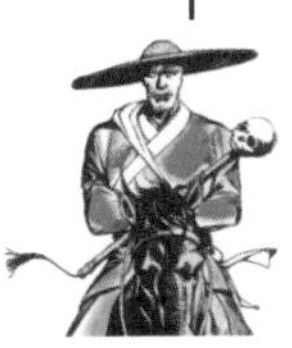

Phoenix & Dragon

Phoenix: Wife of Dragon and Servant of Nameless. Childless, she and her husband seek an answer from Mud Buddha.
Technique: Phoenix from the Heavens
Weapon: Phoenix Arrow

Dragon: Husband of Phoenix and member of the Five Sons of Elation Sect. Childless, he and his wife seek an answer from Mud Buddha.
Technique: Revealing the Dragon
Weapon: Dragon Blade

Duan-Lang

Duan-Lang: Son of Master Duan
Weapon: Inherits the Flame Kylin Sword

Guan-Seven

Guan Seven: Master of Lien Stronghold. He battles Cloud, who believes a traitor to Conquer is hiding in the Stronghold.
Technique: Chopping Knife
Weapon: Horse Knife

Tian

Tian: Cloud's servant. He was defeated by Cloud many years ago and must live as his servant. He is a loyal servant, but deep inside he dreams of defeating Cloud and regaining his honor.
Technique: Legion of Skulls
Weapon: Skull Shaft

Chapter 5: As Wind And Cloud Emerge

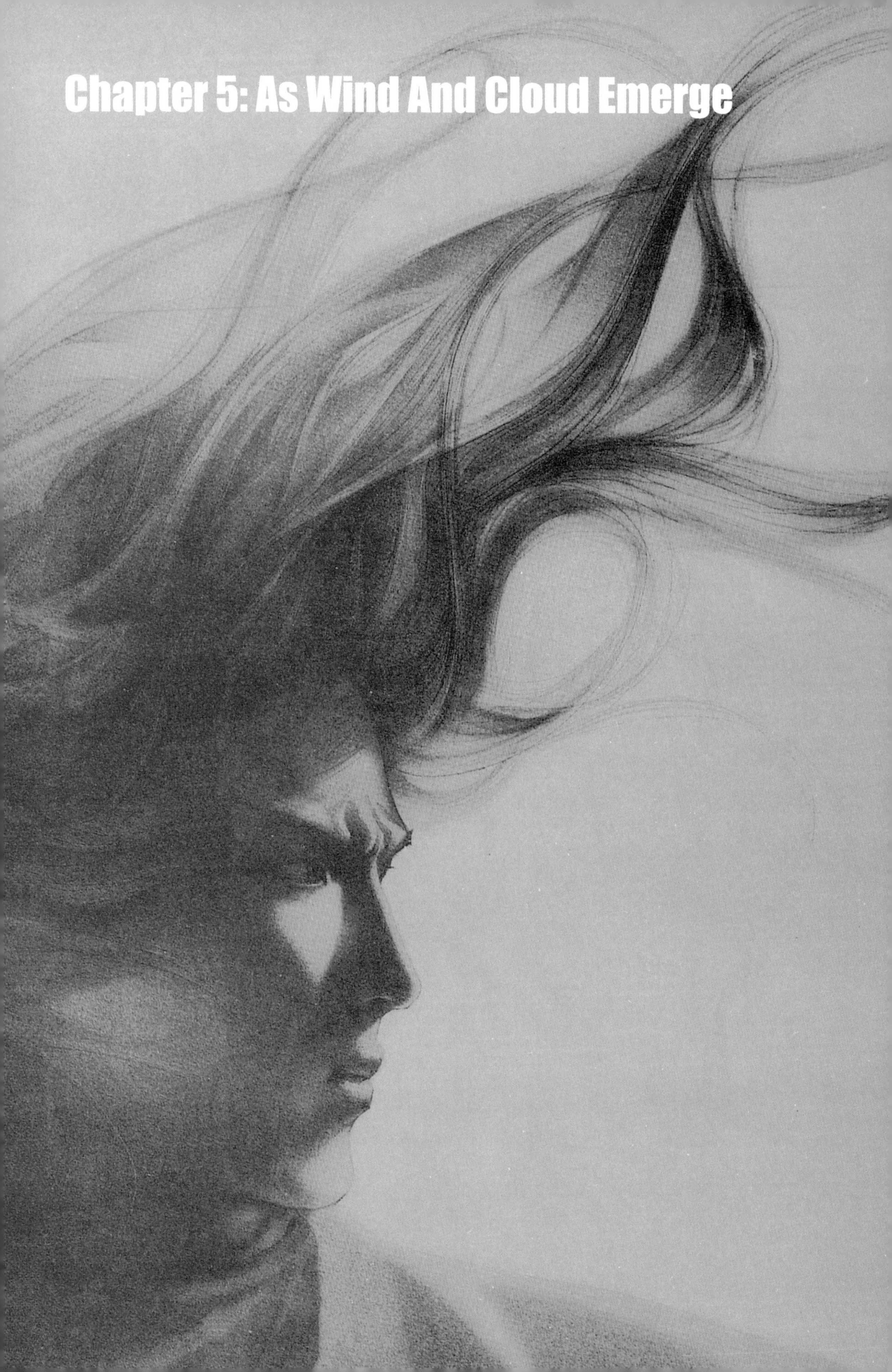

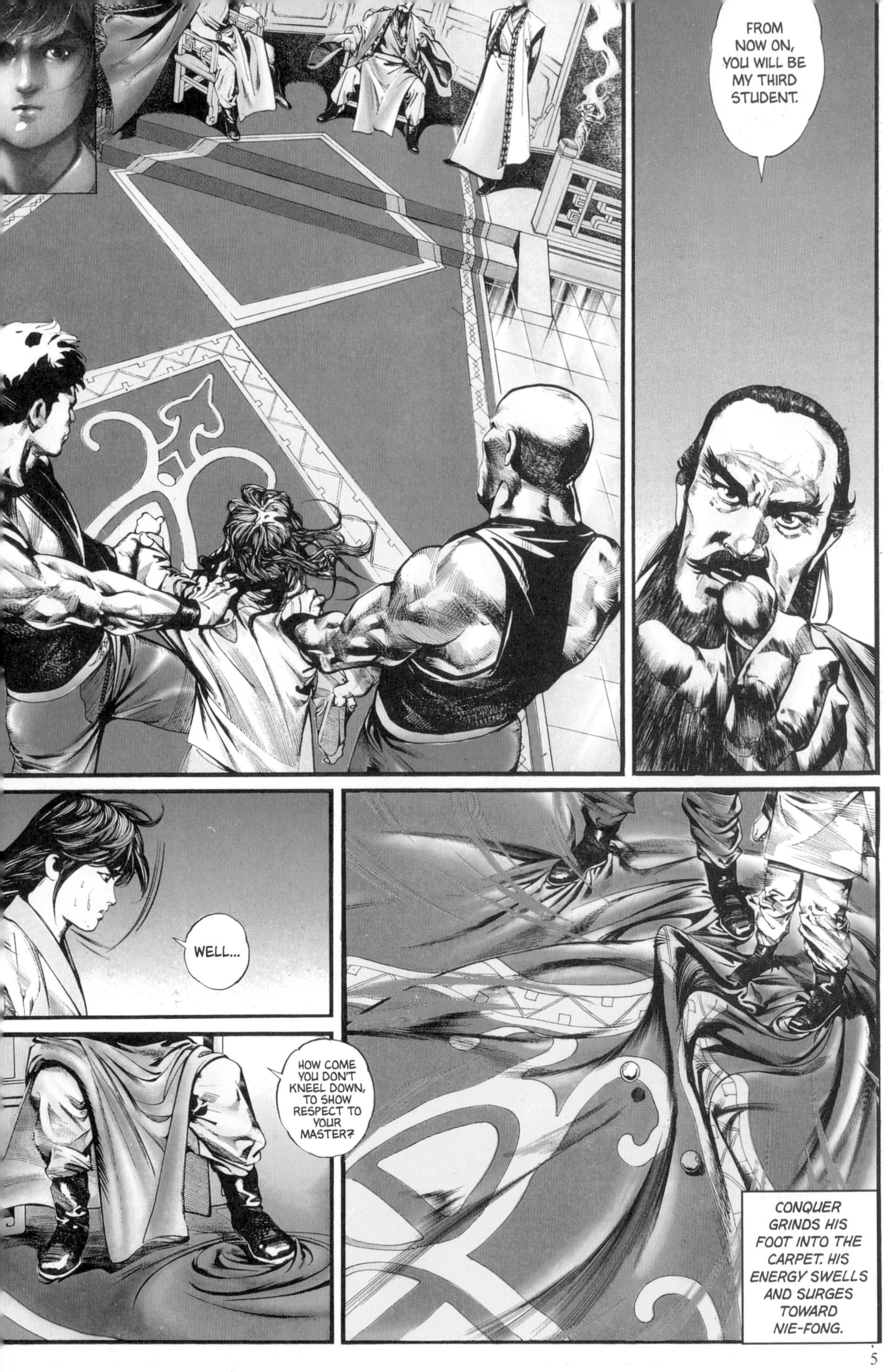
FROM NOW ON, YOU WILL BE MY THIRD STUDENT.
WELL...
HOW COME YOU DON'T KNEEL DOWN, TO SHOW RESPECT TO YOUR MASTER?
CONQUER GRINDS HIS FOOT INTO THE CARPET. HIS ENERGY SWELLS AND SURGES TOWARD NIE-FONG.

THWACK

WITH BROKEN KNEES, NIE-FONG CAN NOT RESIST THE POWER. HELPLESS, HE FALLS TO THE GROUND.

NOBODY CAN DENY THE MASTER'S WISHES.

IN GREAT PAIN, NIE-FONG STILL REMAINS SILENT.

WHAT A TOUGH KID. CONQUER SHOULD BE GLAD TO HAVE A STUDENT LIKE HIM.

SON, TAKE YOUR THIRD BROTHER TO STORM RIDERS PAVILION.

YES, SIR.

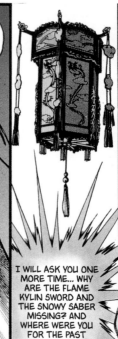

SPEAK.

I WILL ASK YOU ONE MORE TIME... WHY ARE THE FLAME KYLIN SWORD AND THE SNOWY SABER MISSING? AND WHERE WERE YOU FOR THE PAST FEW DAYS?

MASTER... I CANNOT REMEMBER ANYTHING. PLEASE DON'T ASK ME AGAIN!

BU-JING-YUN LOOKS DISTRAUGHT. WHAT HAPPENED TO HIM WHILE HE WAS ON LE-SHAN MOUNTAIN?

MASTE[R] DON'T A[SK] ME AGA[IN] I CAN[T] REMEM[BER] ANYTHI[NG] I DON[T] WANT [TO] REMEM[BER] IT ANYM[ORE]

6

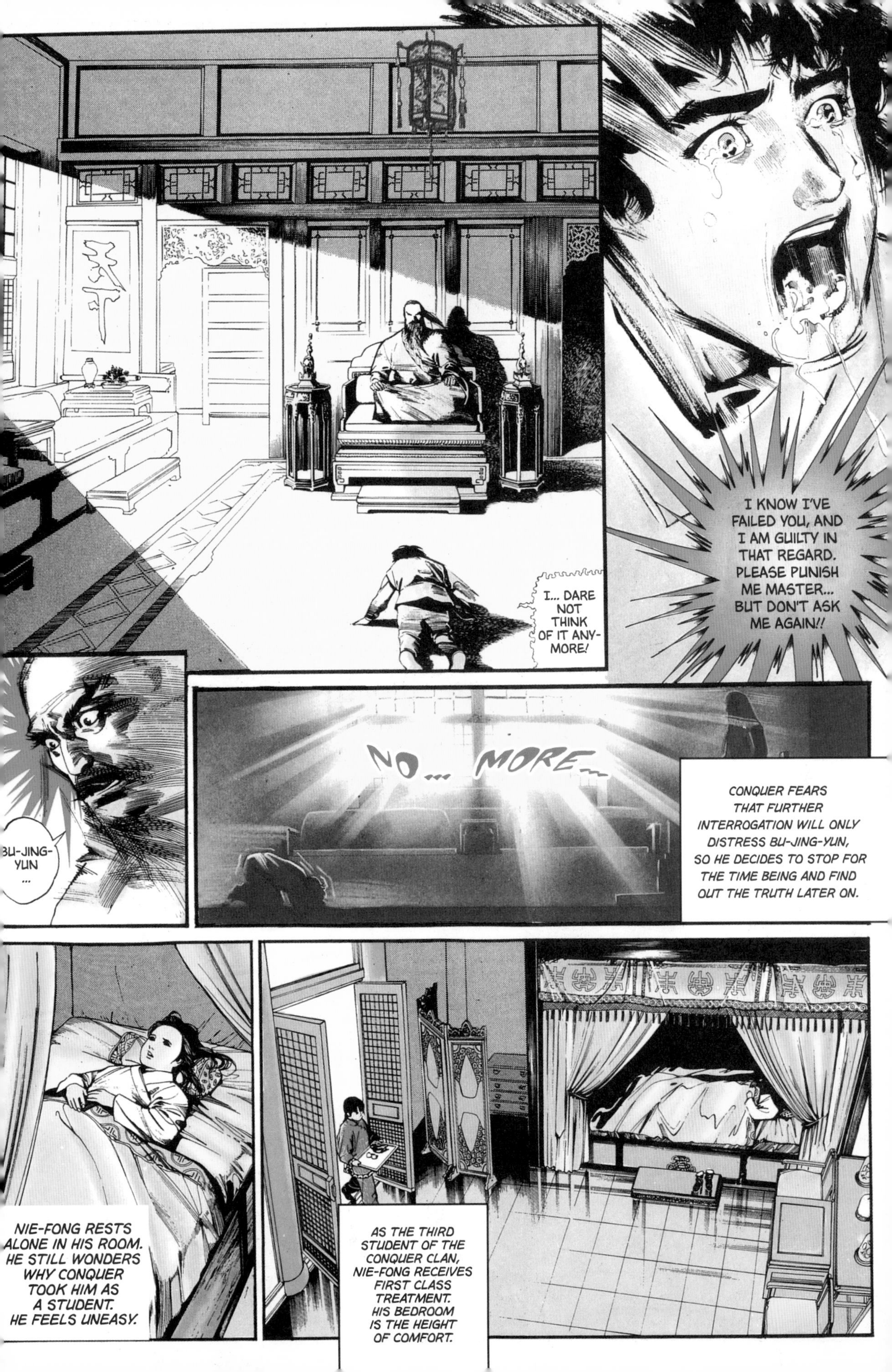
I... DARE NOT THINK OF IT ANY-MORE!
I KNOW I'VE FAILED YOU, AND I AM GUILTY IN THAT REGARD. PLEASE PUNISH ME MASTER... BUT DON'T ASK ME AGAIN!!
BU-JING-YUN ...
NO... MORE...
CONQUER FEARS THAT FURTHER INTERROGATION WILL ONLY DISTRESS BU-JING-YUN, SO HE DECIDES TO STOP FOR THE TIME BEING AND FIND OUT THE TRUTH LATER ON.
NIE-FONG RESTS ALONE IN HIS ROOM. HE STILL WONDERS WHY CONQUER TOOK HIM AS A STUDENT. HE FEELS UNEASY.
AS THE THIRD STUDENT OF THE CONQUER CLAN, NIE-FONG RECEIVES FIRST CLASS TREATMENT. HIS BEDROOM IS THE HEIGHT OF COMFORT.

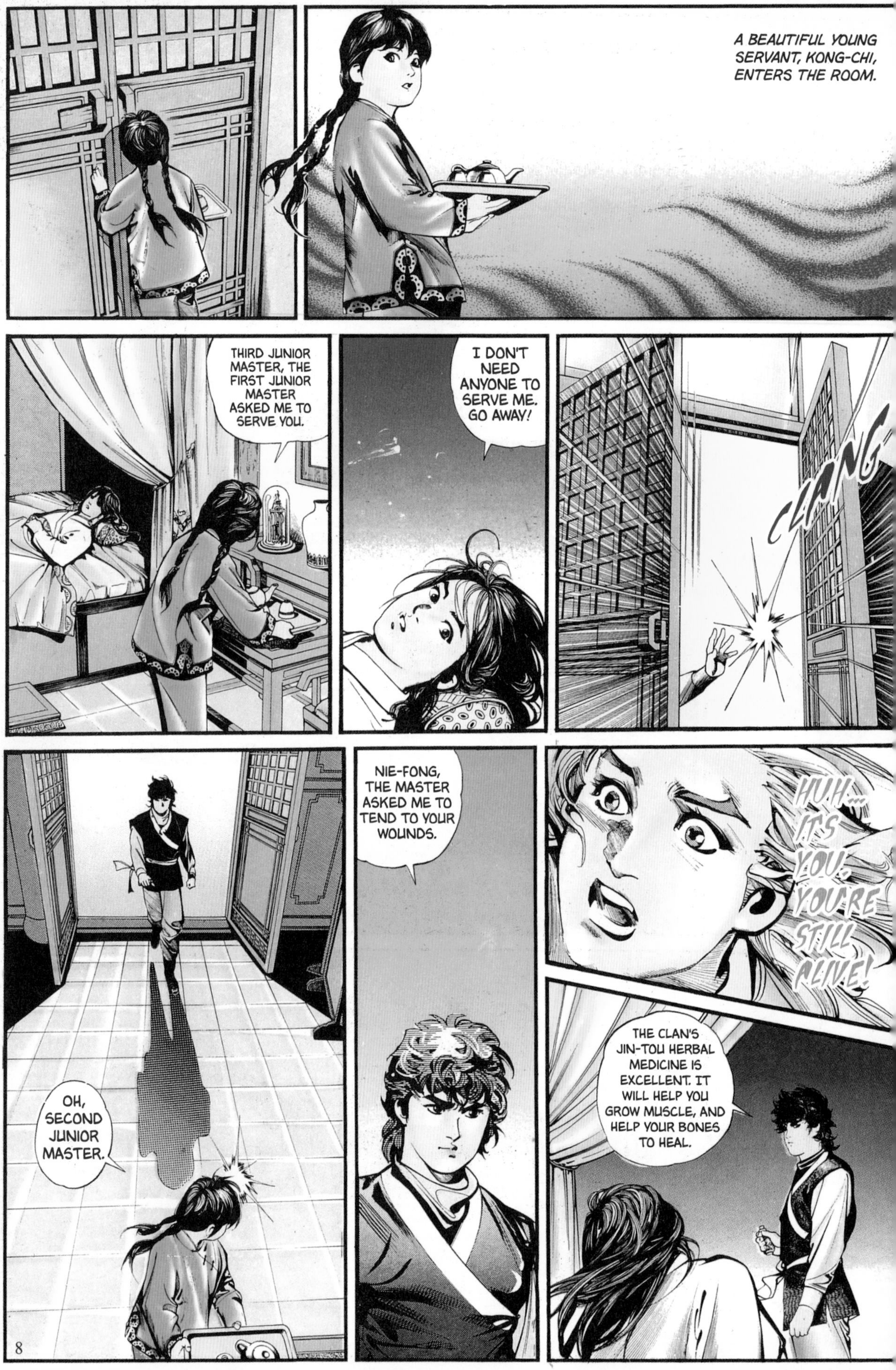
A BEAUTIFUL YOUNG SERVANT, KONG-CHI, ENTERS THE ROOM.
THIRD JUNIOR MASTER, THE FIRST JUNIOR MASTER ASKED ME TO SERVE YOU.
I DON'T NEED ANYONE TO SERVE ME. GO AWAY!
CLANG
OH, SECOND JUNIOR MASTER.
NIE-FONG, THE MASTER ASKED ME TO TEND TO YOUR WOUNDS.
HUH... IT'S YOU. YOU'RE STILL ALIVE!
THE CLAN'S JIN-TOU HERBAL MEDICINE IS EXCELLENT. IT WILL HELP YOU GROW MUSCLE, AND HELP YOUR BONES TO HEAL.

IT'S GOOD TO KNOW YOU'RE ALL RIGHT. WHAT HAPPENED TO MY DAD AND MASTER DUAN?

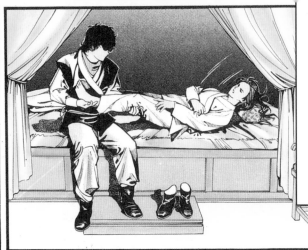

BU-JING-YUN HAS BEEN HEADSTRONG SINCE CHILDHOOD, AND DOESN'T MINGLE WITH OTHERS. HE REMAINS QUIET WHILE HE TENDS TO WIND'S WOUNDS AND IGNORES HIS QUESTIONS.

I REALLY WANT TO KNOW WHAT HAPPENED IN LIN-YIN CAVE. TELL ME, PLEASE!

QUIET!

AGGH

THIRD JUNIOR MASTER, HE'S RESETTING YOUR BONES. PLEASE, TRY TO COPE WITH THE PAIN.

9

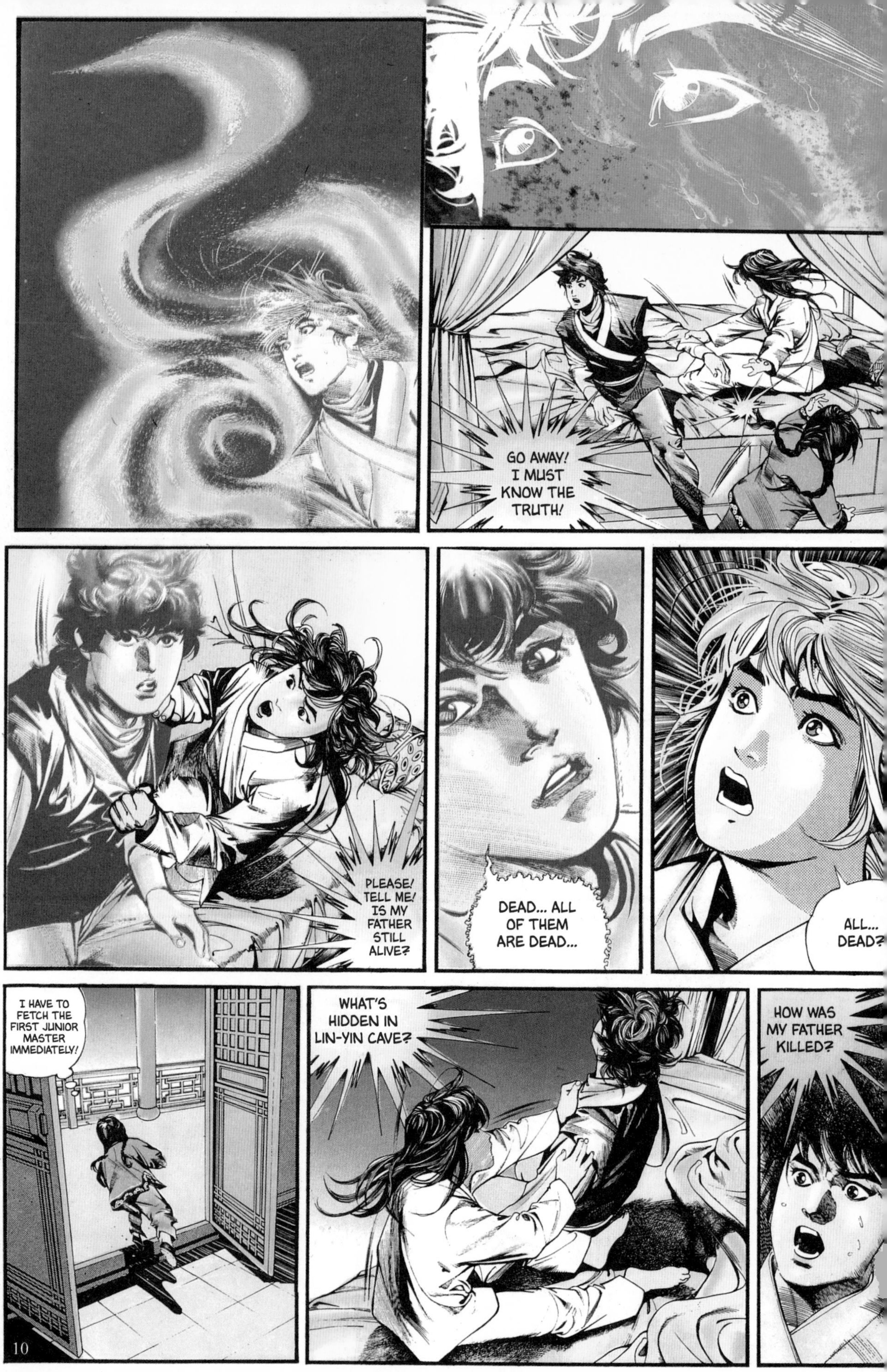
GO AWAY! I MUST KNOW THE TRUTH!
PLEASE! TELL ME! IS MY FATHER STILL ALIVE?
DEAD... ALL OF THEM ARE DEAD...
ALL... DEAD?
I HAVE TO FETCH THE FIRST JUNIOR MASTER IMMEDIATELY!
WHAT'S HIDDEN IN LIN-YIN CAVE?
HOW WAS MY FATHER KILLED?

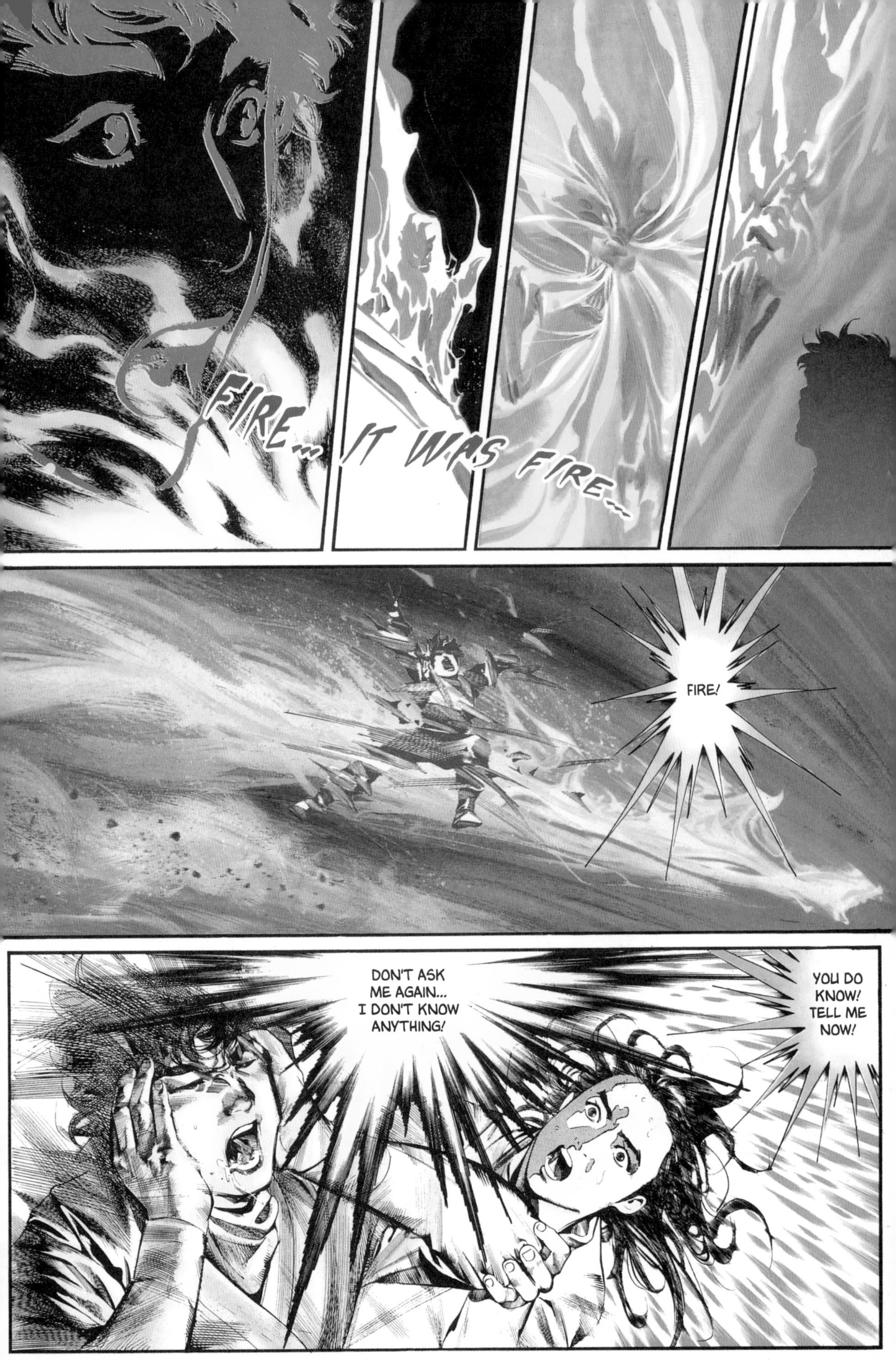
FIRE... IT WAS FIRE...
FIRE!
DON'T ASK ME AGAIN... I DON'T KNOW ANYTHING!
YOU DO KNOW! TELL ME NOW!

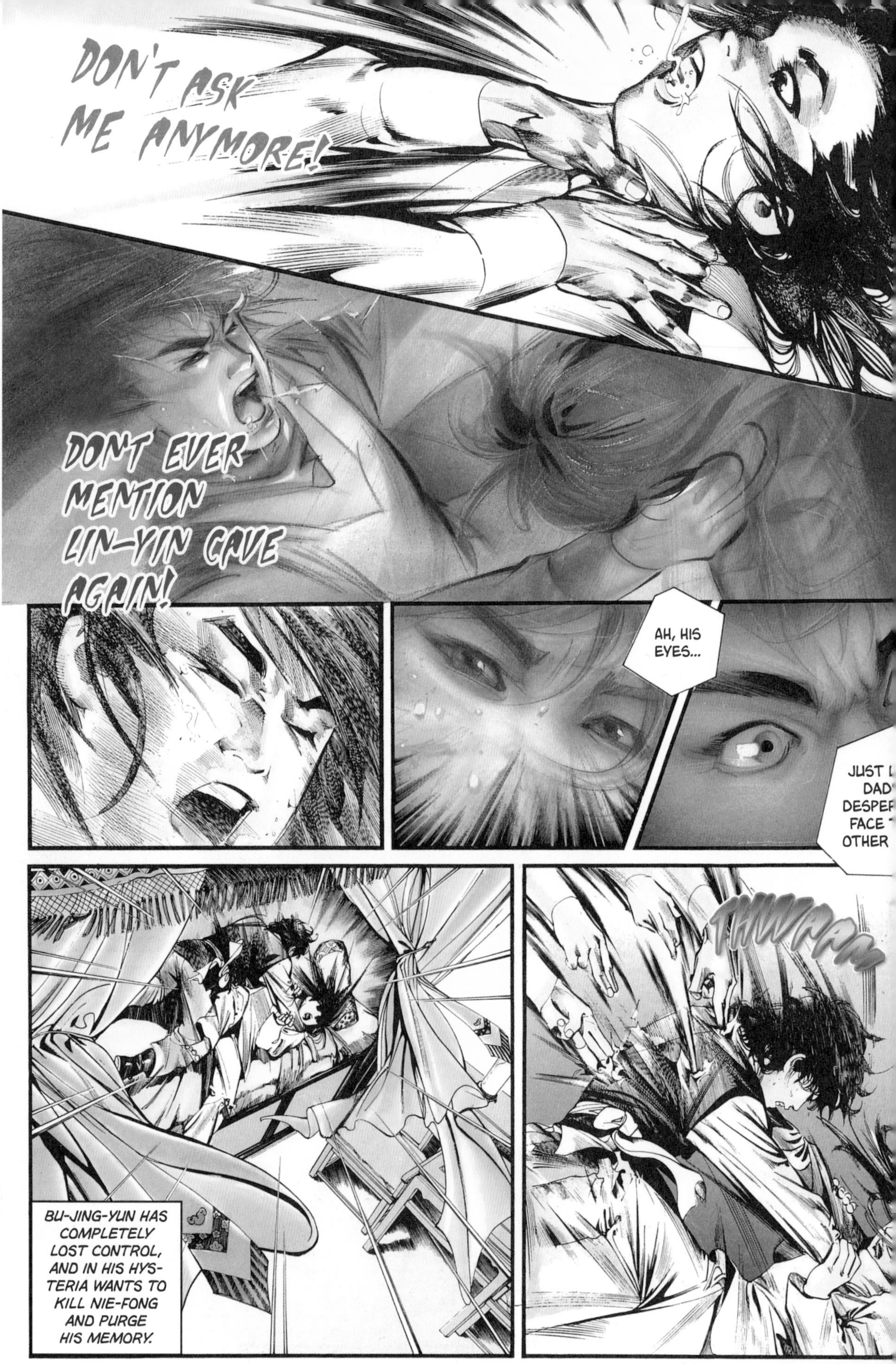
DON'T ASK ME ANYMORE!
DON'T EVER MENTION LIN-YIN CAVE AGAIN!
AH, HIS EYES...
BU-JING-YUN HAS COMPLETELY LOST CONTROL, AND IN HIS HYSTERIA WANTS TO KILL NIE-FONG AND PURGE HIS MEMORY.

BU-JING-YUN HAS BEEN HIT ON A NERVE PRESSURE POINT. NIE-FONG IS SAFE.

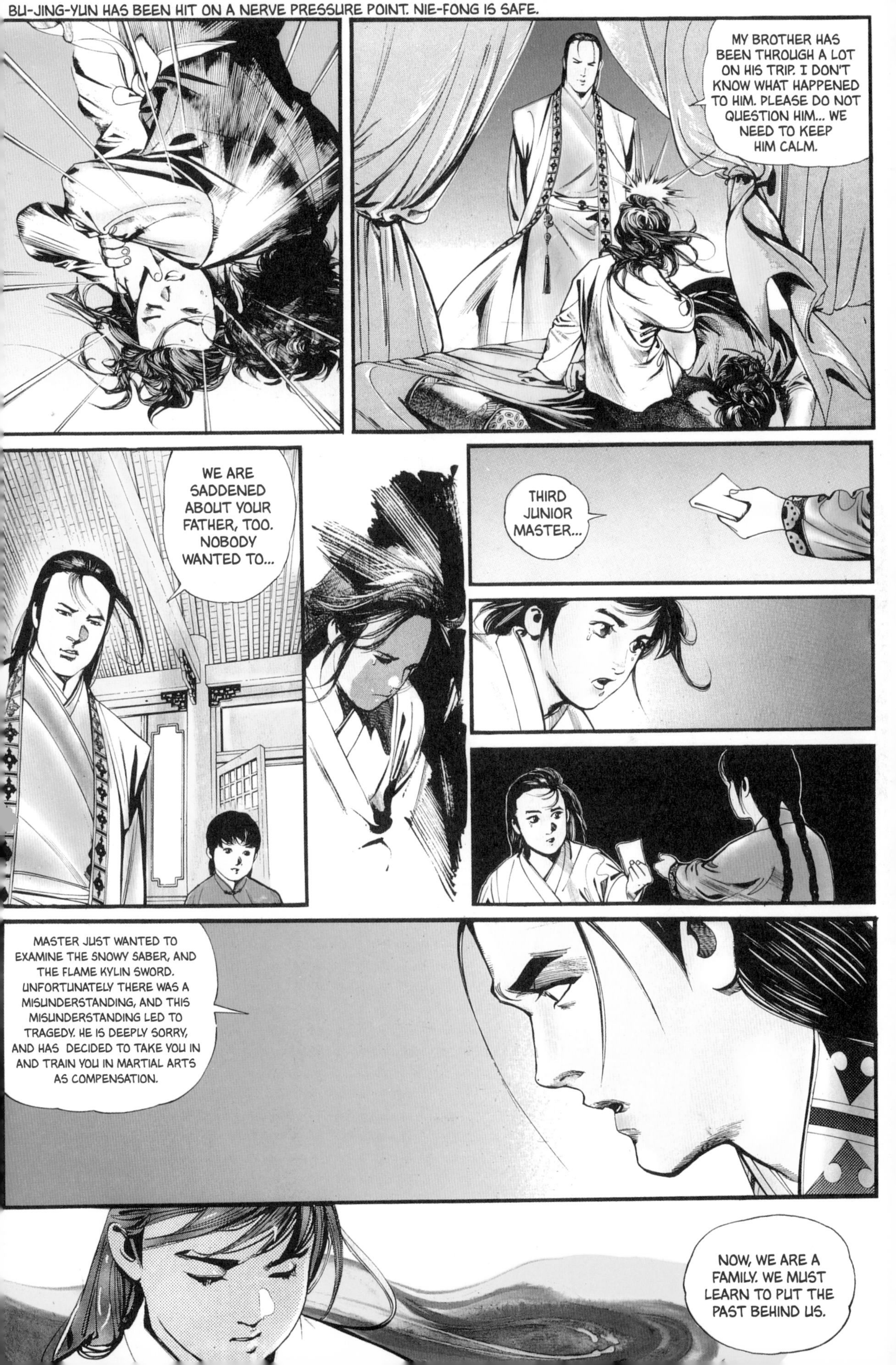
MY BROTHER HAS BEEN THROUGH A LOT ON HIS TRIP. I DON'T KNOW WHAT HAPPENED TO HIM. PLEASE DO NOT QUESTION HIM... WE NEED TO KEEP HIM CALM.
WE ARE SADDENED ABOUT YOUR FATHER, TOO. NOBODY WANTED TO...
THIRD JUNIOR MASTER...
MASTER JUST WANTED TO EXAMINE THE SNOWY SABER, AND THE FLAME KYLIN SWORD. UNFORTUNATELY THERE WAS A MISUNDERSTANDING, AND THIS MISUNDERSTANDING LED TO TRAGEDY. HE IS DEEPLY SORRY, AND HAS DECIDED TO TAKE YOU IN AND TRAIN YOU IN MARTIAL ARTS AS COMPENSATION.
NOW, WE ARE A FAMILY. WE MUST LEARN TO PUT THE PAST BEHIND US.

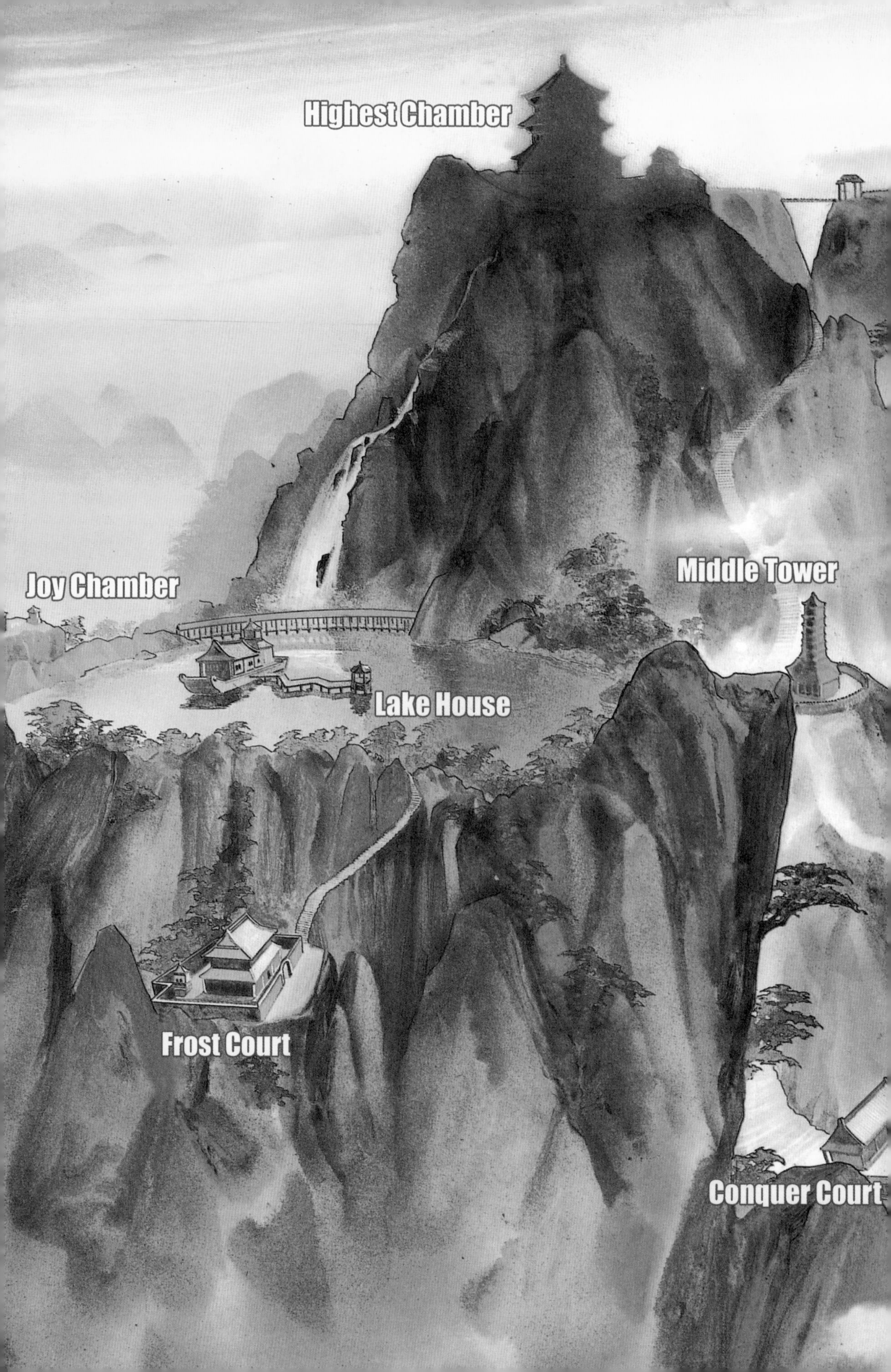
Highest Chamber
Joy Chamber
Middle Tower
Lake House
Frost Court
Conquer Court

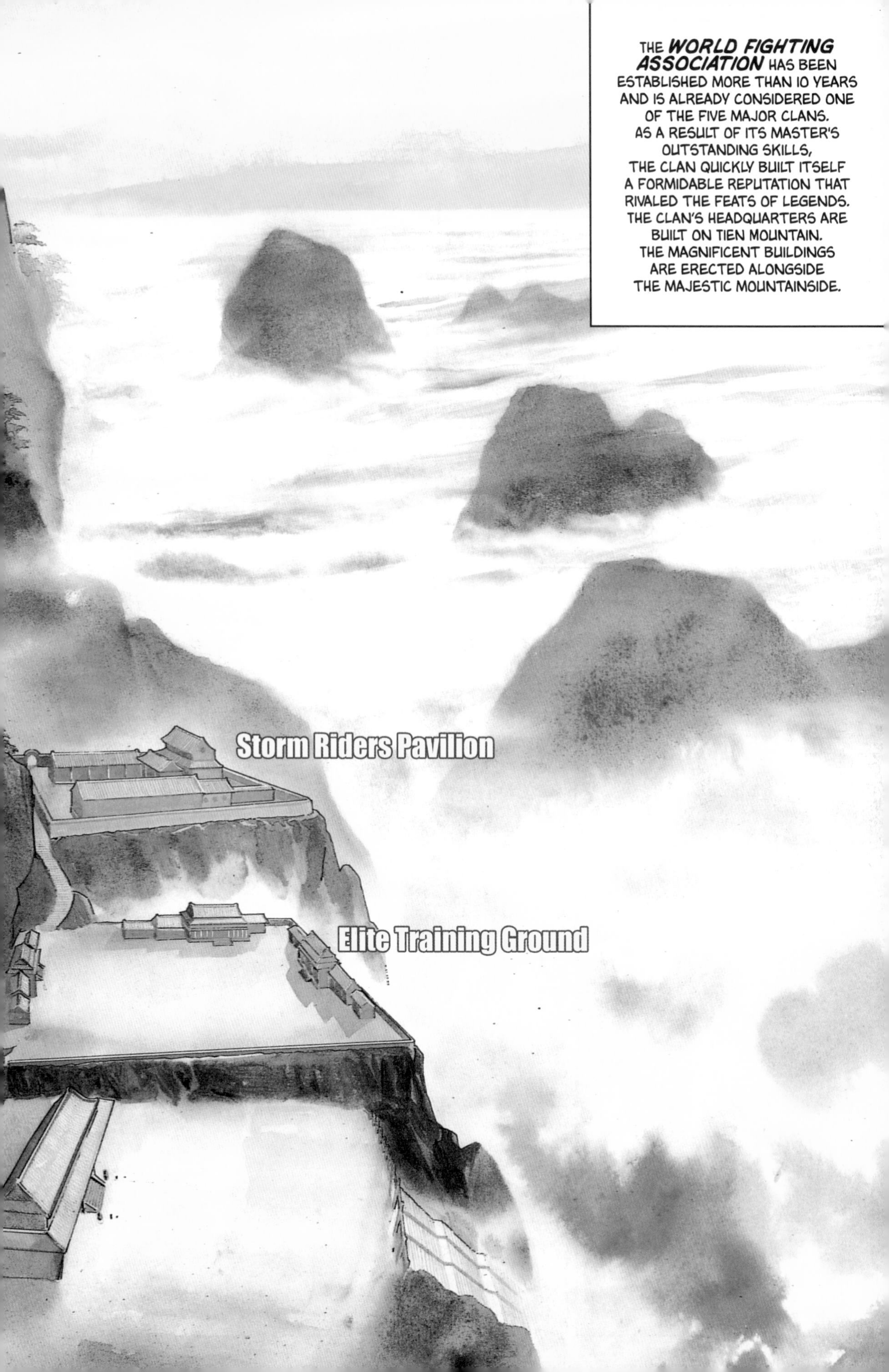
THE WORLD FIGHTING ASSOCIATION HAS BEEN ESTABLISHED MORE THAN 10 YEARS AND IS ALREADY CONSIDERED ONE OF THE FIVE MAJOR CLANS. AS A RESULT OF ITS MASTER'S OUTSTANDING SKILLS, THE CLAN QUICKLY BUILT ITSELF A FORMIDABLE REPUTATION THAT RIVALED THE FEATS OF LEGENDS. THE CLAN'S HEADQUARTERS ARE BUILT ON TIEN MOUNTAIN. THE MAGNIFICENT BUILDINGS ARE ERECTED ALONGSIDE THE MAJESTIC MOUNTAINSIDE.
Storm Riders Pavilion
Elite Training Ground

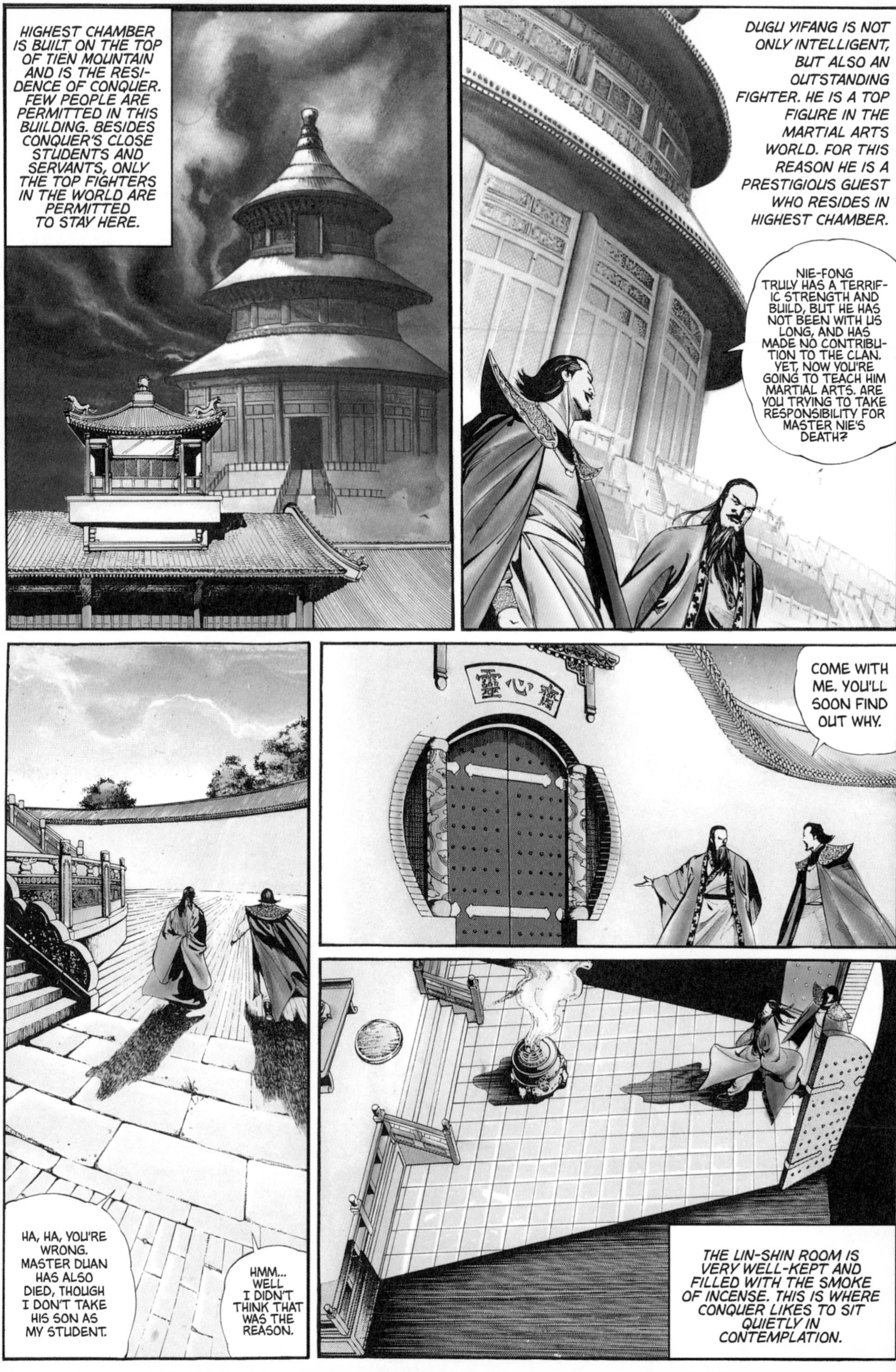
HIGHEST CHAMBER IS BUILT ON THE TOP OF TIEN MOUNTAIN AND IS THE RESI-DENCE OF CONQUER. FEW PEOPLE ARE PERMITTED IN THIS BUILDING. BESIDES CONQUER'S CLOSE STUDENTS AND SERVANTS, ONLY THE TOP FIGHTERS IN THE WORLD ARE PERMITTED TO STAY HERE.
DUGU YIFANG IS NOT ONLY INTELLIGENT, BUT ALSO AN OUTSTANDING FIGHTER. HE IS A TOP FIGURE IN THE MARTIAL ARTS WORLD. FOR THIS REASON HE IS A PRESTIGIOUS GUEST WHO RESIDES IN HIGHEST CHAMBER.
NIE-FONG TRULY HAS A TERRIF-IC STRENGTH AND BUILD, BUT HE HAS NOT BEEN WITH US LONG, AND HAS MADE NO CONTRIBU-TION TO THE CLAN. YET, NOW YOU'RE GOING TO TEACH HIM MARTIAL ARTS. ARE YOU TRYING TO TAKE RESPONSIBILITY FOR MASTER NIE'S DEATH?
HA, HA, YOU'RE WRONG. MASTER DUAN HAS ALSO DIED, THOUGH I DON'T TAKE HIS SON AS MY STUDENT.
HMM... WELL I DIDN'T THINK THAT WAS THE REASON.
靈心齋
COME WITH ME. YOU'LL SOON FIND OUT WHY.
THE LIN-SHIN ROOM IS VERY WELL-KEPT AND FILLED WITH THE SMOKE OF INCENSE. THIS IS WHERE CONQUER LIKES TO SIT QUIETLY IN CONTEMPLATION.

"THE GOLDEN-SCALED CREATURE CAN NEVER BE CONFINED IN THE POND, AND WILL GROW INTO A DRAGON, AS WIND AND CLOUD EMERGE." WHAT DOES THIS MEAN?

THIS IS MY DESTINY, AS FORETOLD BY THE PROPHET, MUD BUDDHA, YEARS AGO.

IT MEANS, THAT WITH WIND AND CLOUD* IN THE WORLD FIGHTING ASSOCIATION AND UNDER MY CARE, I WILL SOAR ABOVE THE SKY. I SAVED WIND, AND MY SECOND STUDENT CLOUD. NOW, I HAVE HARNESSED THE POWER OF BOTH THE WIND AND CLOUDS. MY DAY IS COMING SOON.

HMM, HE HAS GROWN QUITE AMBITIOUS. I HAVE A DANGEROUS PARTNER NOW. I MUST PROCEED WITH CAUTION.

HA, WIND AND [CLOUD] EMERGE. YOU HAVE [OUTSTA]NDING STUDENTS, [WHO WI]LL BUILD UP YOUR [POWER] AND STRIKE DOWN [Y]OUR FOES. TRULY [EX]CELLENT. [CON]GRATULATIONS!

CONQUER ALWAYS RELIES ON ABILITIES AND STRENGTH... BUT HE ALSO BELIEVES IN THE WORDS OF A FORTUNETELLER. CAN IT BE THAT MUD BUDDHA IS REALLY ABLE TO FORESEE PEOPLE'S DESTINIES?

[NIE-]FONG: FONG MEANS WIND IN CHINESE, HE IS KNOWN AS WIND.
[BU]NG-YUN: YUN MEANS CLOUD IN CHINESE, AND HE IS KNOWN AS CLOUD.

17

6 years later

NIE-FONG (WIND) AND BU-JING-YUN (CLOUD) HAVE BOTH BECOME TREMENDOUS FIGHTERS.

IN BOTH HEAVEN AND EARTH, I AM THE ONLY MASTER OF THE WORLD FIGHTING ASSOCIATION WHICH HAS DEVELOPED RAPIDLY OVER A SHORT PERIOD OF TIME AND NOW STANDS AT THE TOP OF THE MARTIAL ARTS WORLD.

I HAVE T... MOST OU... STANDIN... PEOPLE A... COMMAND T... UTMOST... LOYALTY. TH... IS NOTHING... THE WOR... BEYOND M... REACH NO...

I AM UNIVERSALLY REVERED AND HAVE NEVER MET ANY SERIOUS OBSTACLES. NOTHING IN THE WORLD CAN THREATEN MY POSITION NOW.

I... FIRM... BELI... IT...

BUT...

WHAT HAP-PENED TODA... PROVES THA... I CAN STILL B... SURPRISED... IT SHOWS M... THAT NOT... EVERYTHING... IS ALWAYS A... IT SEEMS.

IN FRO... OF ME... IS A BLEE... ING HUM... HEAD!

THE HEAD O... DUGU YIFAN...

18

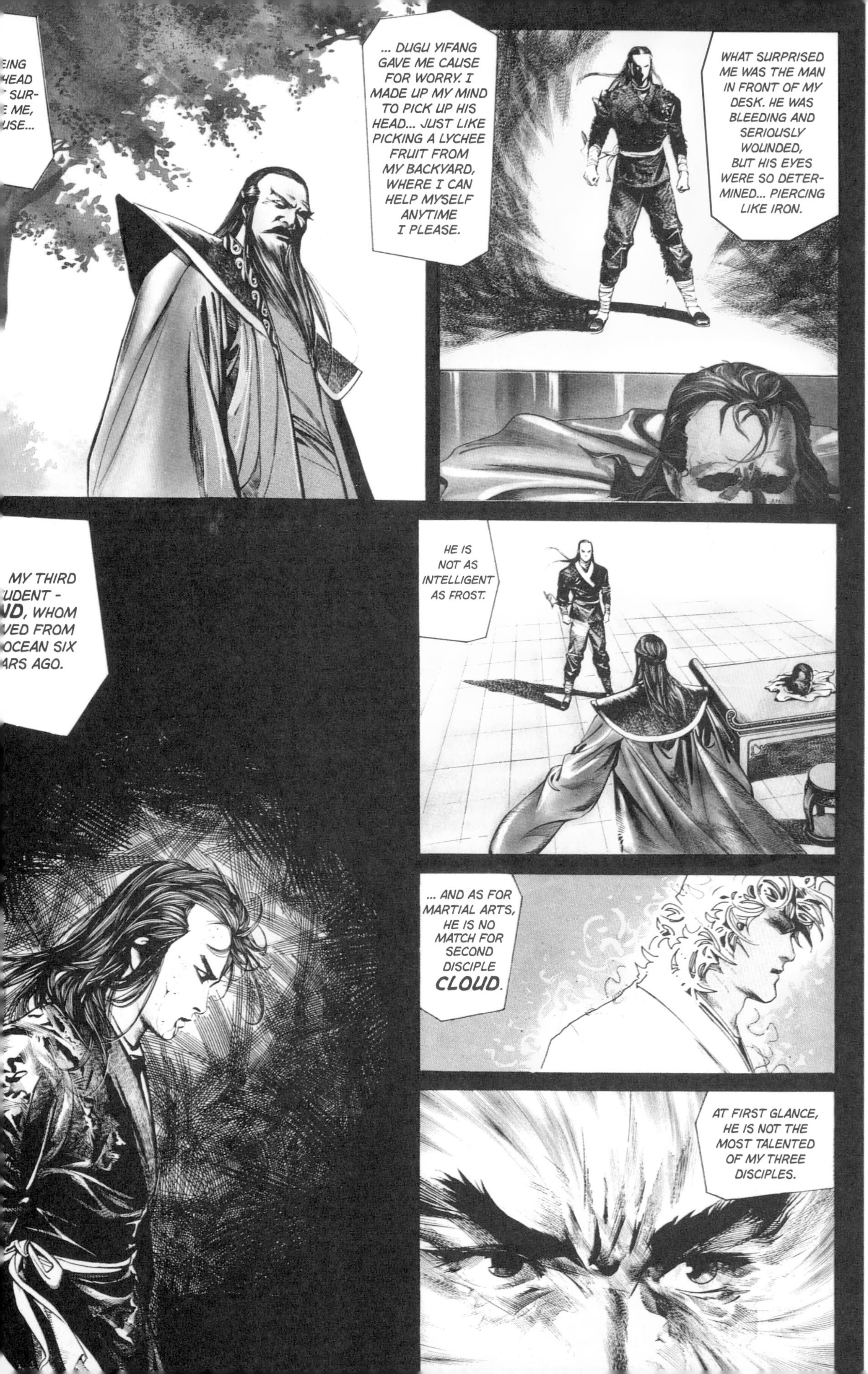
EING HEAD SUR- E ME, USE...
... DUGU YIFANG GAVE ME CAUSE FOR WORRY. I MADE UP MY MIND TO PICK UP HIS HEAD... JUST LIKE PICKING A LYCHEE FRUIT FROM MY BACKYARD, WHERE I CAN HELP MYSELF ANYTIME I PLEASE.
WHAT SURPRISED ME WAS THE MAN IN FRONT OF MY DESK. HE WAS BLEEDING AND SERIOUSLY WOUNDED, BUT HIS EYES WERE SO DETERMINED... PIERCING LIKE IRON.
MY THIRD UDENT - ND, WHOM VED FROM OCEAN SIX ARS AGO.
HE IS NOT AS INTELLIGENT AS FROST.
... AND AS FOR MARTIAL ARTS, HE IS NO MATCH FOR SECOND DISCIPLE CLOUD.
AT FIRST GLANCE, HE IS NOT THE MOST TALENTED OF MY THREE DISCIPLES.

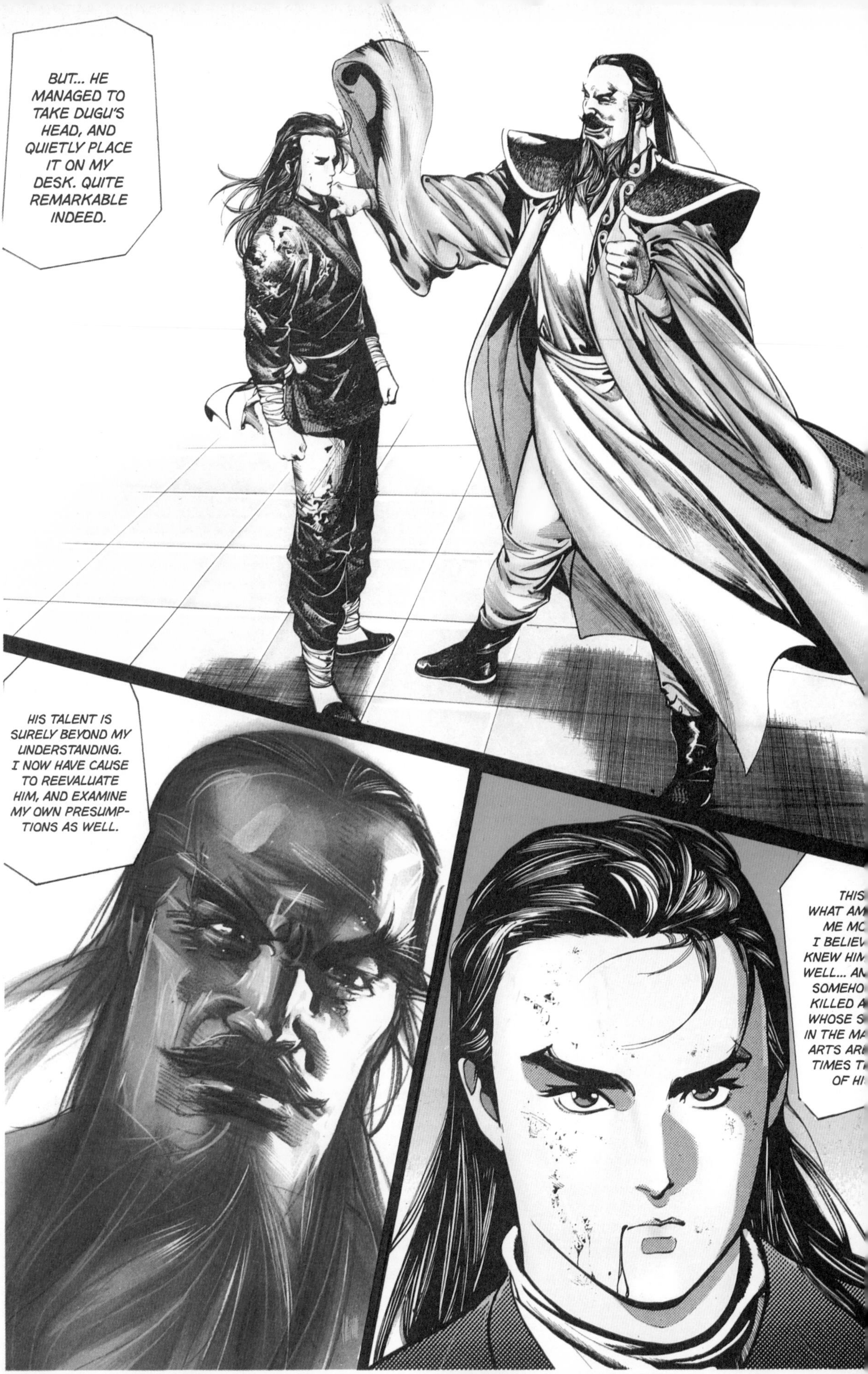
BUT... HE MANAGED TO TAKE DUGU'S HEAD, AND QUIETLY PLACE IT ON MY DESK. QUITE REMARKABLE INDEED.
HIS TALENT IS SURELY BEYOND MY UNDERSTANDING. I NOW HAVE CAUSE TO REEVALUATE HIM, AND EXAMINE MY OWN PRESUMPTIONS AS WELL.
THIS WHAT AM ME MC I BELIEV KNEW HIM WELL... AN SOMEHO KILLED A WHOSE S IN THE MA ARTS AR TIMES T OF HI

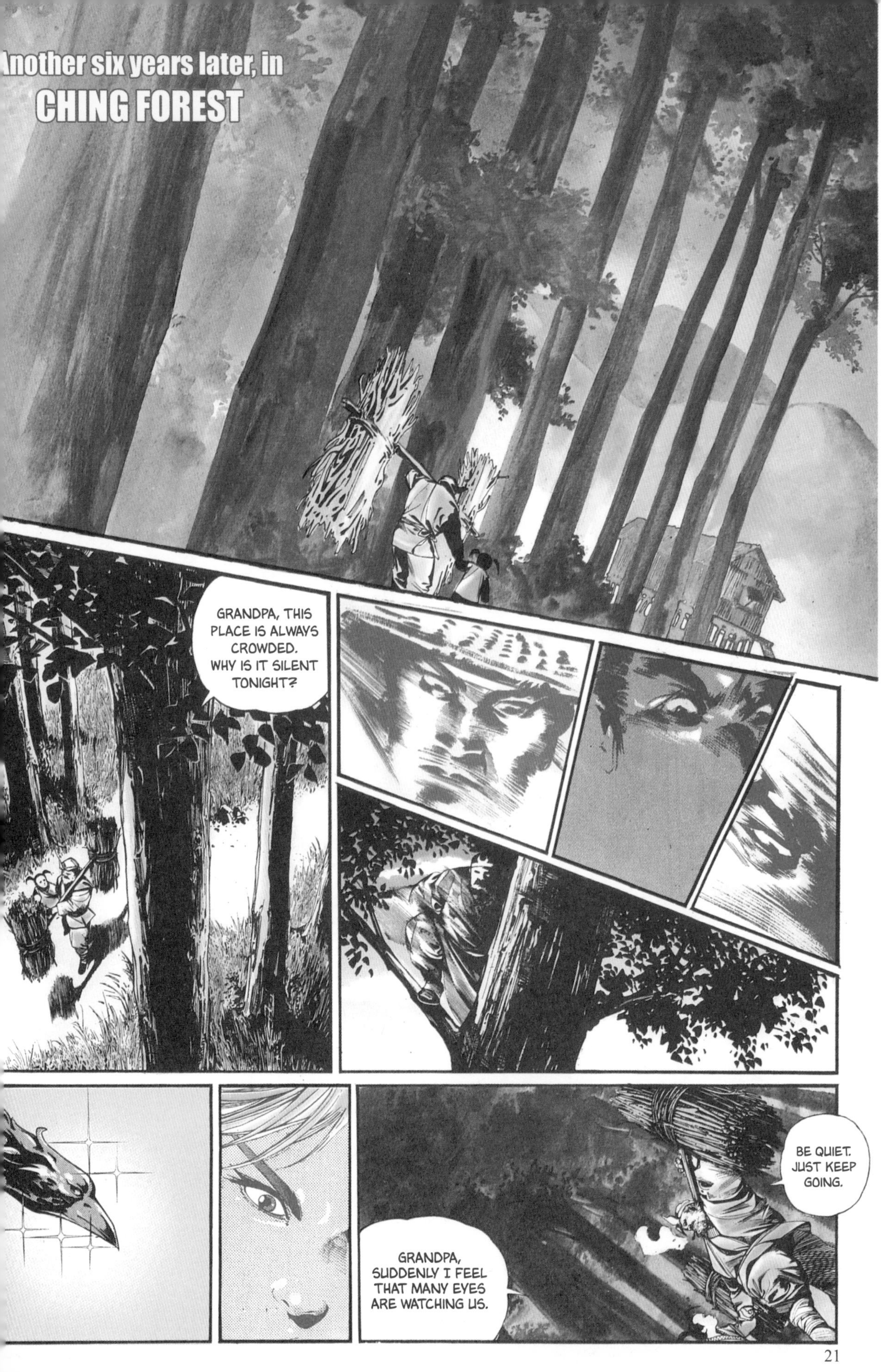
Another six years later, in
CHING FOREST
GRANDPA, THIS PLACE IS ALWAYS CROWDED. WHY IS IT SILENT TONIGHT?
BE QUIET. JUST KEEP GOING.
GRANDPA, SUDDENLY I FEEL THAT MANY EYES ARE WATCHING US.

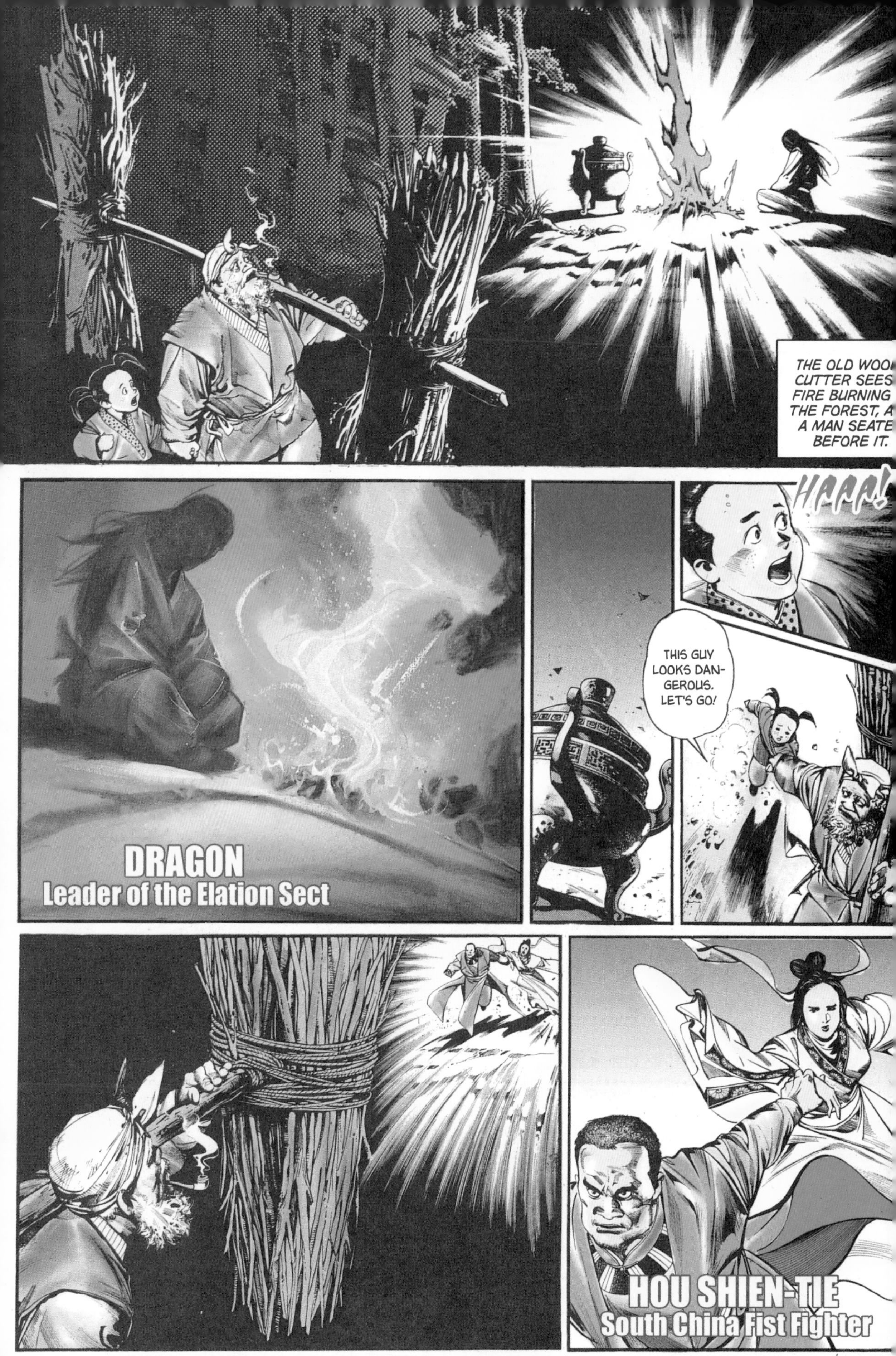
THE OLD WOO
CUTTER SEES
FIRE BURNING
THE FOREST, A
A MAN SEATE
BEFORE IT.
HPPP!
DRAGON
Leader of the Elation Sect
THIS GUY LOOKS DAN- GEROUS. LET'S GO!
HOU SHIEN-TIE
South China Fist Fighter

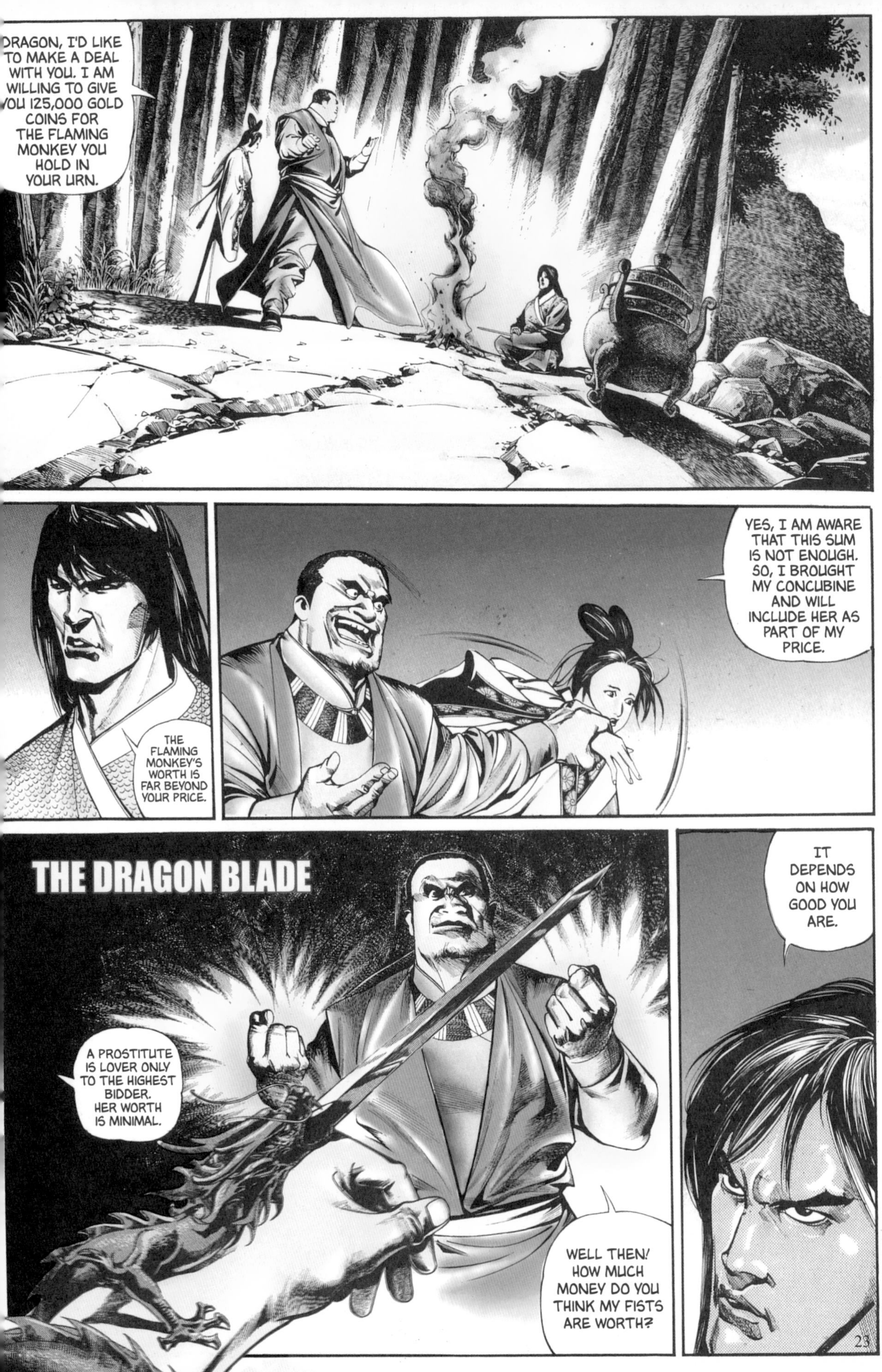

DRAGON, I'D LIKE TO MAKE A DEAL WITH YOU. I AM WILLING TO GIVE YOU 125,000 GOLD COINS FOR THE FLAMING MONKEY YOU HOLD IN YOUR URN.
YES, I AM AWARE THAT THIS SUM IS NOT ENOUGH. SO, I BROUGHT MY CONCUBINE AND WILL INCLUDE HER AS PART OF MY PRICE.
THE FLAMING MONKEY'S WORTH IS FAR BEYOND YOUR PRICE.
A PROSTITUTE IS LOVER ONLY TO THE HIGHEST BIDDER. HER WORTH IS MINIMAL.
THE DRAGON BLADE
WELL THEN! HOW MUCH MONEY DO YOU THINK MY FISTS ARE WORTH?
IT DEPENDS ON HOW GOOD YOU ARE.

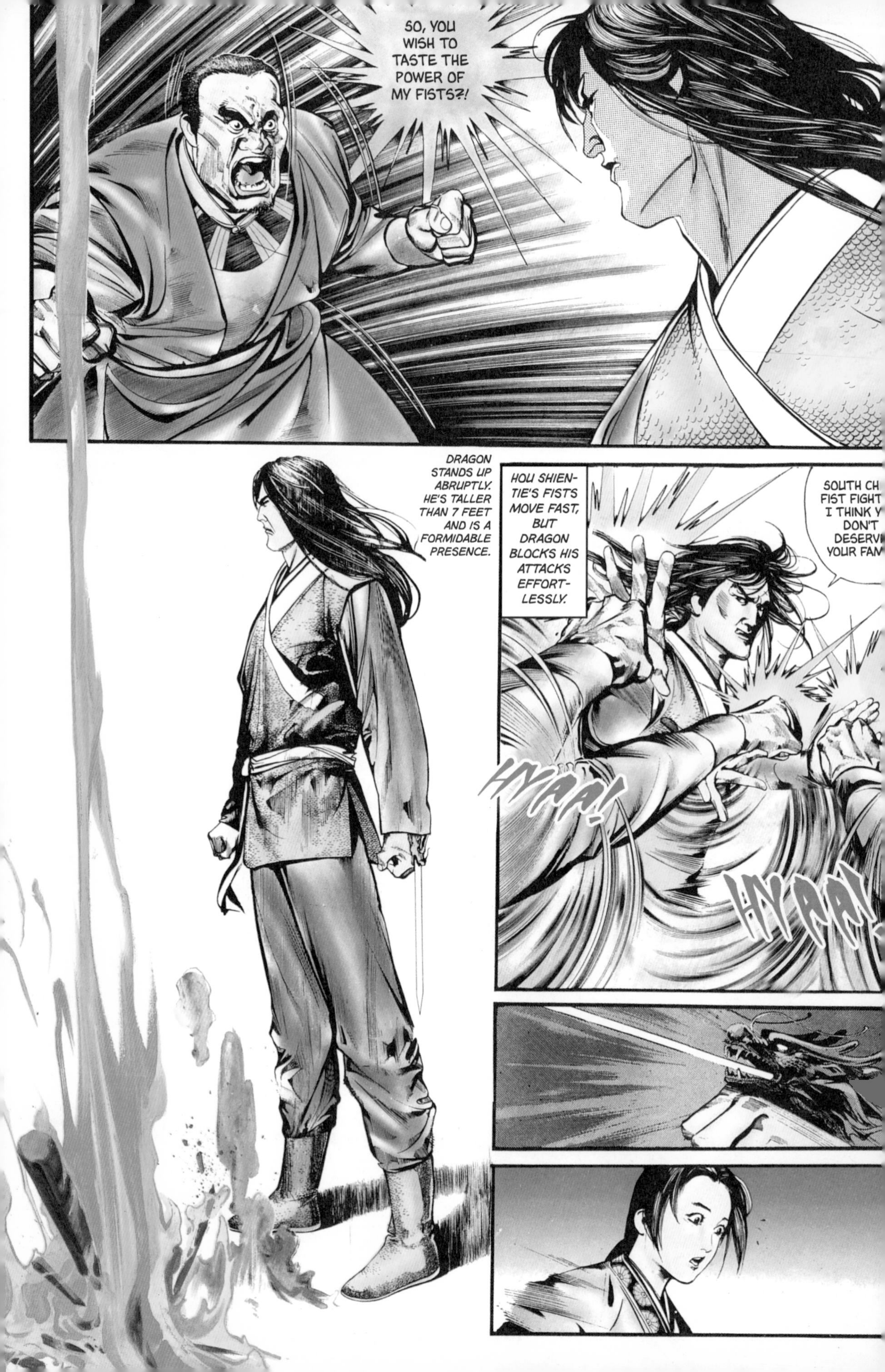
SO, YOU WISH TO TASTE THE POWER OF MY FISTS?!
DRAGON STANDS UP ABRUPTLY. HE'S TALLER THAN 7 FEET AND IS A FORMIDABLE PRESENCE.
HOU SHIEN-TIE'S FISTS MOVE FAST, BUT DRAGON BLOCKS HIS ATTACKS EFFORTLESSLY.
SOUTH CH
FIST FIGHT
I THINK Y
DON'T
DESERV
YOUR FAM
HYAA!
HYAA!

HOENIX ARROW

THE FIERCE FIGHT CONTINUES IN THE FOREST. THERE IS A SHARP ARROWHEAD HIDDEN ON THE EDGE OF THE SCENE, AIMED AT DRAGON. NO ONE KNOWS WHOSE HAND CONTROLS ITS DEADLY POINT...

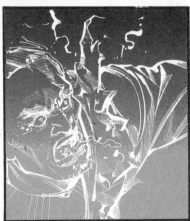

WHAT KIND OF SOUTH CHINA FIST FIGHTER ARE YOU? YOU'RE ONLY GOOD AT TALK. YOU'RE NO MATCH EVEN FOR FROST OF THE WORLD FIGHTING ASSOCIATION, WHO USES THE SKY FROST FIST WITH GREATER SKILL.

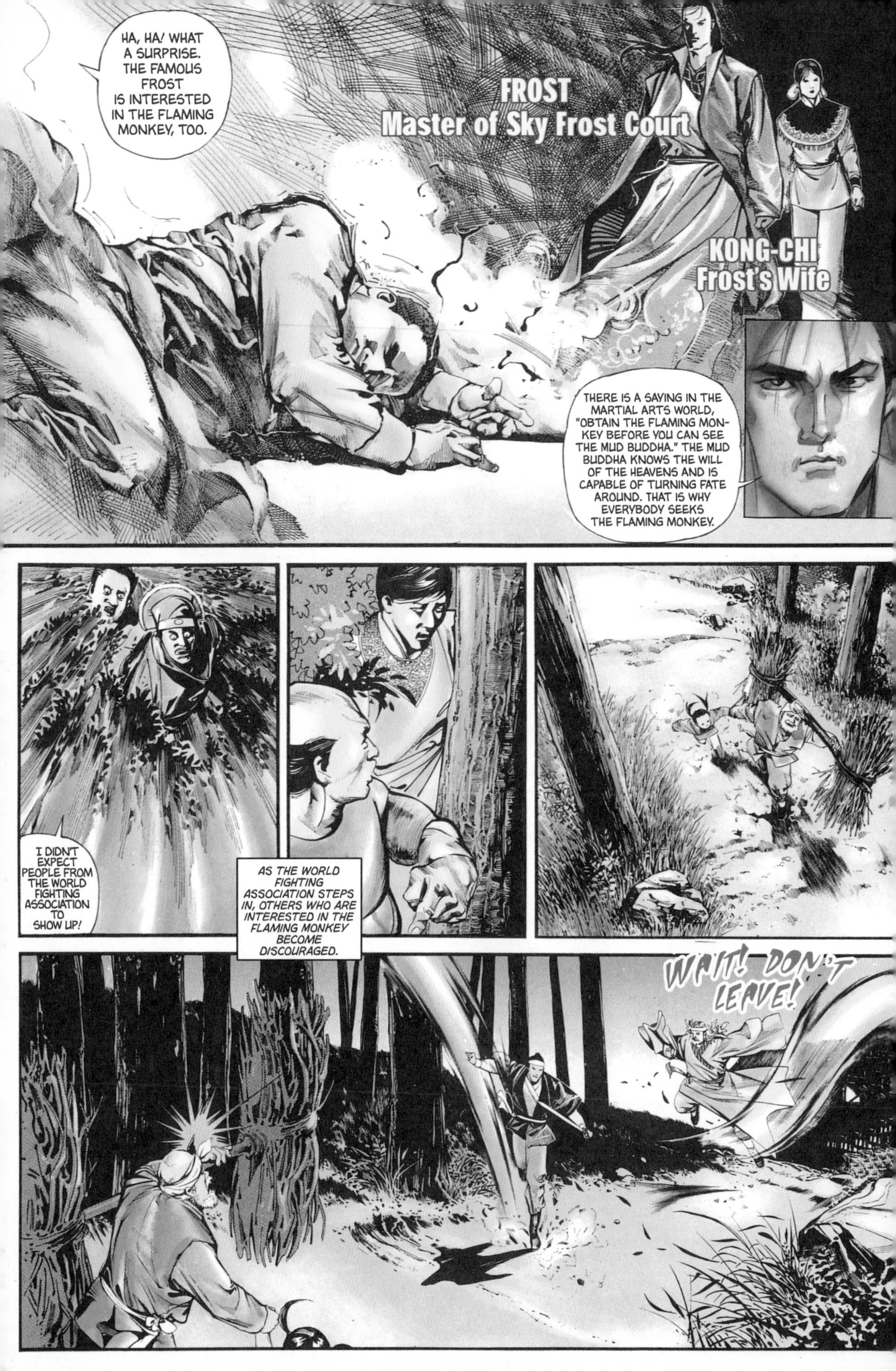
HA, HA! WHAT A SURPRISE. THE FAMOUS FROST IS INTERESTED IN THE FLAMING MONKEY, TOO.
FROST
Master of Sky Frost Court
KONG-CHI
Frost's Wife
THERE IS A SAYING IN THE MARTIAL ARTS WORLD, "OBTAIN THE FLAMING MONKEY BEFORE YOU CAN SEE THE MUD BUDDHA." THE MUD BUDDHA KNOWS THE WILL OF THE HEAVENS AND IS CAPABLE OF TURNING FATE AROUND. THAT IS WHY EVERYBODY SEEKS THE FLAMING MONKEY.
I DIDN'T EXPECT PEOPLE FROM THE WORLD FIGHTING ASSOCIATION TO SHOW UP!
AS THE WORLD FIGHTING ASSOCIATION STEPS IN, OTHERS WHO ARE INTERESTED IN THE FLAMING MONKEY BECOME DISCOURAGED.
WAIT! DON'T LEAVE!

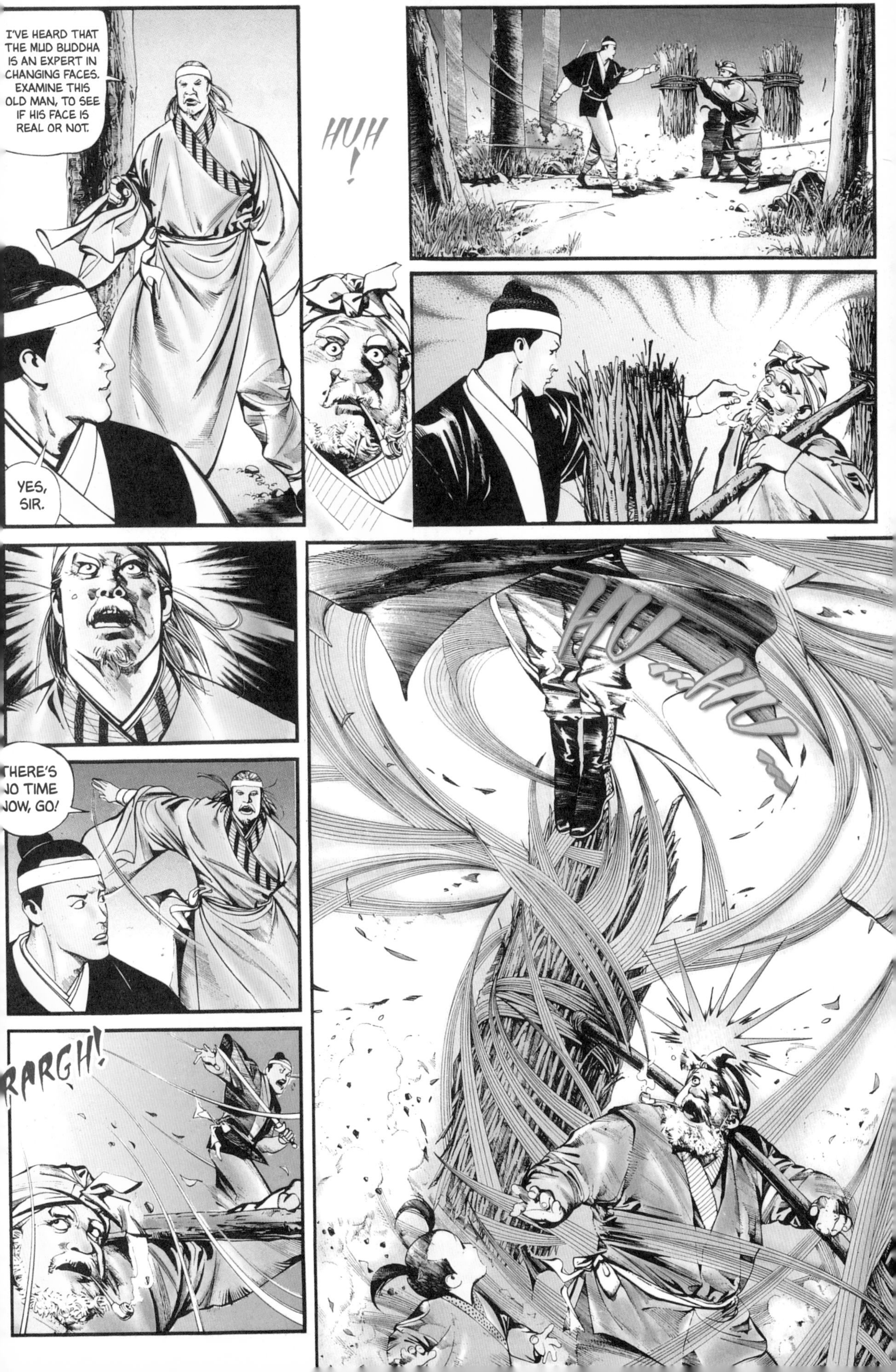
I'VE HEARD THAT THE MUD BUDDHA IS AN EXPERT IN CHANGING FACES. EXAMINE THIS OLD MAN, TO SEE IF HIS FACE IS REAL OR NOT.
YES, SIR.
HUH!
THERE'S NO TIME NOW, GO!
RARGH!
HU...HU...

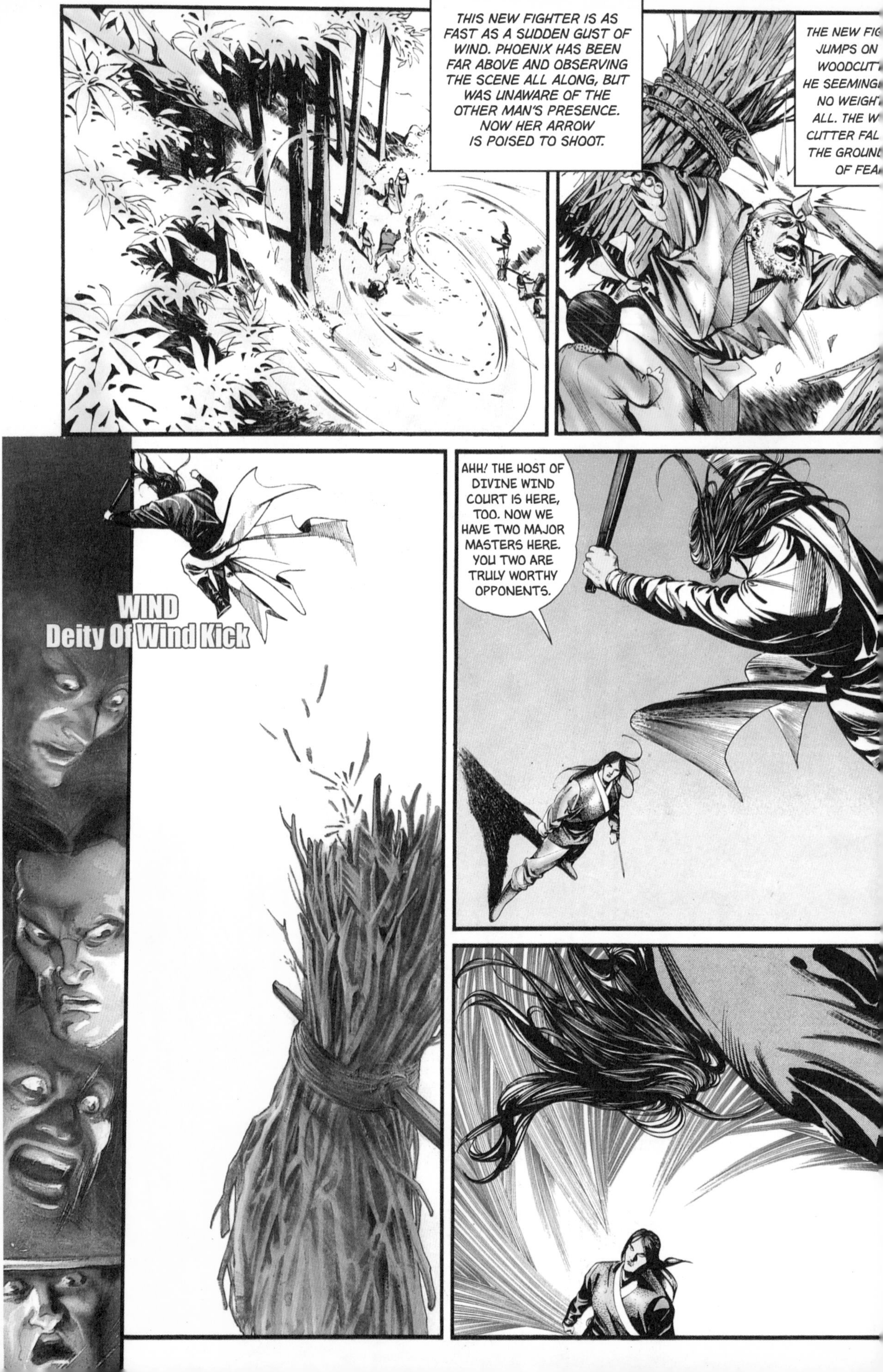
THIS NEW FIGHTER IS AS FAST AS A SUDDEN GUST OF WIND. PHOENIX HAS BEEN FAR ABOVE AND OBSERVING THE SCENE ALL ALONG, BUT WAS UNAWARE OF THE OTHER MAN'S PRESENCE. NOW HER ARROW IS POISED TO SHOOT.
THE NEW FIG JUMPS ON WOODCUTT HE SEEMING NO WEIGHT ALL. THE W CUTTER FAL THE GROUNL OF FEA
WIND
Deity Of Wind Kick
AHH! THE HOST OF DIVINE WIND COURT IS HERE, TOO. NOW WE HAVE TWO MAJOR MASTERS HERE. YOU TWO ARE TRULY WORTHY OPPONENTS.

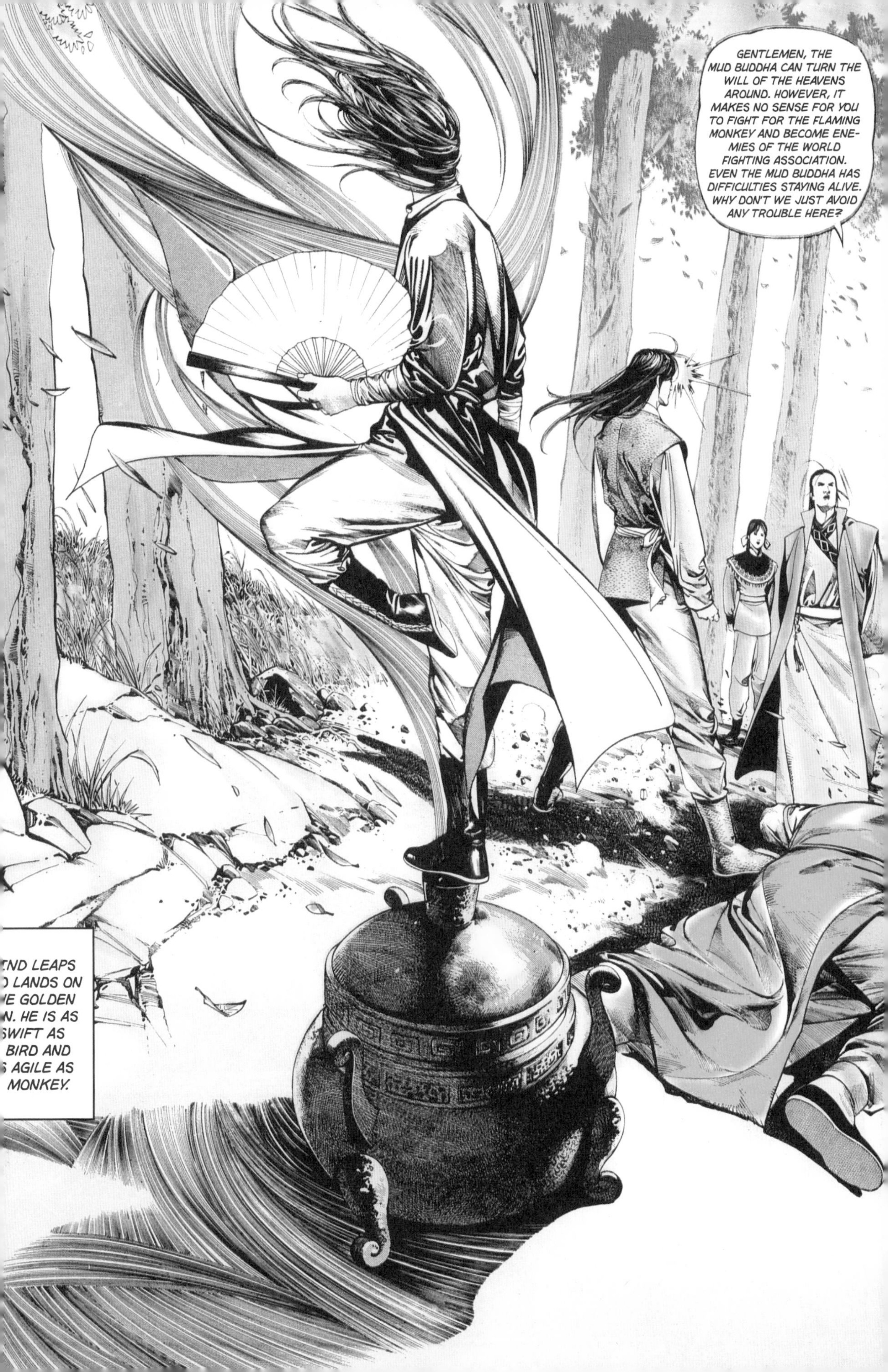
GENTLEMEN, THE MUD BUDDHA CAN TURN THE WILL OF THE HEAVENS AROUND. HOWEVER, IT MAKES NO SENSE FOR YOU TO FIGHT FOR THE FLAMING MONKEY AND BECOME ENEMIES OF THE WORLD FIGHTING ASSOCIATION. EVEN THE MUD BUDDHA HAS DIFFICULTIES STAYING ALIVE. WHY DON'T WE JUST AVOID ANY TROUBLE HERE?
ND LEAPS
LANDS ON
E GOLDEN
N. HE IS AS
SWIFT AS
BIRD AND
AGILE AS
MONKEY.

YEARS AGO, CONQUER FOUNDED THE WORLD FIGHTING ASSOCIATION. HE BUILT UP HIS EMPIRE THROUGH THE POWER OF HIS OUTSTANDING TECHNIQUES - SKY FROST FIST, REPELLING PALM, AND DEITY OF WIND KICK.

LATER ON, CONQ... PASSED DOWN... MARTIAL ARTS SK... TO 3 STUDENT... FROST, THE HEA... SKY FROST COD... CLOUD, THE HEA... FLYING CLOUD... COURT, AND WI... THE HEAD OF DIV... WIND COURT. ... THREE STUDEN... STUDIED VERY HA... GRASP THE ESSE... OF EACH SKILL...

FROST JOINED THE CLAN FIRST, AND IS THE FAVORITE OF CONQUER. HE DIRECTS THE CLAN'S INTERNAL AFFAIRS AND HAS CONSIDERABLE POWER, BUT REMAINS QUIET IN THE OUTSIDE WORLD. BECAUSE OF THIS QUIET DEMEANOR, HE HAS NOT ACHIEVED THE SAME DEGREE OF FAME AS WIND AND CLOUD.

CONQUER SENT TWO MA... TERS TO FIGHT FOR T... FLAMING MONKEY. T... WORLD FIGHTING ASSOCIATION DESPERAT... WANTS POSSESSION OF... FLAMING MONKEY. WIN... PRESENCE DISCOURAG... THE OTHERS WHO PURS...

HMF! THE WORLD FIGHTING ASSOCIATION IS A BIG AND POWERFUL CLAN, BUT THAT DOESN'T MEAN YOU MAY DO AS YOU PLEASE. YOU NEED TO CHECK WITH THE ELATION SECT FIRST.

OH?!

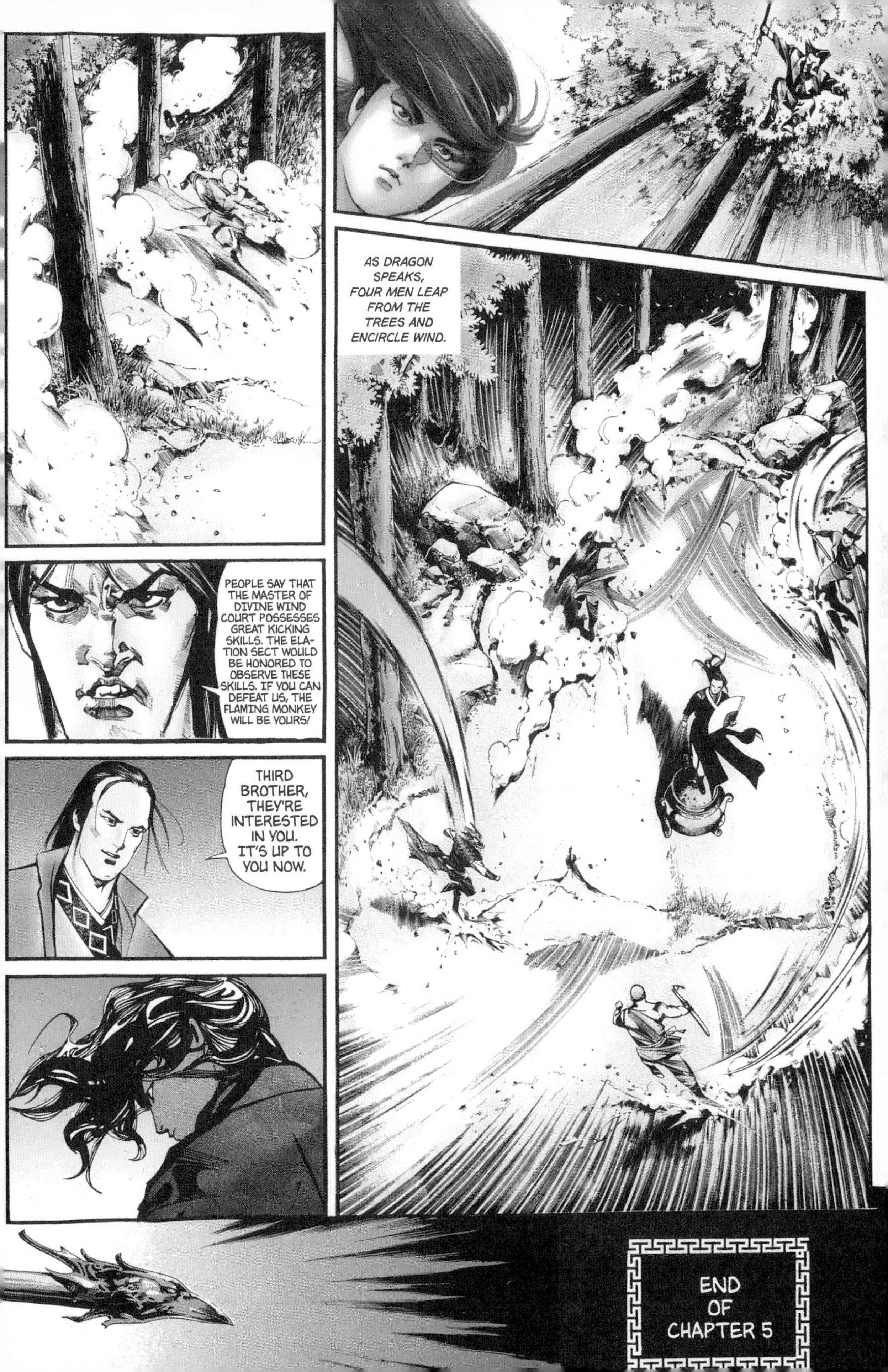
AS DRAGON SPEAKS, FOUR MEN LEAP FROM THE TREES AND ENCIRCLE WIND.
PEOPLE SAY THAT THE MASTER OF DIVINE WIND COURT POSSESSES GREAT KICKING SKILLS. THE ELATION SECT WOULD BE HONORED TO OBSERVE THESE SKILLS. IF YOU CAN DEFEAT US, THE FLAMING MONKEY WILL BE YOURS!
THIRD BROTHER, THEY'RE INTERESTED IN YOU. IT'S UP TO YOU NOW.
END OF CHAPTER 5

Chapter 6: Swifter Than Blade Or Arrow

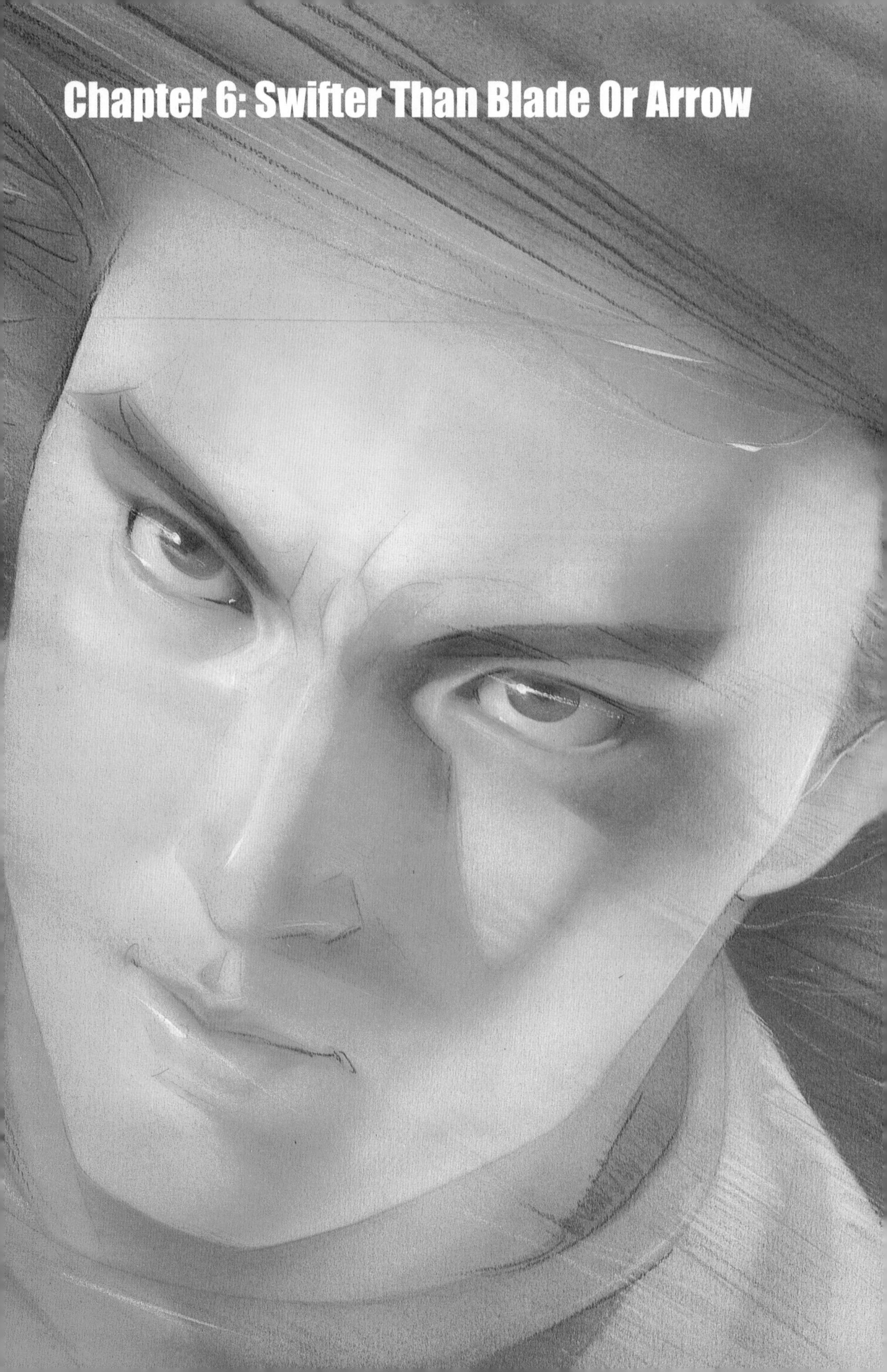

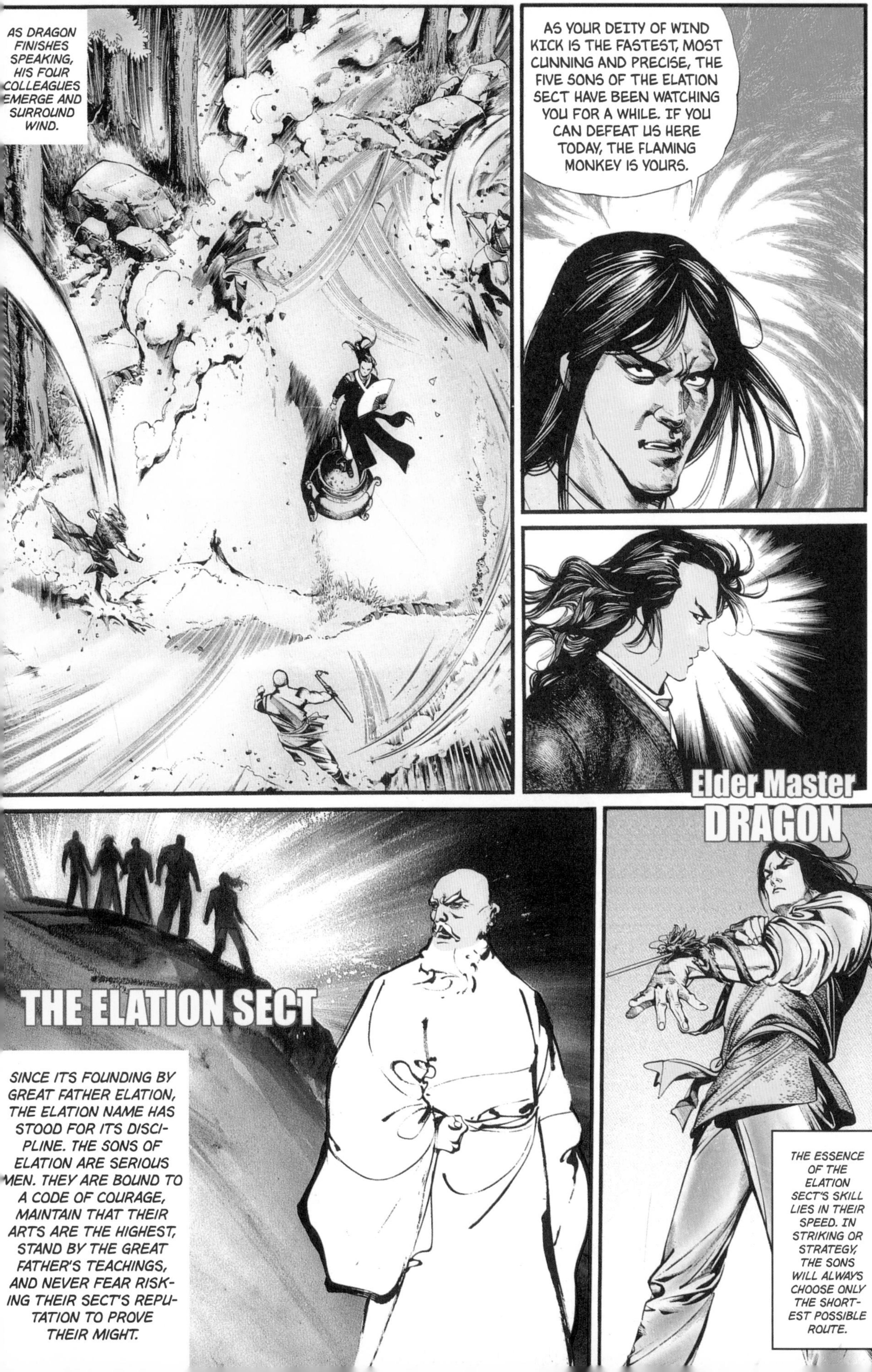
AS DRAGON FINISHES SPEAKING, HIS FOUR COLLEAGUES EMERGE AND SURROUND WIND.
AS YOUR DEITY OF WIND KICK IS THE FASTEST, MOST CUNNING AND PRECISE, THE FIVE SONS OF THE ELATION SECT HAVE BEEN WATCHING YOU FOR A WHILE. IF YOU CAN DEFEAT US HERE TODAY, THE FLAMING MONKEY IS YOURS.
Elder Master DRAGON
THE ELATION SECT
SINCE ITS FOUNDING BY GREAT FATHER ELATION, THE ELATION NAME HAS STOOD FOR ITS DISCI-PLINE. THE SONS OF ELATION ARE SERIOUS MEN. THEY ARE BOUND TO A CODE OF COURAGE, MAINTAIN THAT THEIR ARTS ARE THE HIGHEST, STAND BY THE GREAT FATHER'S TEACHINGS, AND NEVER FEAR RISK-ING THEIR SECT'S REPU-TATION TO PROVE THEIR MIGHT.
THE ESSENCE OF THE ELATION SECT'S SKILL LIES IN THEIR SPEED. IN STRIKING OR STRATEGY, THE SONS WILL ALWAYS CHOOSE ONLY THE SHORT-EST POSSIBLE ROUTE.

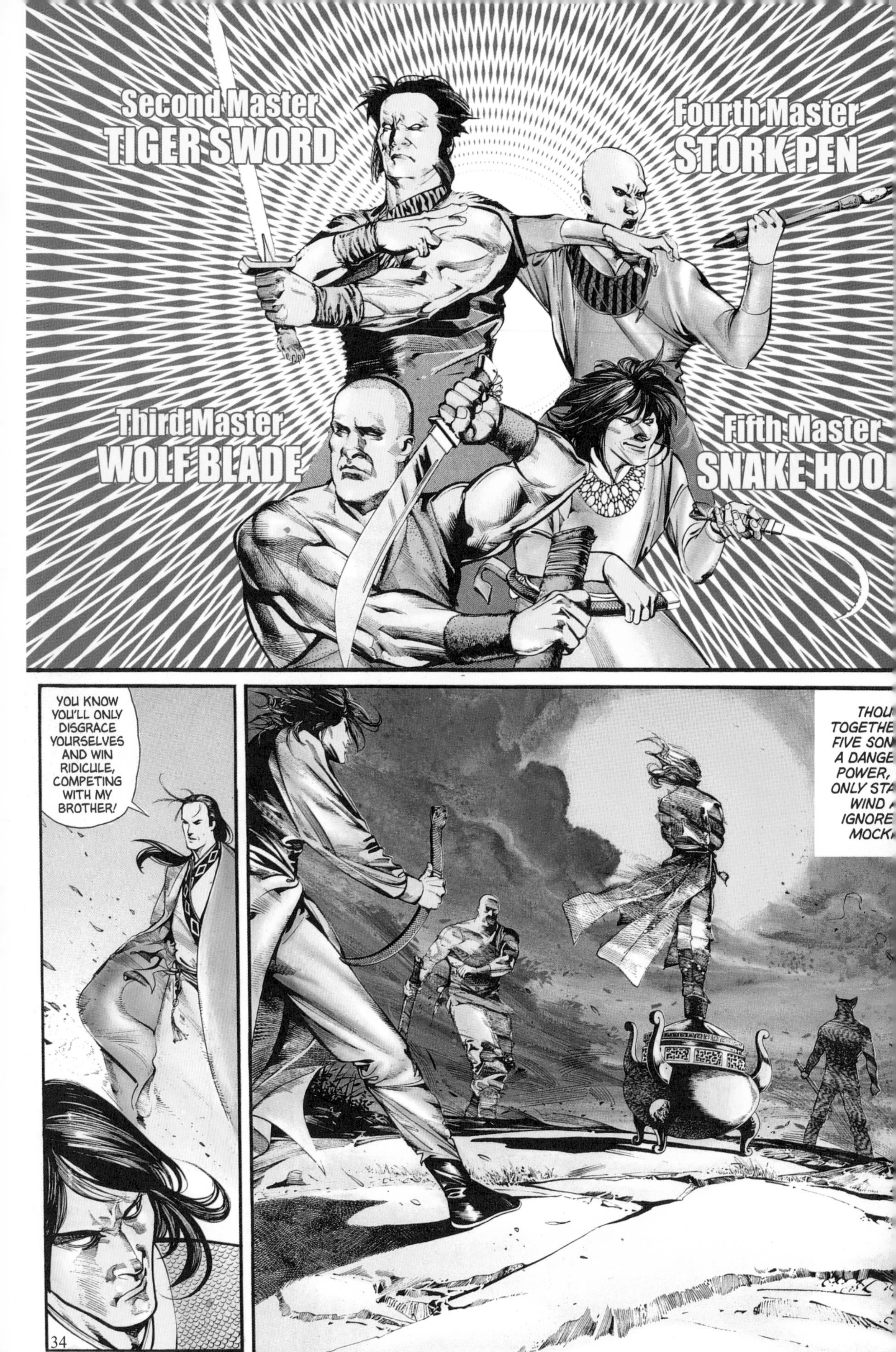
Second Master
TIGER SWORD
Fourth Master
STORK PEN
Third Master
WOLF BLADE
Fifth Master
SNAKE HOO
YOU KNOW YOU'LL ONLY DISGRACE YOURSELVES AND WIN RIDICULE, COMPETING WITH MY BROTHER!
THOU TOGETHE FIVE SON A DANGE POWER, ONLY STA WIND A IGNORE MOCK

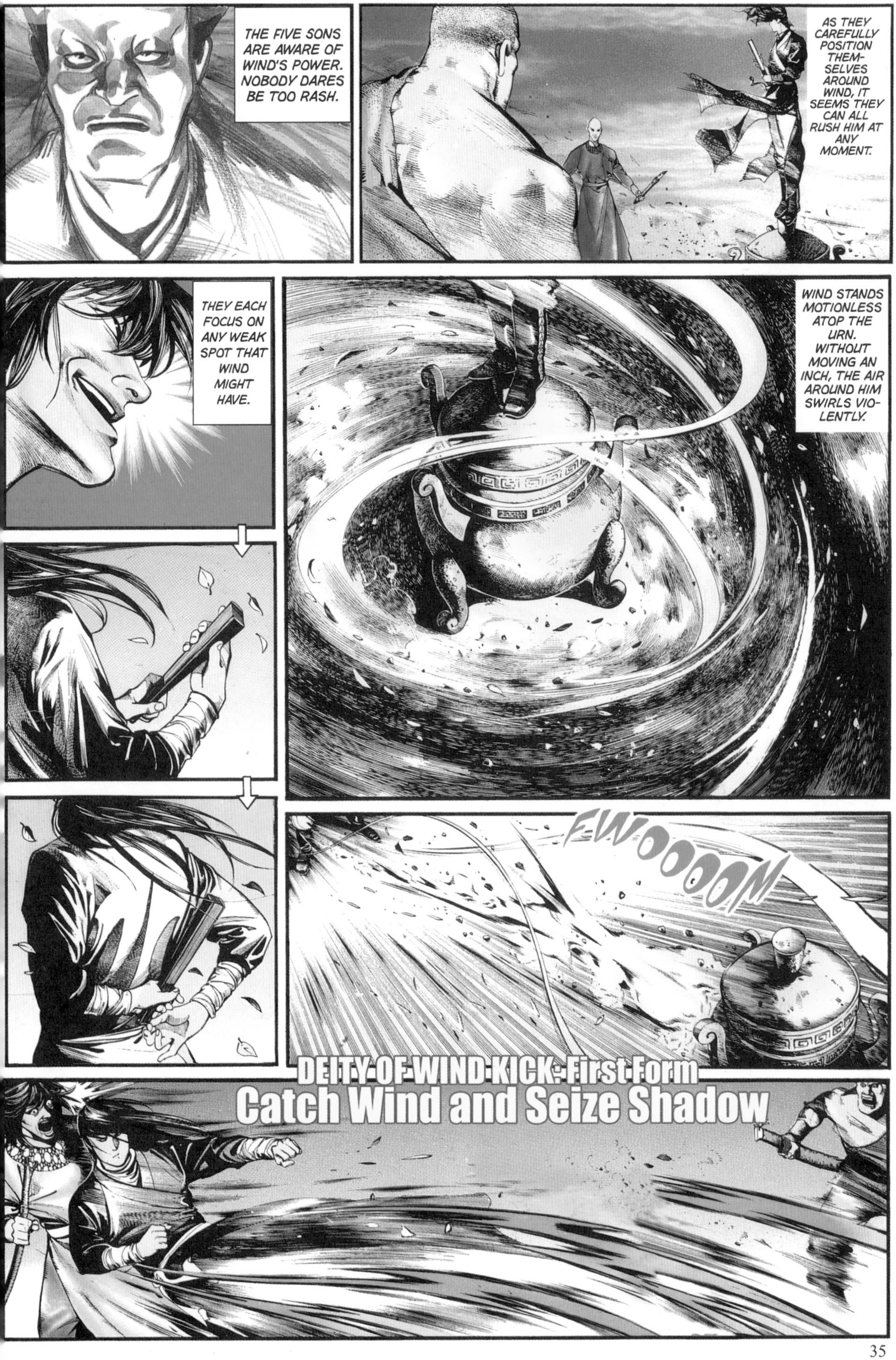
THE FIVE SONS ARE AWARE OF WIND'S POWER. NOBODY DARES BE TOO RASH.
AS THEY CAREFULLY POSITION THEM-SELVES AROUND WIND, IT SEEMS THEY CAN ALL RUSH HIM AT ANY MOMENT.
THEY EACH FOCUS ON ANY WEAK SPOT THAT WIND MIGHT HAVE.
WIND STANDS MOTIONLESS ATOP THE URN. WITHOUT MOVING AN INCH, THE AIR AROUND HIM SWIRLS VIO-LENTLY.
FWOOOOM
DEITY OF WIND KICK: First Form
Catch Wind and Seize Shadow

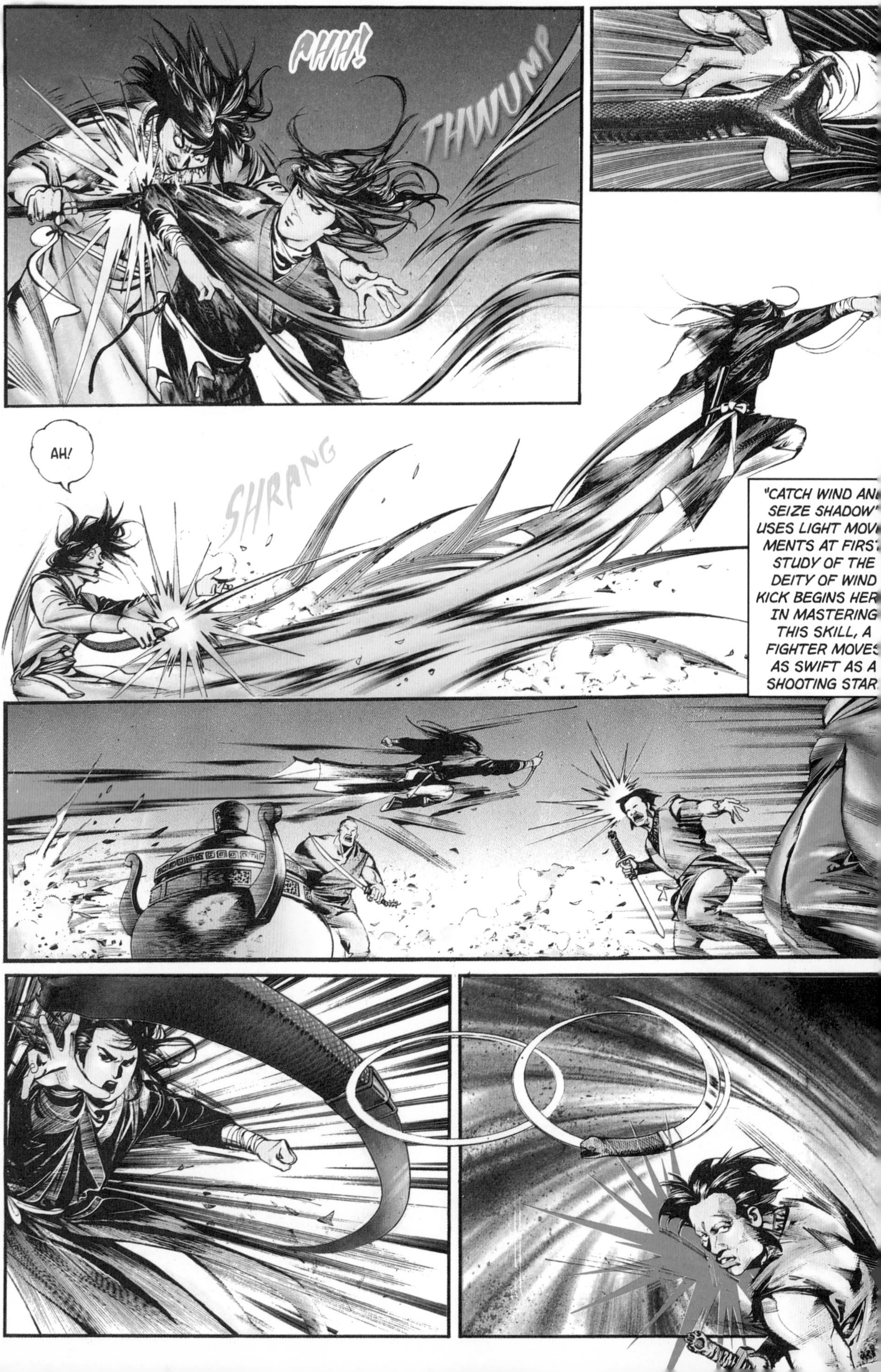
AHH!
THWUMP
AH!
SHRANG
"CATCH WIND AN
SEIZE SHADOW"
USES LIGHT MOV
MENTS AT FIRST
STUDY OF THE
DEITY OF WIND
KICK BEGINS HER
IN MASTERING
THIS SKILL, A
FIGHTER MOVES
AS SWIFT AS A
SHOOTING STAR

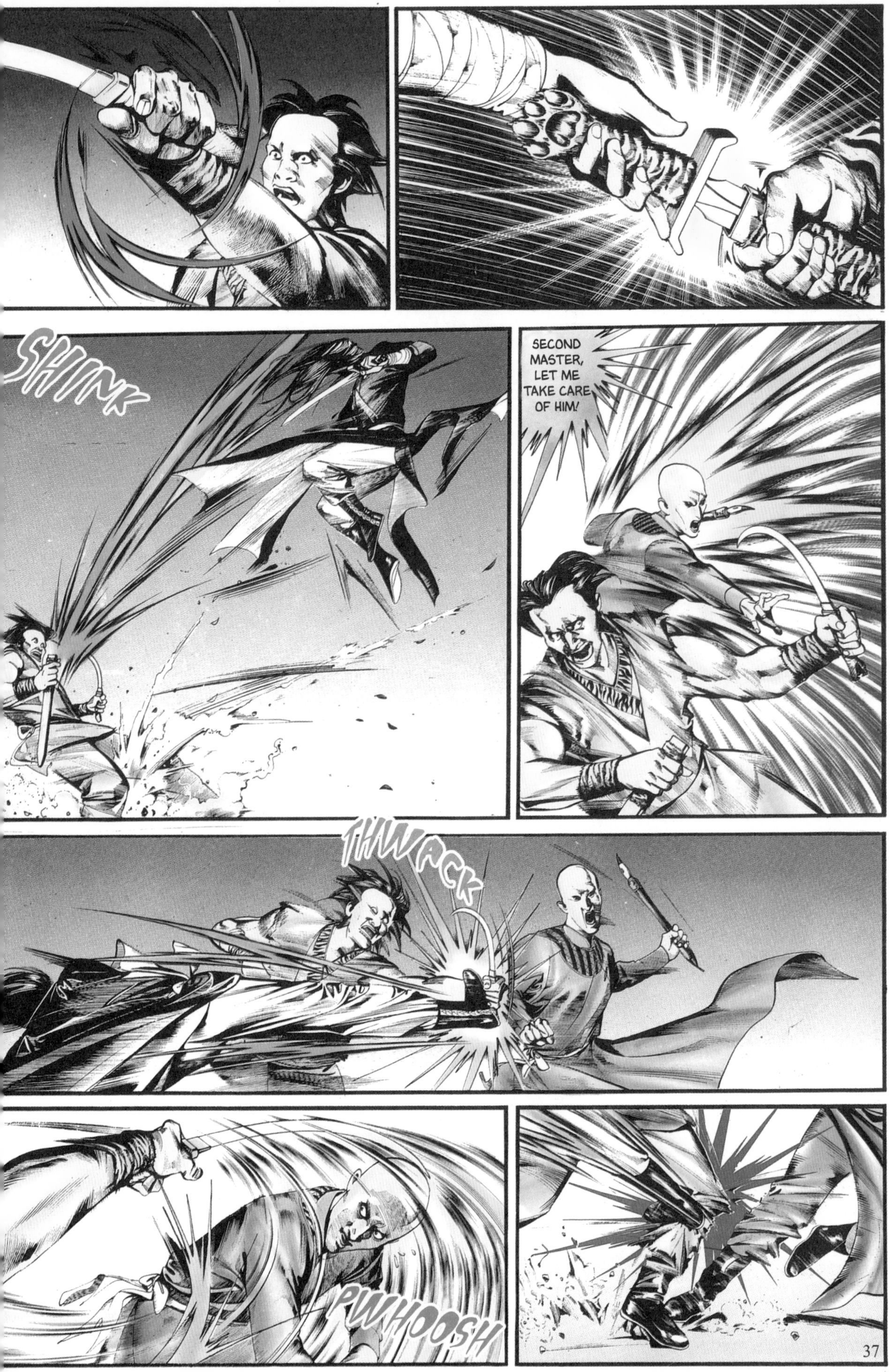
SHINK
SECOND MASTER, LET ME TAKE CARE OF HIM!
THWACK
PWHOOSH

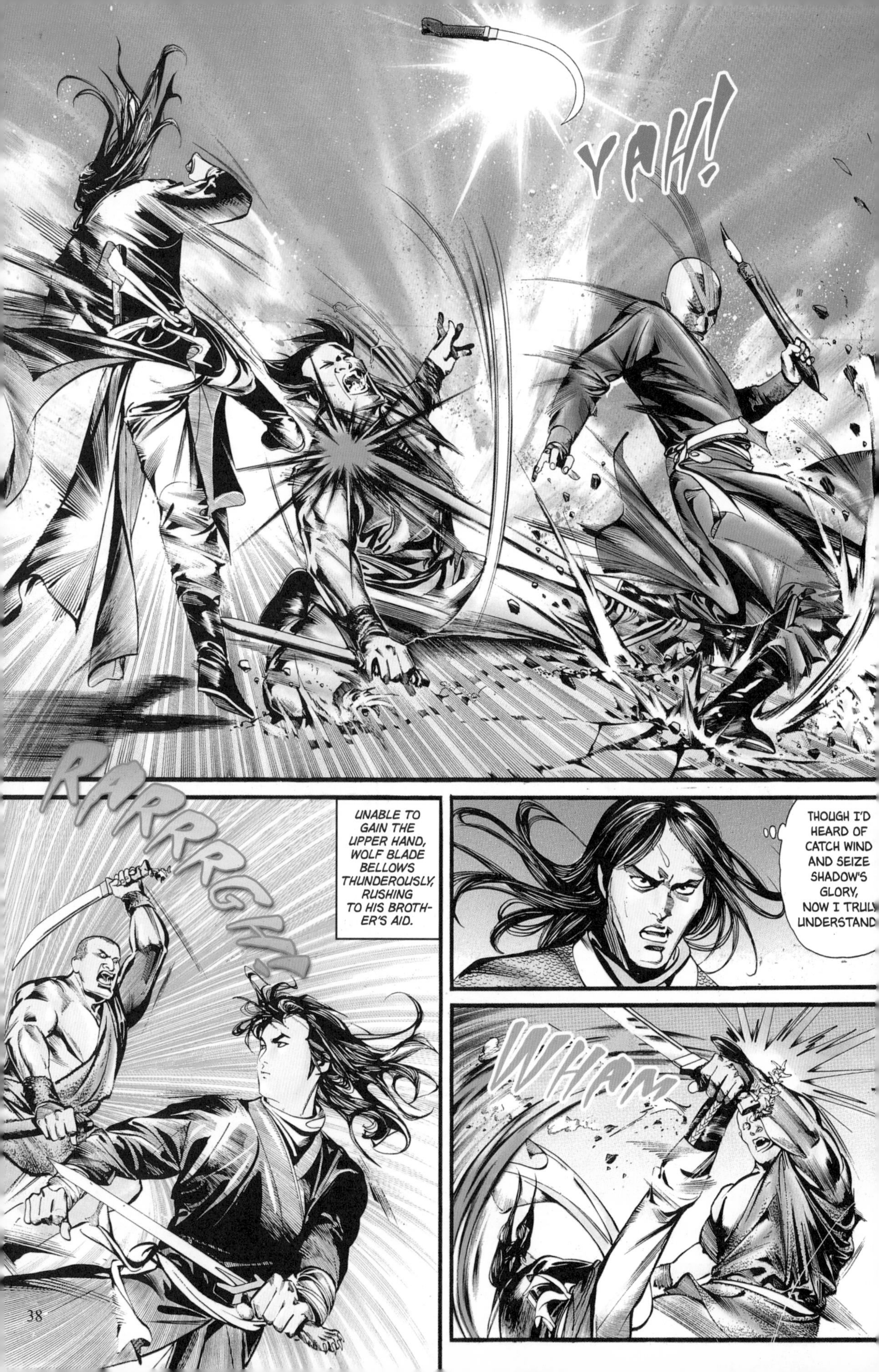
YAH!
RARRRGH!!
UNABLE TO GAIN THE UPPER HAND, WOLF BLADE BELLOWS THUNDEROUSLY, RUSHING TO HIS BROTHER'S AID.
THOUGH I'D HEARD OF CATCH WIND AND SEIZE SHADOW'S GLORY, NOW I TRULY UNDERSTAND.
WHAM

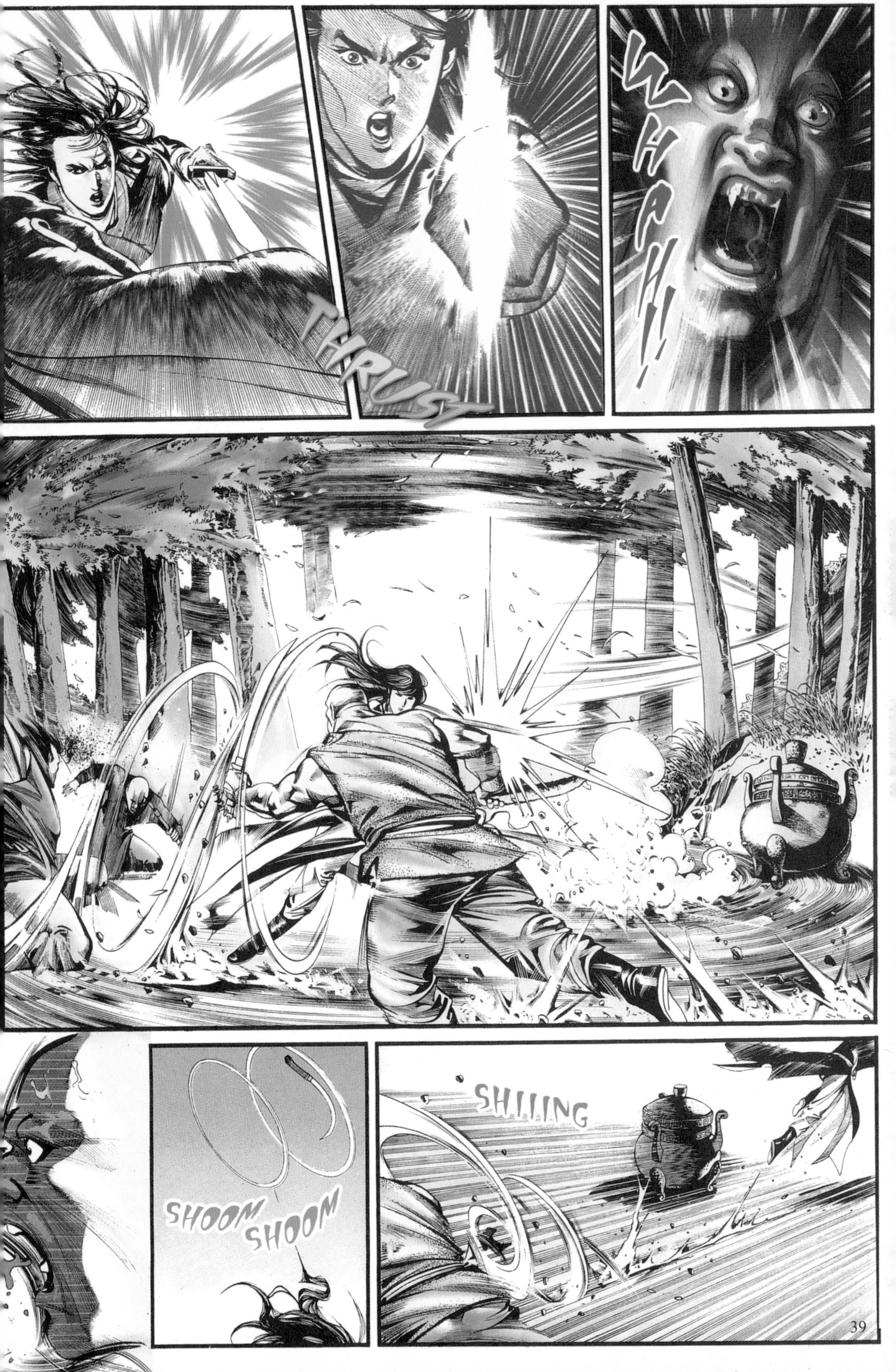
THRUST
WHAH!!
SHOOM SHOOM
SHIIING

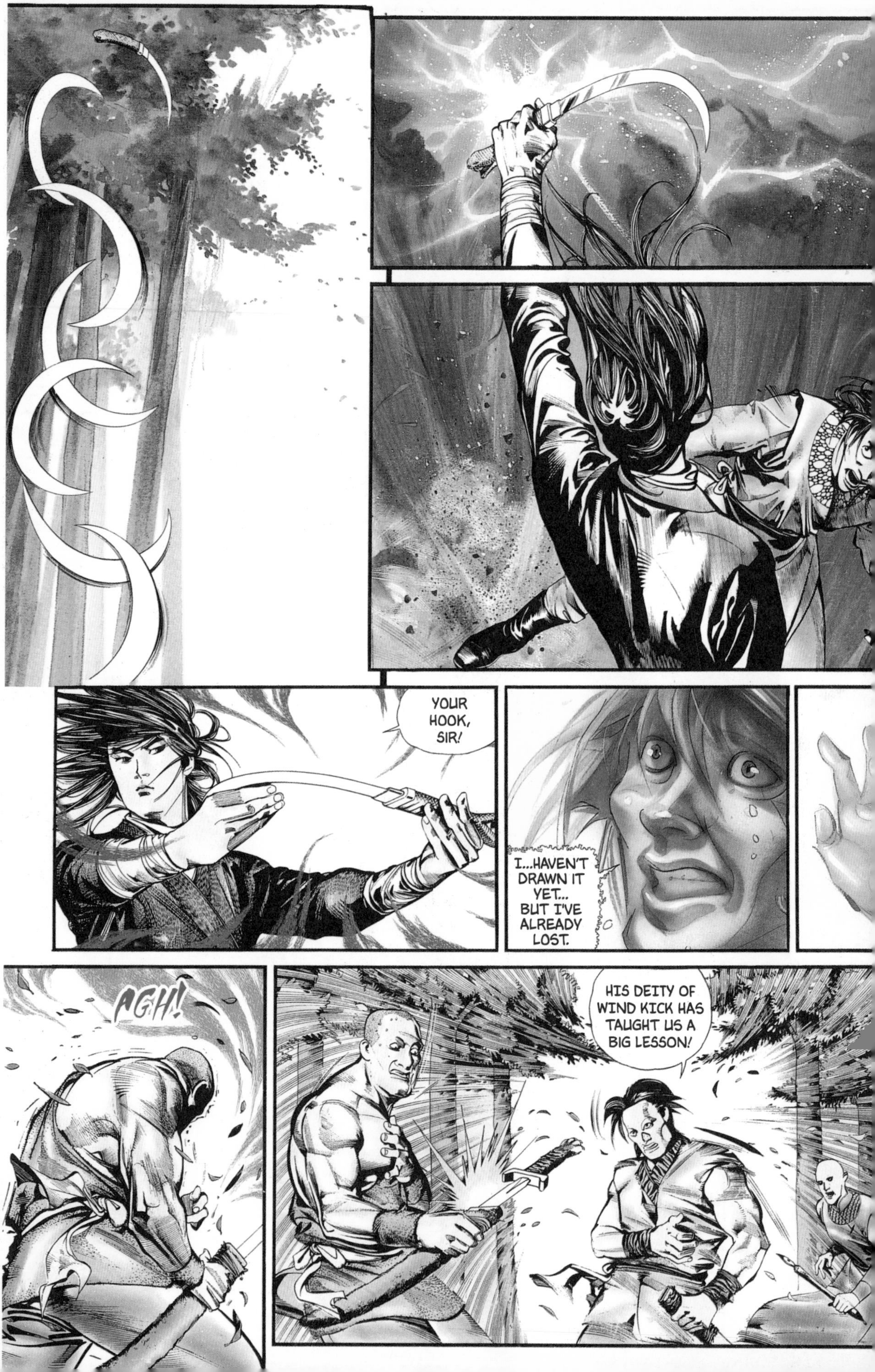
YOUR HOOK, SIR!
I...HAVEN'T DRAWN IT YET... BUT I'VE ALREADY LOST.
AGH!
HIS DEITY OF WIND KICK HAS TAUGHT US A BIG LESSON!

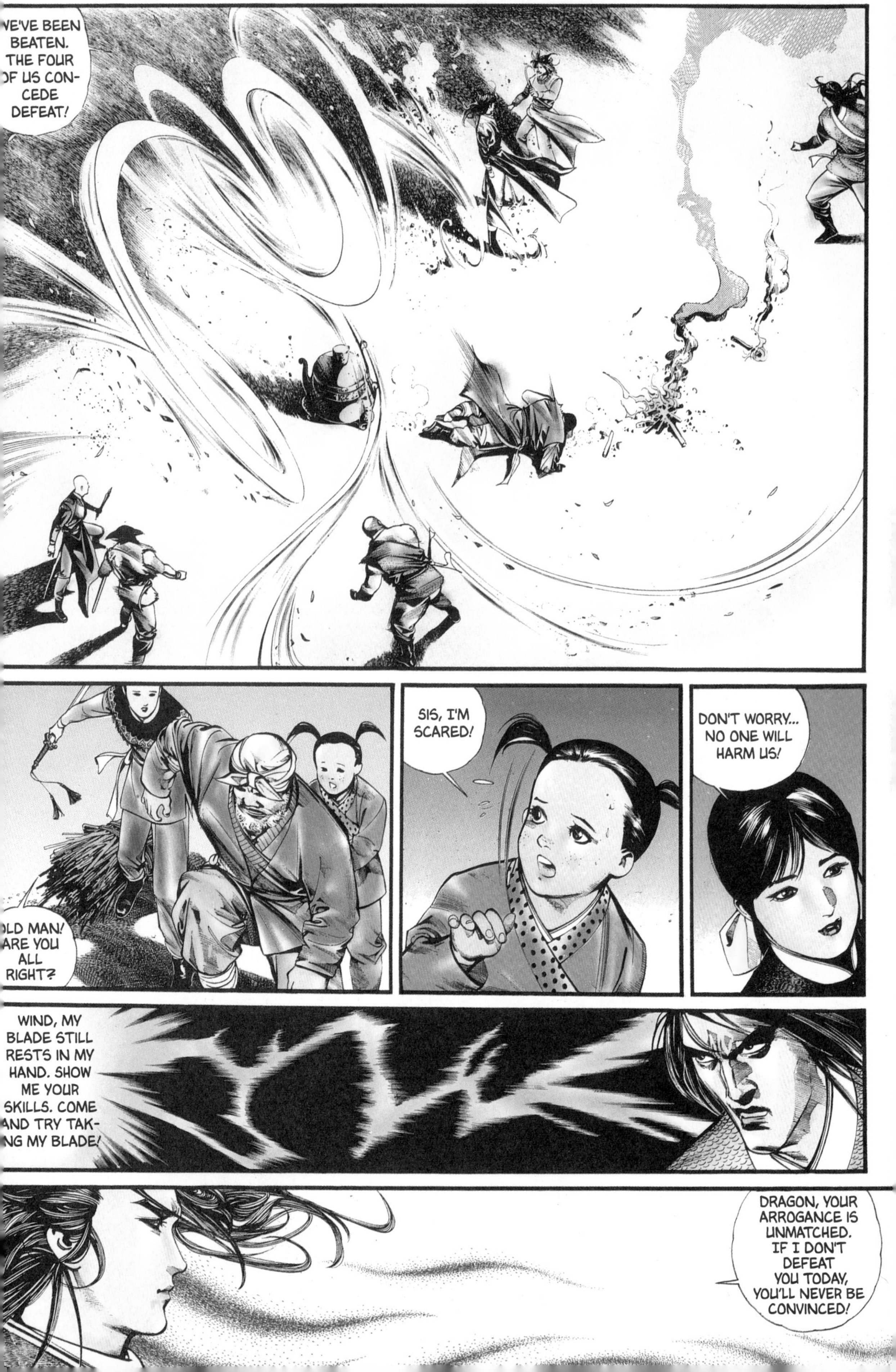
WE'VE BEEN BEATEN. THE FOUR OF US CONCEDE DEFEAT!
OLD MAN! ARE YOU ALL RIGHT?
SIS, I'M SCARED!
DON'T WORRY... NO ONE WILL HARM US!
WIND, MY BLADE STILL RESTS IN MY HAND. SHOW ME YOUR SKILLS. COME AND TRY TAKING MY BLADE!
DRAGON, YOUR ARROGANCE IS UNMATCHED. IF I DON'T DEFEAT YOU TODAY, YOU'LL NEVER BE CONVINCED!

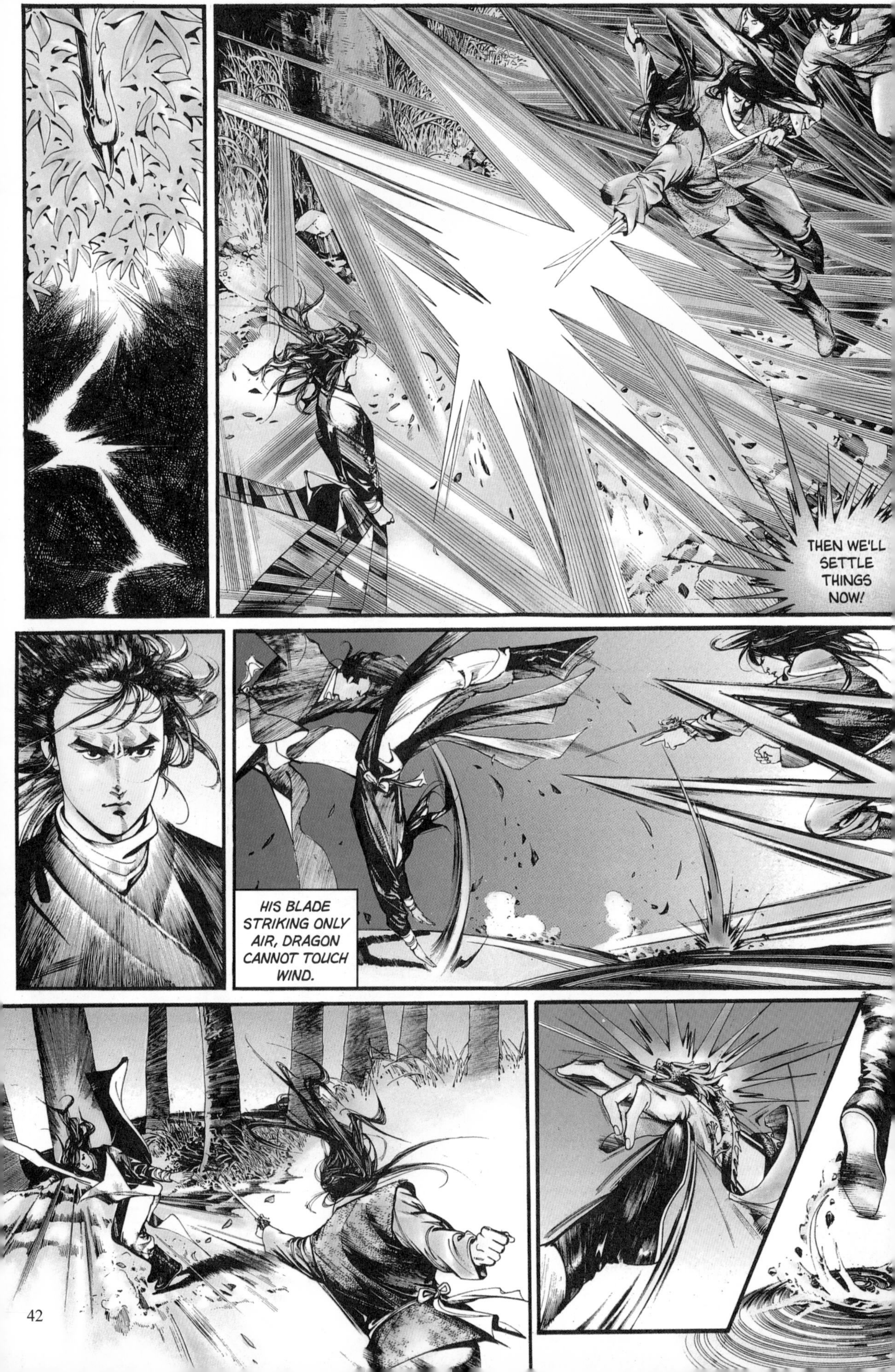
THEN WE'LL SETTLE THINGS NOW!
HIS BLADE STRIKING ONLY AIR, DRAGON CANNOT TOUCH WIND.

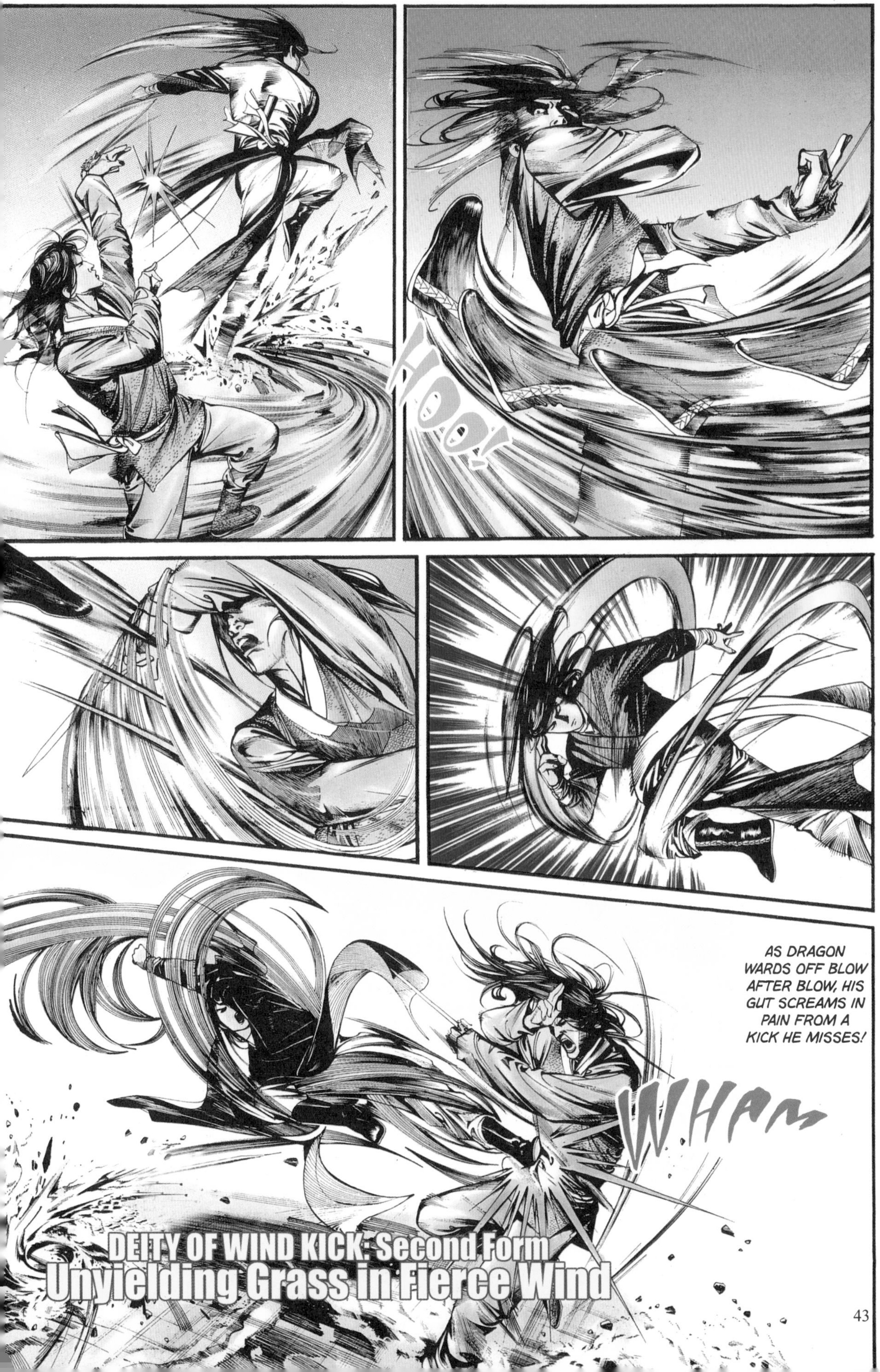
HOO!
AS DRAGON WARDS OFF BLOW AFTER BLOW, HIS GUT SCREAMS IN PAIN FROM A KICK HE MISSES!
WHAM
DEITY OF WIND KICK: Second Form
Unyielding Grass in Fierce Wind

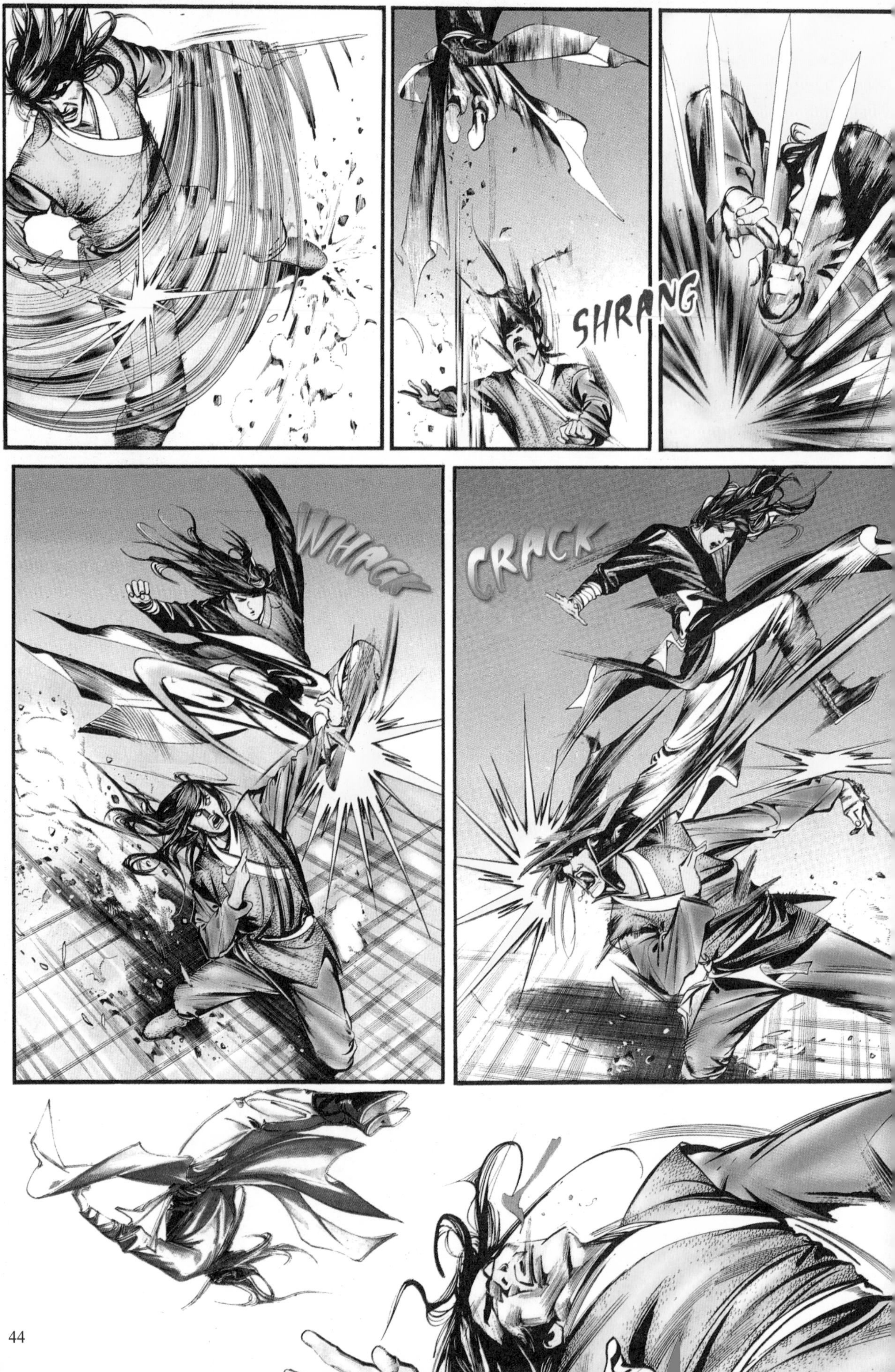
SHRANG
WHACK
CRACK

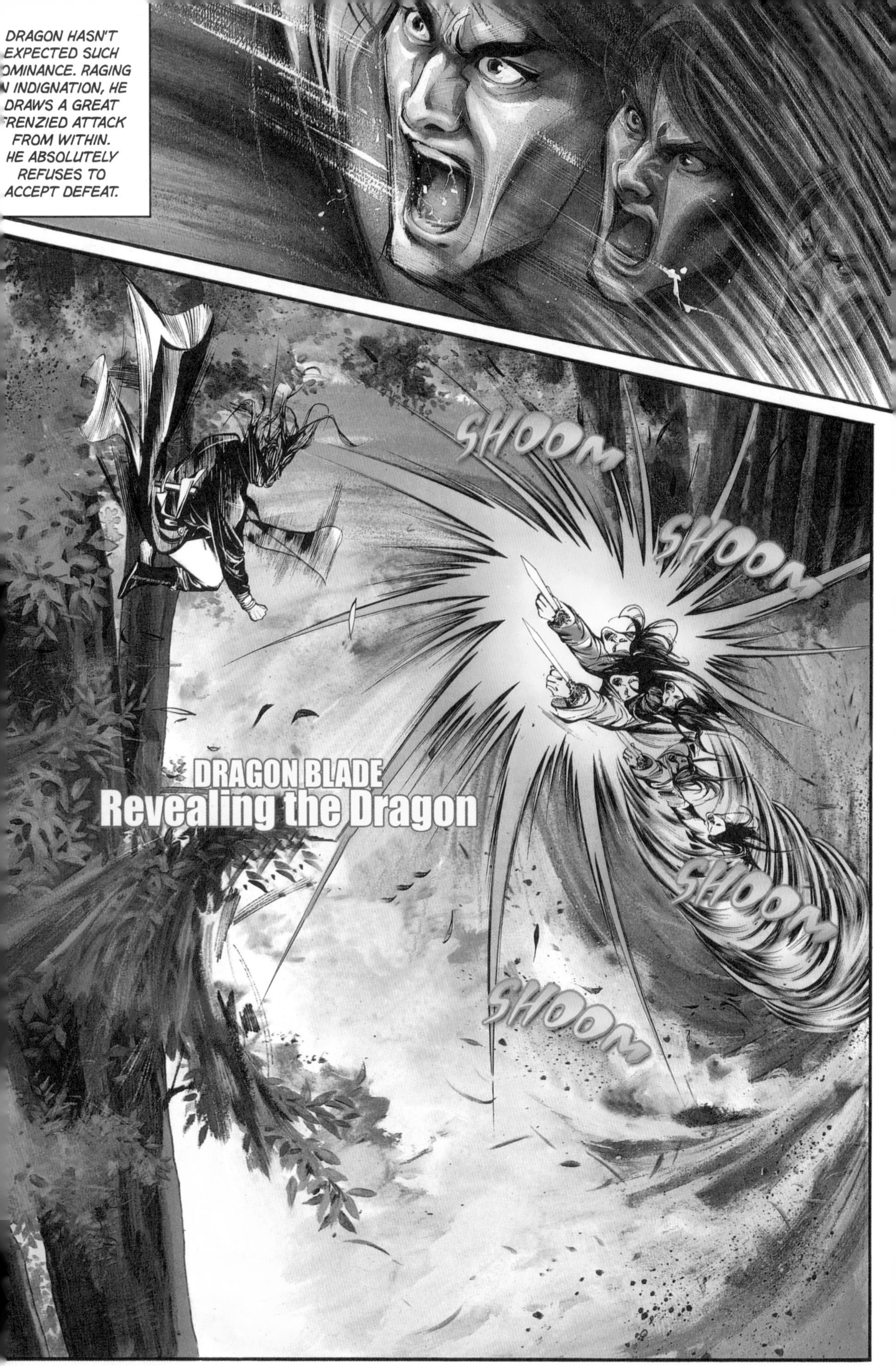
DRAGON HASN'T EXPECTED SUCH OMINANCE. RAGING N INDIGNATION, HE DRAWS A GREAT RENZIED ATTACK FROM WITHIN. HE ABSOLUTELY REFUSES TO ACCEPT DEFEAT.
SHOOM
SHOOM
DRAGON BLADE
Revealing the Dragon
SHOOM
SHOOM

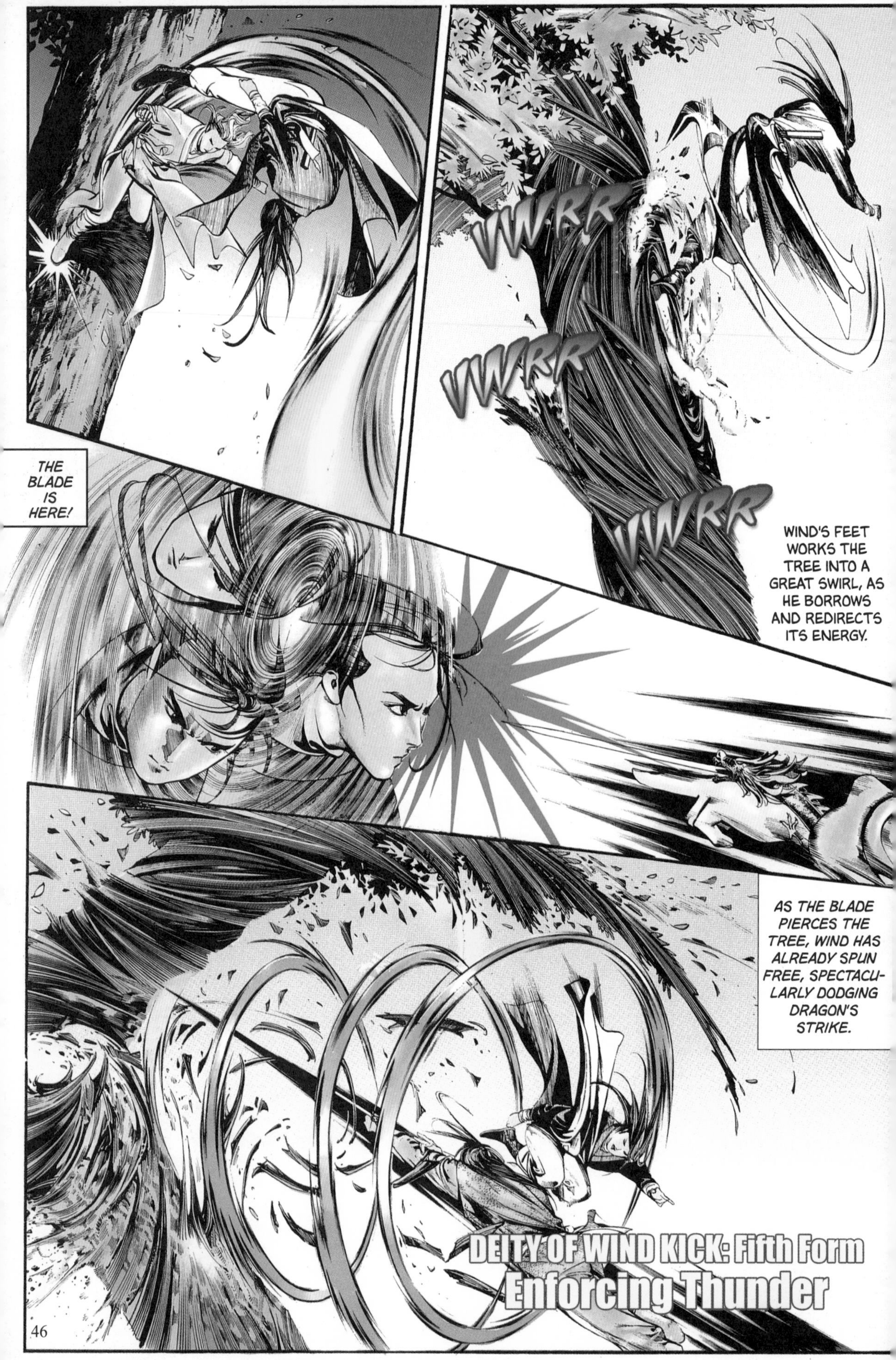
VWRR
VWRR
THE BLADE IS HERE!
VWRR
WIND'S FEET WORKS THE TREE INTO A GREAT SWIRL, AS HE BORROWS AND REDIRECTS ITS ENERGY.
AS THE BLADE PIERCES THE TREE, WIND HAS ALREADY SPUN FREE, SPECTACU-LARLY DODGING DRAGON'S STRIKE.
DEITY OF WIND KICK: Fifth Form
Enforcing Thunder

DESPITE DESPERATELY BATTLING
THE STORM IN FRONT OF HIM,
THE WOOD OVERWHELMS DRAGON
AND FORCES HIM INTO A WILD
DEFENSIVE DANCE.

ENEMY PREOC-
CUPIED WITH RAGE,
HE QUICKLY CAPI-
TALIZES, BELTING
HIM HARD
IN THE SIDE.

OOOF!

WWSHHH!

AS THE FIGHTING
INTENSIFIES,
A PHOENIX ARROW,
LONG IN WAITING,
ABRUPTLY SHOOTS OUT!

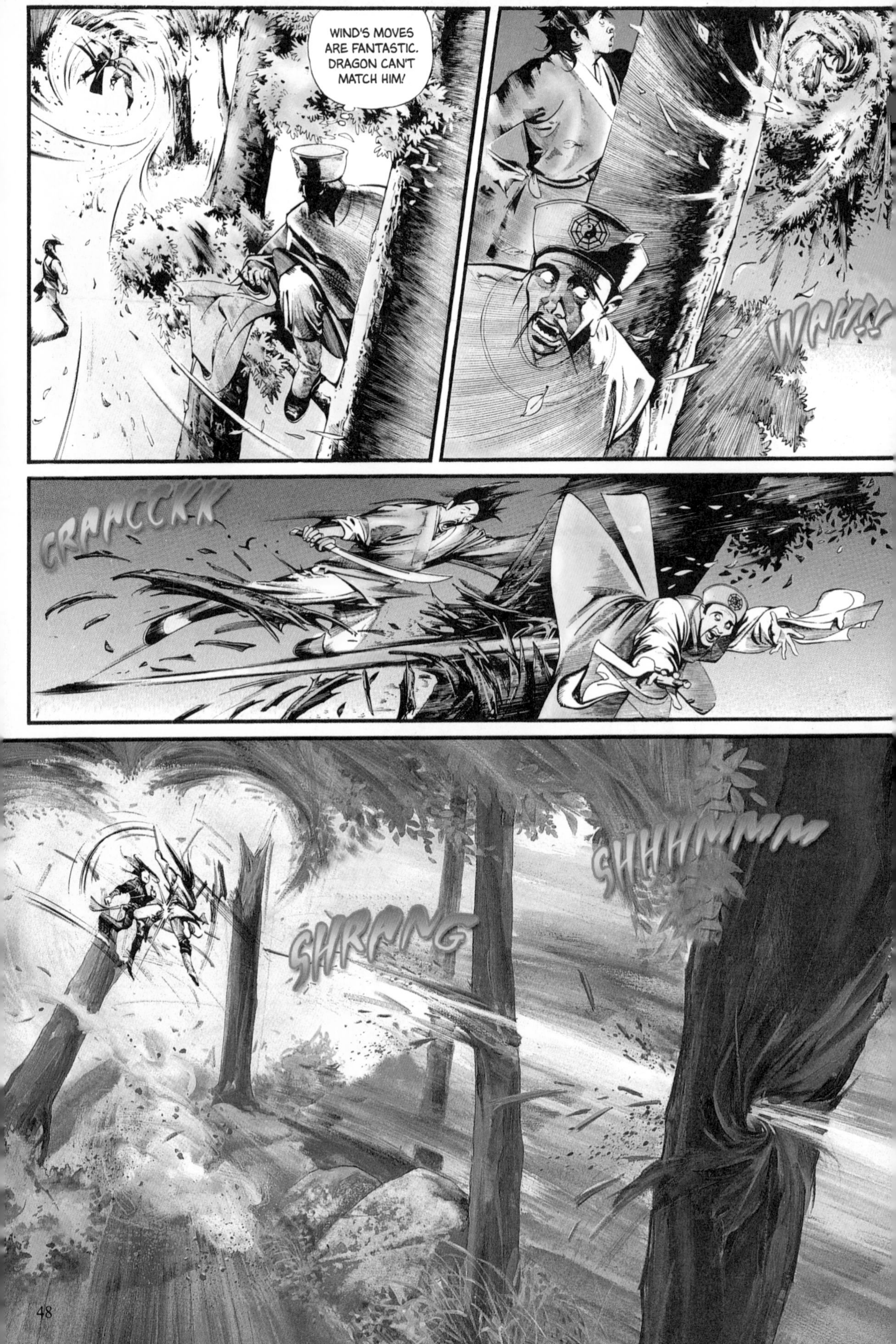
WIND'S MOVES ARE FANTASTIC. DRAGON CAN'T MATCH HIM!
CRAACCKK
SHHHMMM
SHRANG

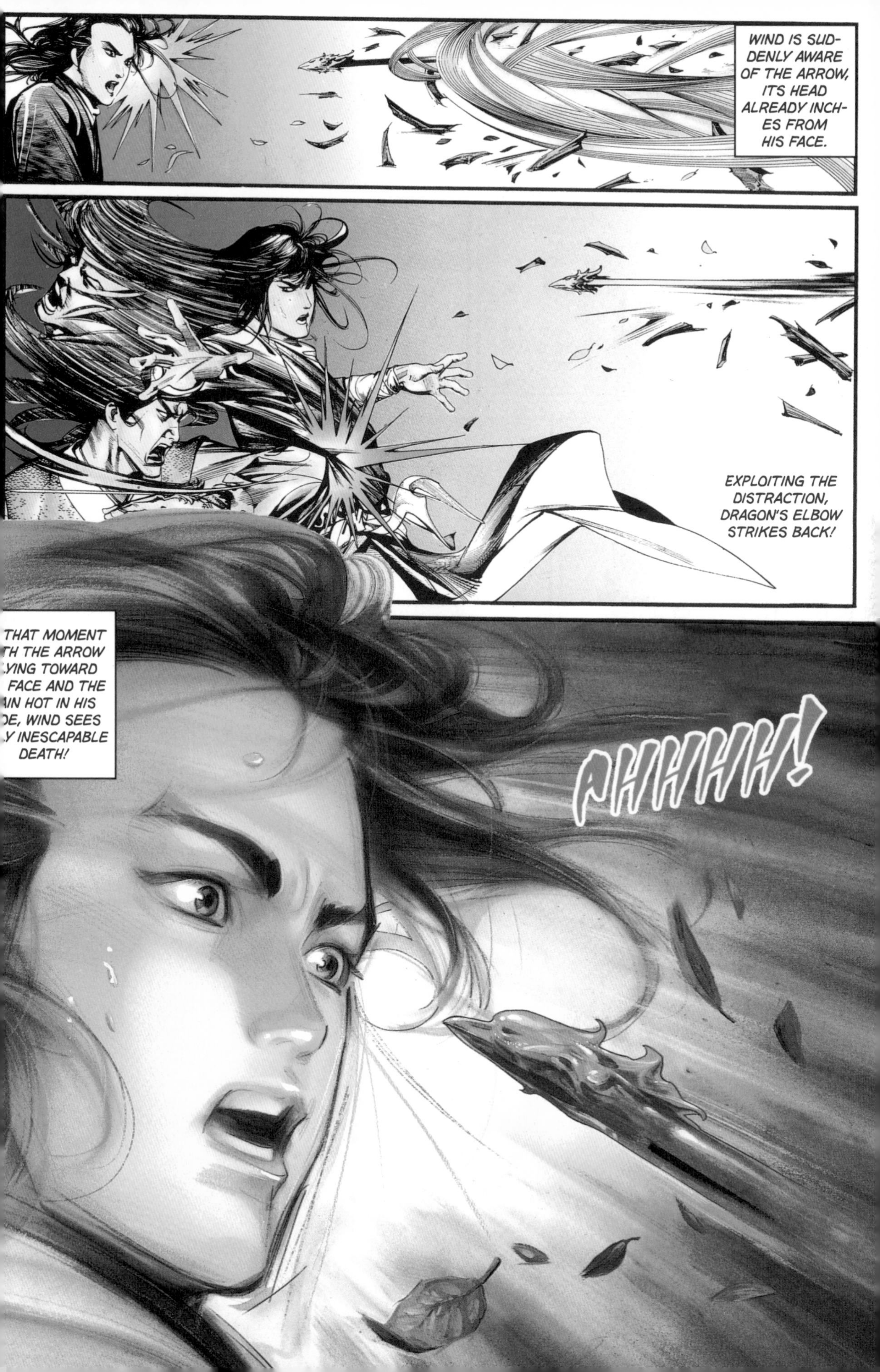
WIND IS SUDDENLY AWARE OF THE ARROW, ITS HEAD ALREADY INCHES FROM HIS FACE.
EXPLOITING THE DISTRACTION, DRAGON'S ELBOW STRIKES BACK!
THAT MOMENT
TH THE ARROW
YING TOWARD
FACE AND THE
AIN HOT IN HIS
DE, WIND SEES
Y INESCAPABLE
DEATH!
AHHHHH!

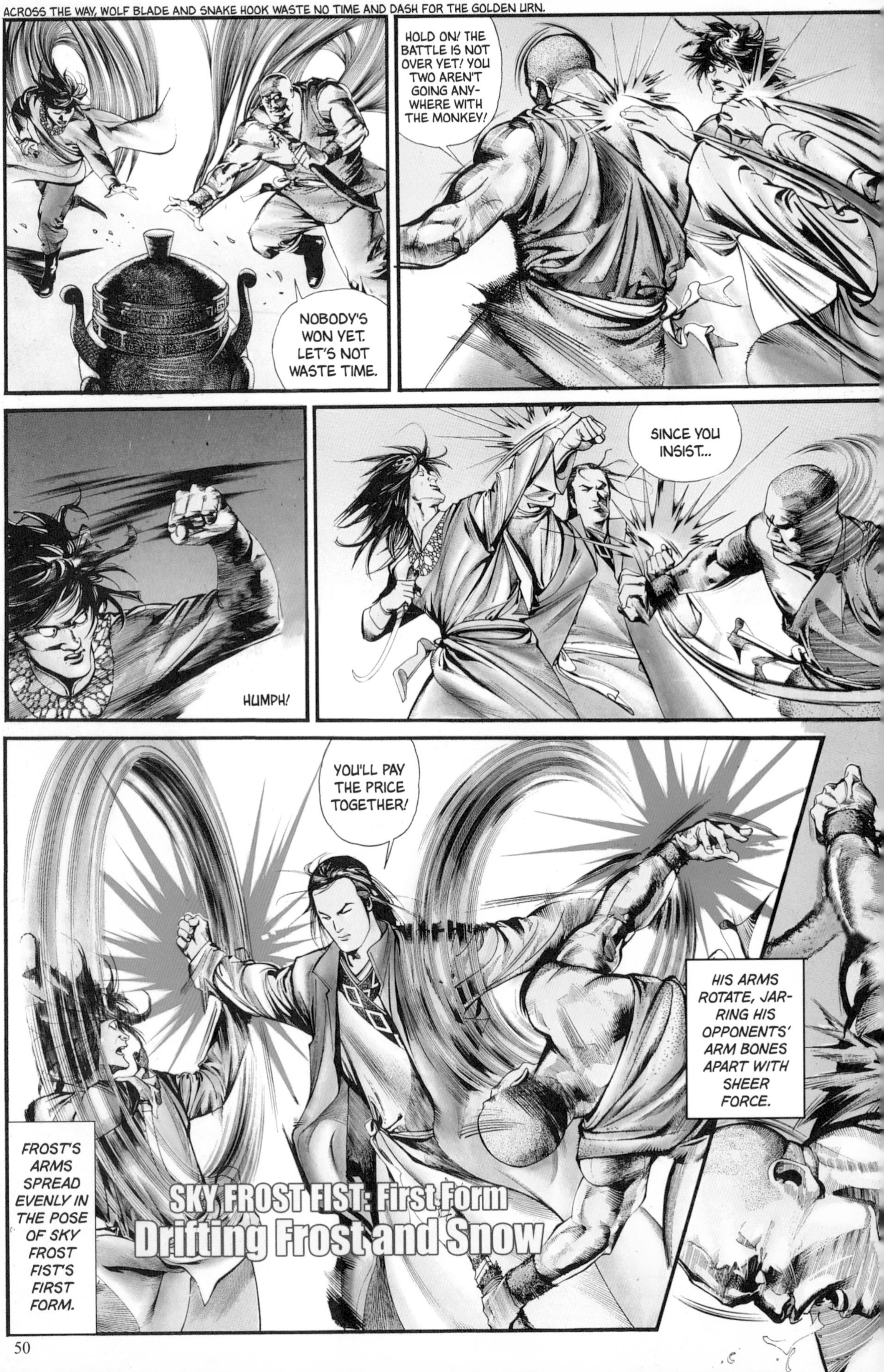
ACROSS THE WAY, WOLF BLADE AND SNAKE HOOK WASTE NO TIME AND DASH FOR THE GOLDEN URN.
NOBODY'S WON YET. LET'S NOT WASTE TIME.
HOLD ON! THE BATTLE IS NOT OVER YET! YOU TWO AREN'T GOING ANYWHERE WITH THE MONKEY!
HUMPH!
SINCE YOU INSIST...
YOU'LL PAY THE PRICE TOGETHER!
HIS ARMS ROTATE, JARRING HIS OPPONENTS' ARM BONES APART WITH SHEER FORCE.
FROST'S ARMS SPREAD EVENLY IN THE POSE OF SKY FROST FIST'S FIRST FORM.
SKY FROST FIST: First Form
Drifting Frost and Snow

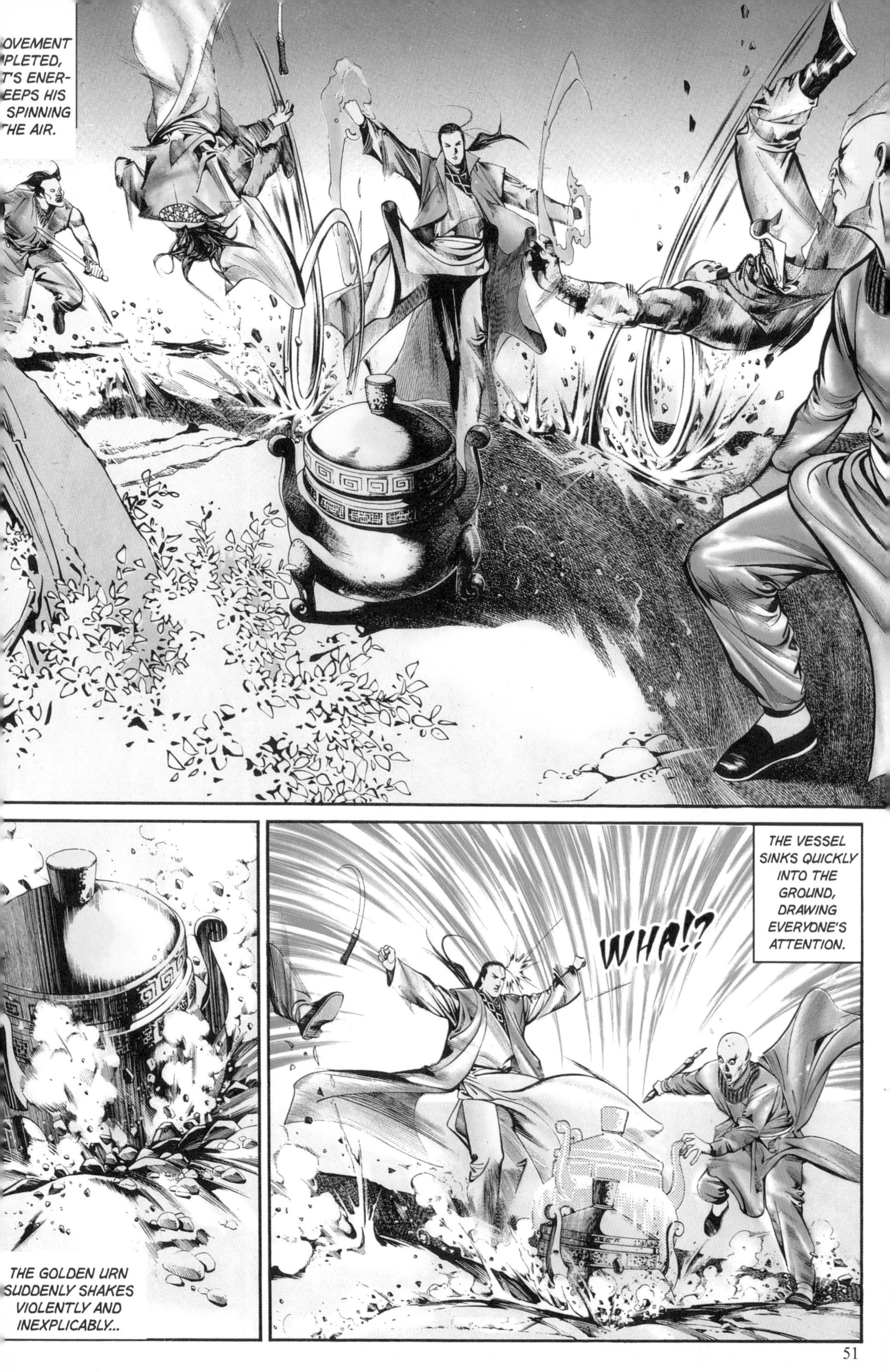
OVEMENT PLETED, T'S ENER- EEPS HIS SPINNING HE AIR.
THE GOLDEN URN SUDDENLY SHAKES VIOLENTLY AND INEXPLICABLY...
THE VESSEL SINKS QUICKLY INTO THE GROUND, DRAWING EVERYONE'S ATTENTION.
WHA!?

MEANWHILE, AT THE FOOT OF TIEN MOUNTAIN, A TORRENTIAL RIVER BECOMES A MAJESTIC, CASCADING WATERFALL.

FWOOSH

IMMERSED IN THE STRONGEST SECTION OF THE DOWNPOUR, WHERE THE WATER STRIKES LIKE A GREAT HAMMER, HE IS UNMOVED BY THE FORCE UPON HIM.

RESTING, BENT ON ALL FOURS IN THE FIERCE FLOW IS A FIGURE WHO BEARS THE OVERWHELMING STRENGTH OF THE WATERFALL.

52

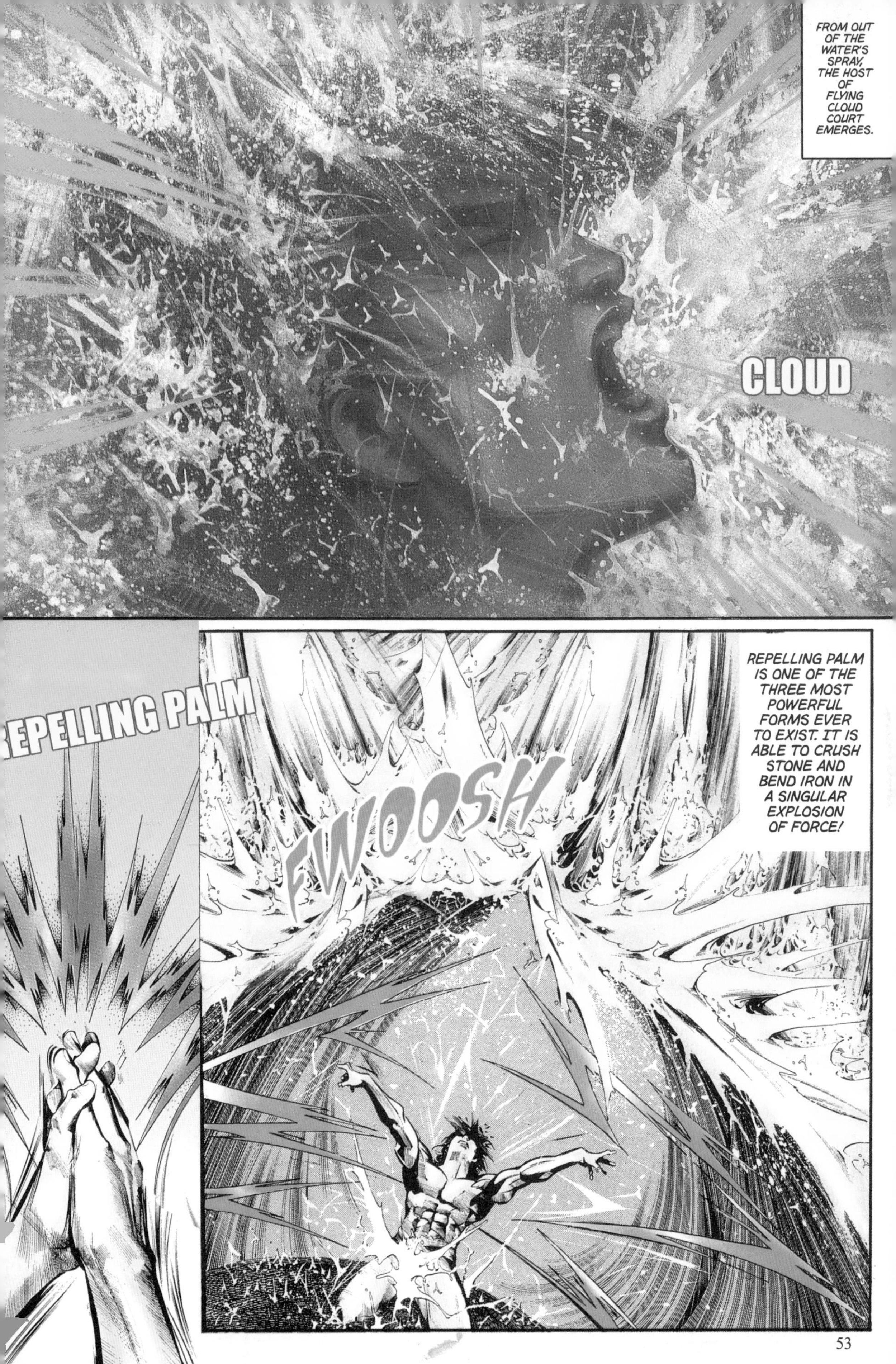
FROM OUT OF THE WATER'S SPRAY, THE HOST OF FLYING CLOUD COURT EMERGES.
CLOUD
REPELLING PALM IS ONE OF THE THREE MOST POWERFUL FORMS EVER TO EXIST. IT IS ABLE TO CRUSH STONE AND BEND IRON IN A SINGULAR EXPLOSION OF FORCE!
FWOOSH
EPELLING PALM

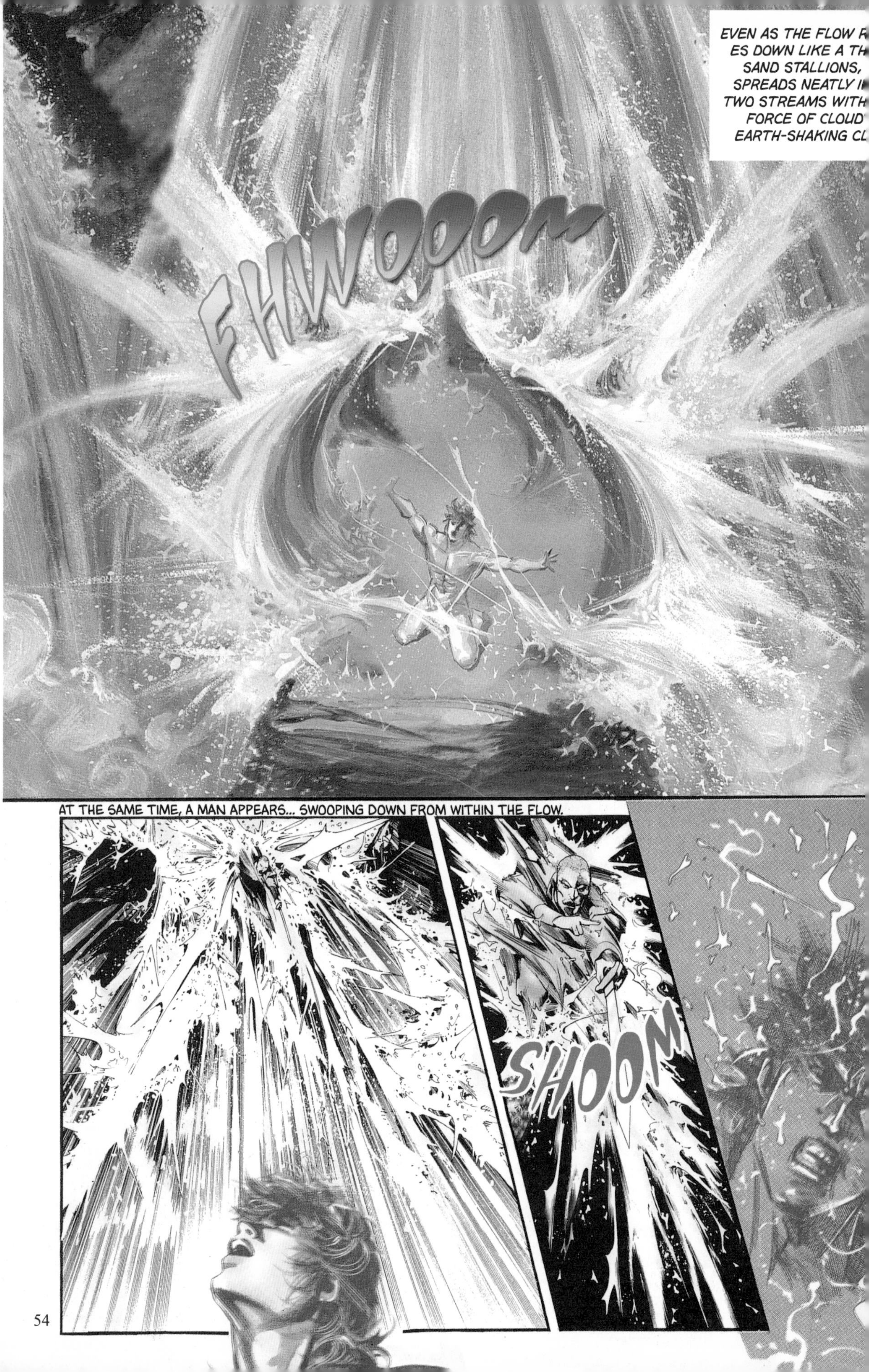
EVEN AS THE FLOW R
ES DOWN LIKE A TH
SAND STALLIONS,
SPREADS NEATLY I
TWO STREAMS WITH
FORCE OF CLOUD
EARTH-SHAKING CL
FHWOOOM
AT THE SAME TIME, A MAN APPEARS... SWOOPING DOWN FROM WITHIN THE FLOW.
SHOOM

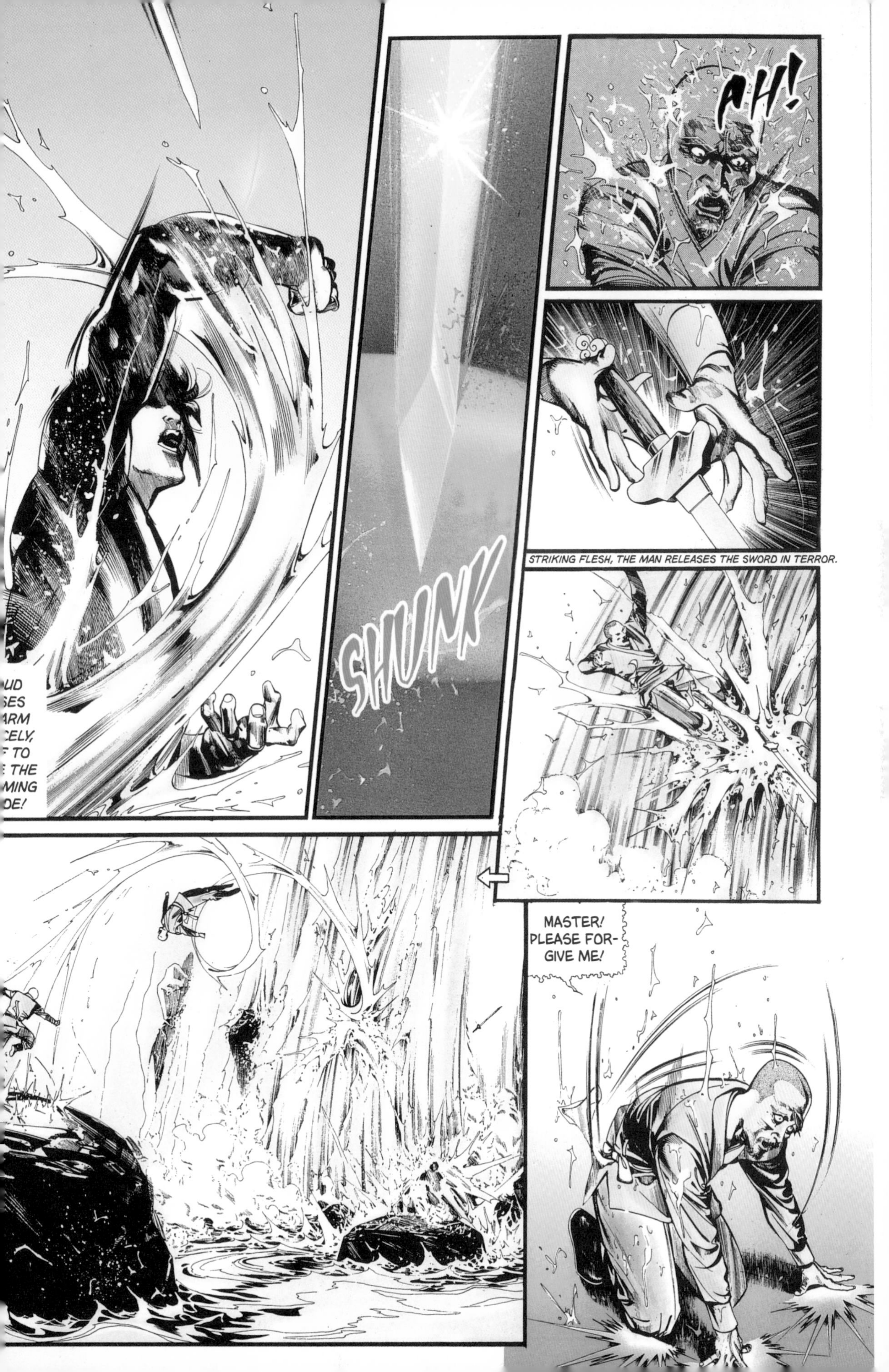
UD
SES
ARM
CELY,
F TO
E THE
MING
DE!
SHUNK
AH!
STRIKING FLESH, THE MAN RELEASES THE SWORD IN TERROR.
MASTER! PLEASE FOR-GIVE ME!

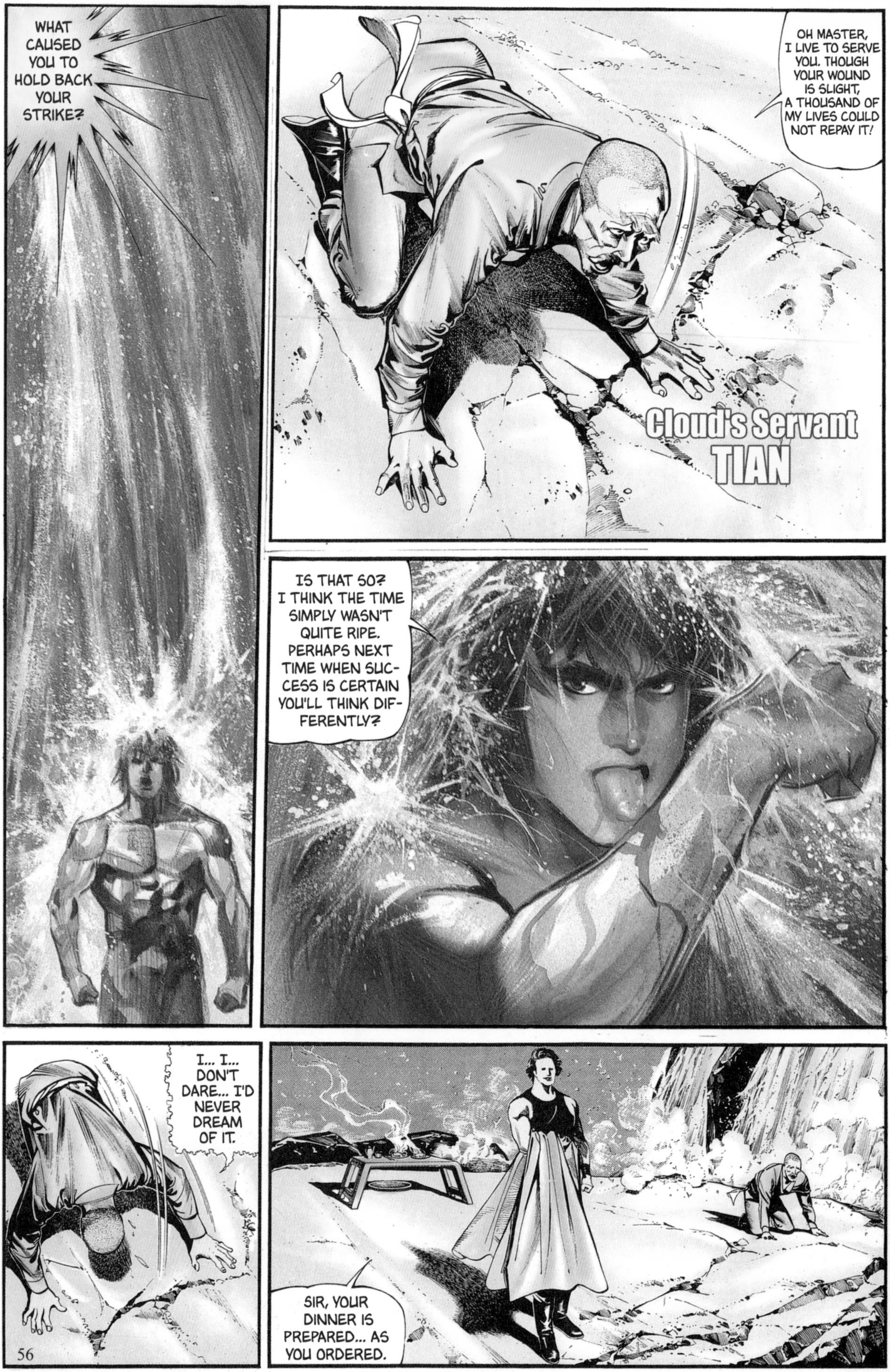
WHAT CAUSED YOU TO HOLD BACK YOUR STRIKE?
OH MASTER, I LIVE TO SERVE YOU. THOUGH YOUR WOUND IS SLIGHT, A THOUSAND OF MY LIVES COULD NOT REPAY IT!
Cloud's Servant
TIAN
IS THAT SO? I THINK THE TIME SIMPLY WASN'T QUITE RIPE. PERHAPS NEXT TIME WHEN SUCCESS IS CERTAIN YOU'LL THINK DIFFERENTLY?
I... I... DON'T DARE... I'D NEVER DREAM OF IT.
SIR, YOUR DINNER IS PREPARED... AS YOU ORDERED.

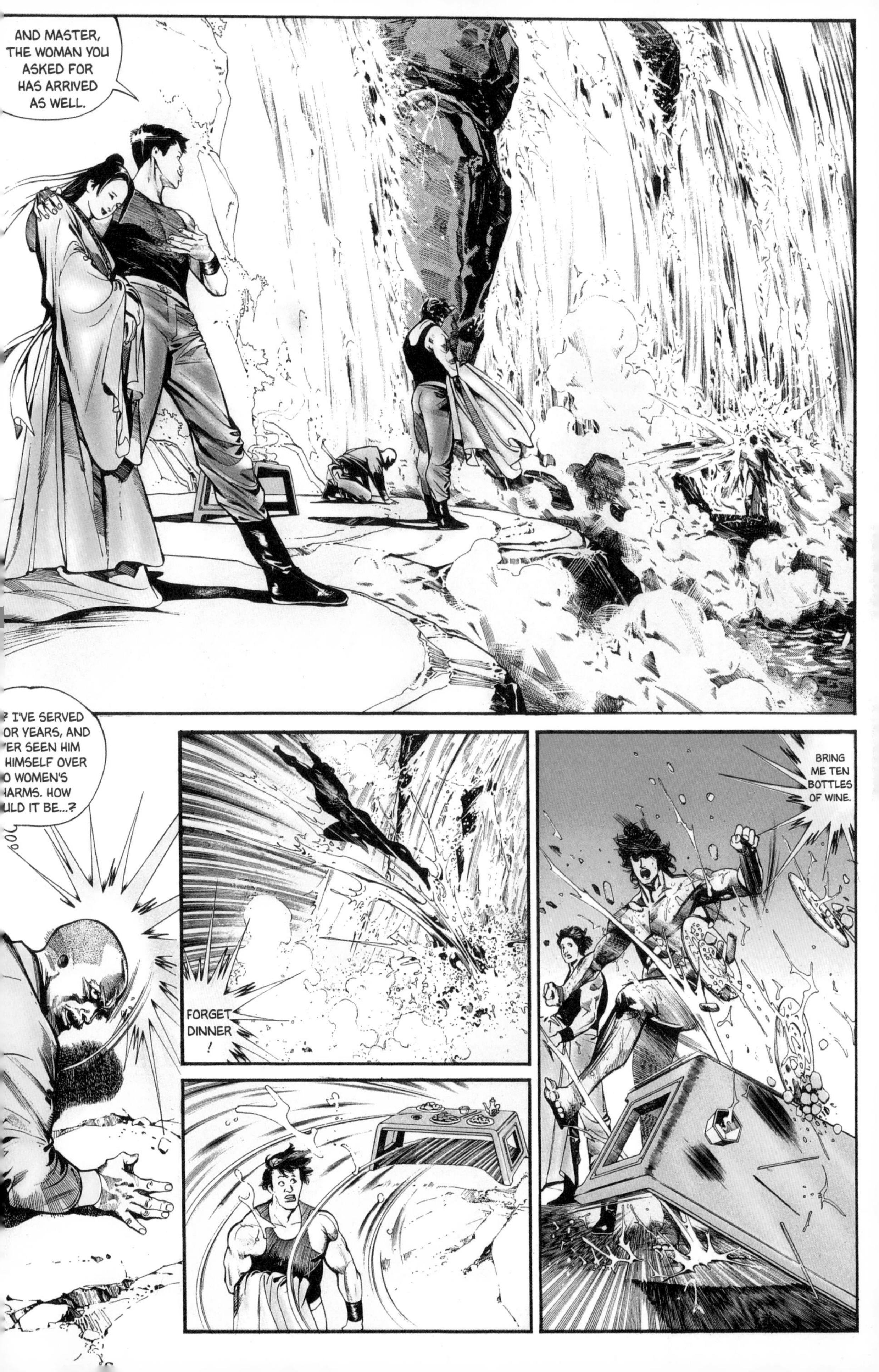
AND MASTER, THE WOMAN YOU ASKED FOR HAS ARRIVED AS WELL.
I'VE SERVED OR YEARS, AND 'ER SEEN HIM HIMSELF OVER O WOMEN'S HARMS. HOW ULD IT BE...?
FORGET DINNER!
BRING ME TEN BOTTLES OF WINE.

AS YOU WISH, MASTER. CALM DOWN, I BEG YOU.

HMPH!

AH, GORGEOUS INDEED!

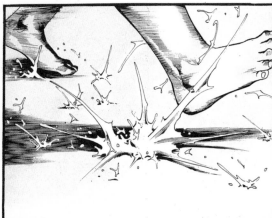

SIR, HER NAME IS YEE. SHE'LL DO EVERYTHING YOU COMMAND.

YES, HUMBLY, MASTER.

FINE THEN, TAKE OF YOUR CLOTHE

58

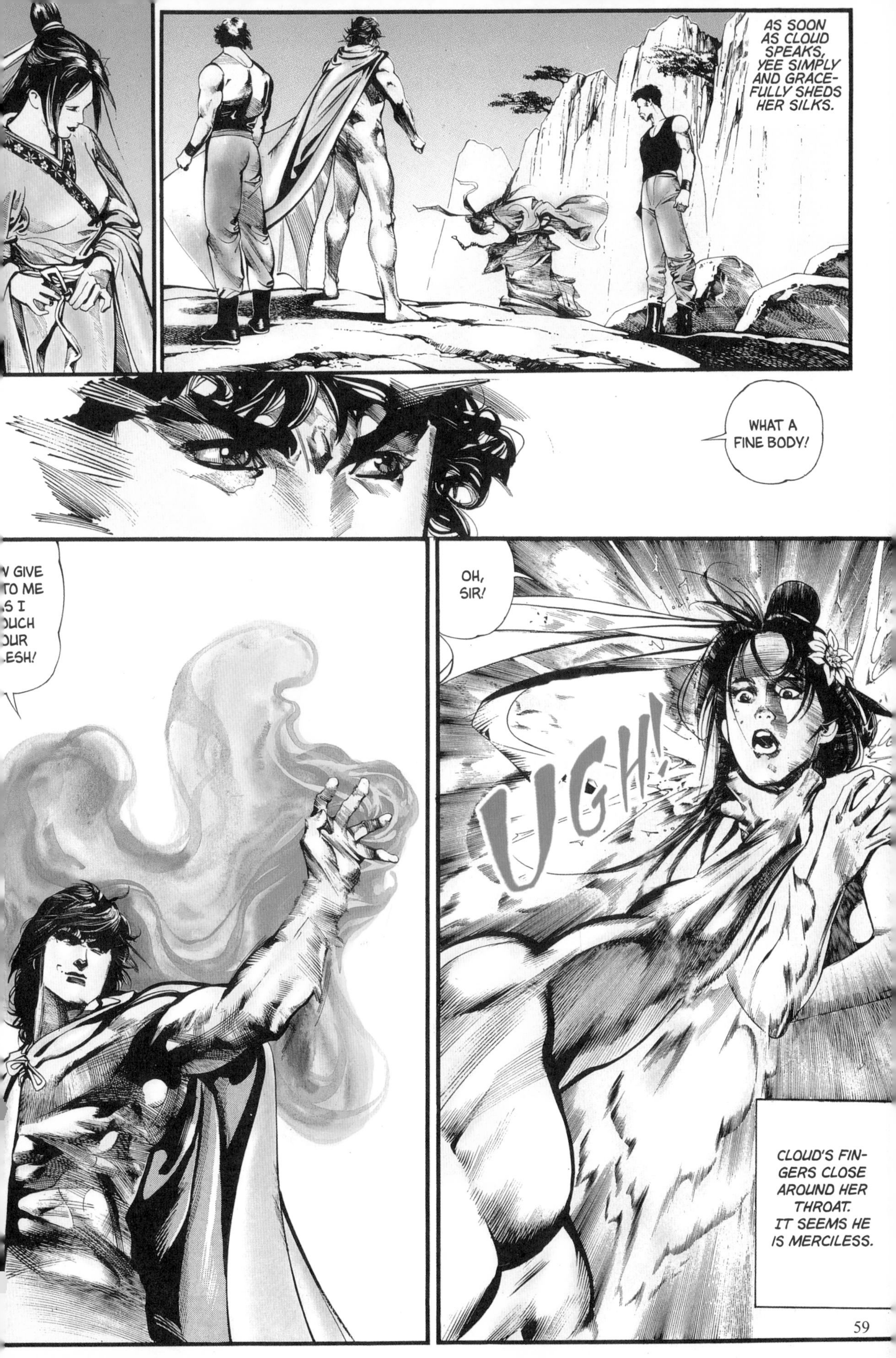
AS SOON AS CLOUD SPEAKS, YEE SIMPLY AND GRACE-FULLY SHEDS HER SILKS.
WHAT A FINE BODY!
V GIVE TO ME S I OUCH OUR ESH!
OH, SIR!
UGH!
CLOUD'S FIN-GERS CLOSE AROUND HER THROAT. IT SEEMS HE IS MERCILESS.

Chapter 7: Dragon Kick

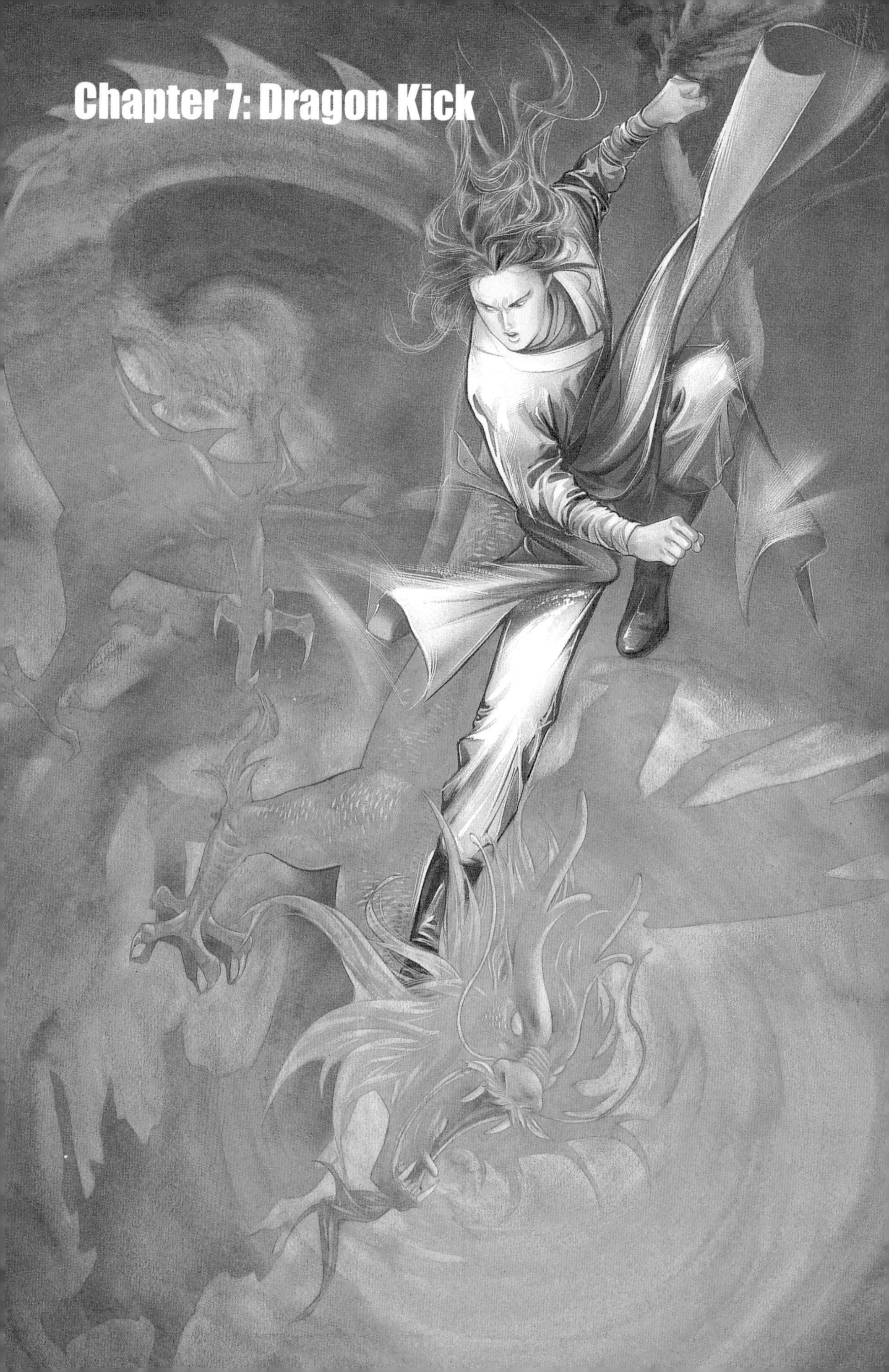

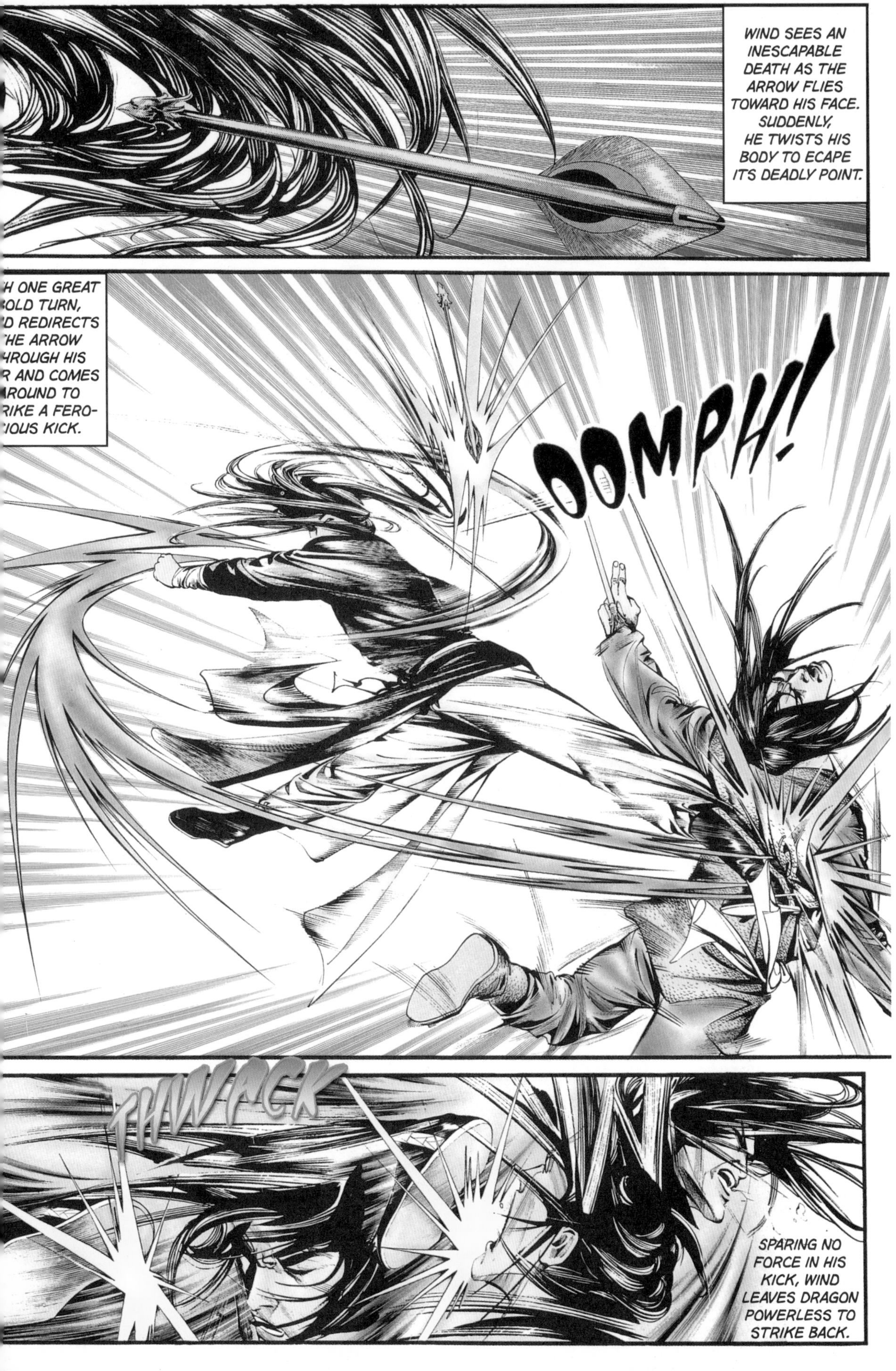
WIND SEES AN INESCAPABLE DEATH AS THE ARROW FLIES TOWARD HIS FACE. SUDDENLY, HE TWISTS HIS BODY TO ECAPE ITS DEADLY POINT.
H ONE GREAT OLD TURN, D REDIRECTS THE ARROW HROUGH HIS R AND COMES AROUND TO RIKE A FERO- CIOUS KICK.
OOMPH!
THWACK
SPARING NO FORCE IN HIS KICK, WIND LEAVES DRAGON POWERLESS TO STRIKE BACK.

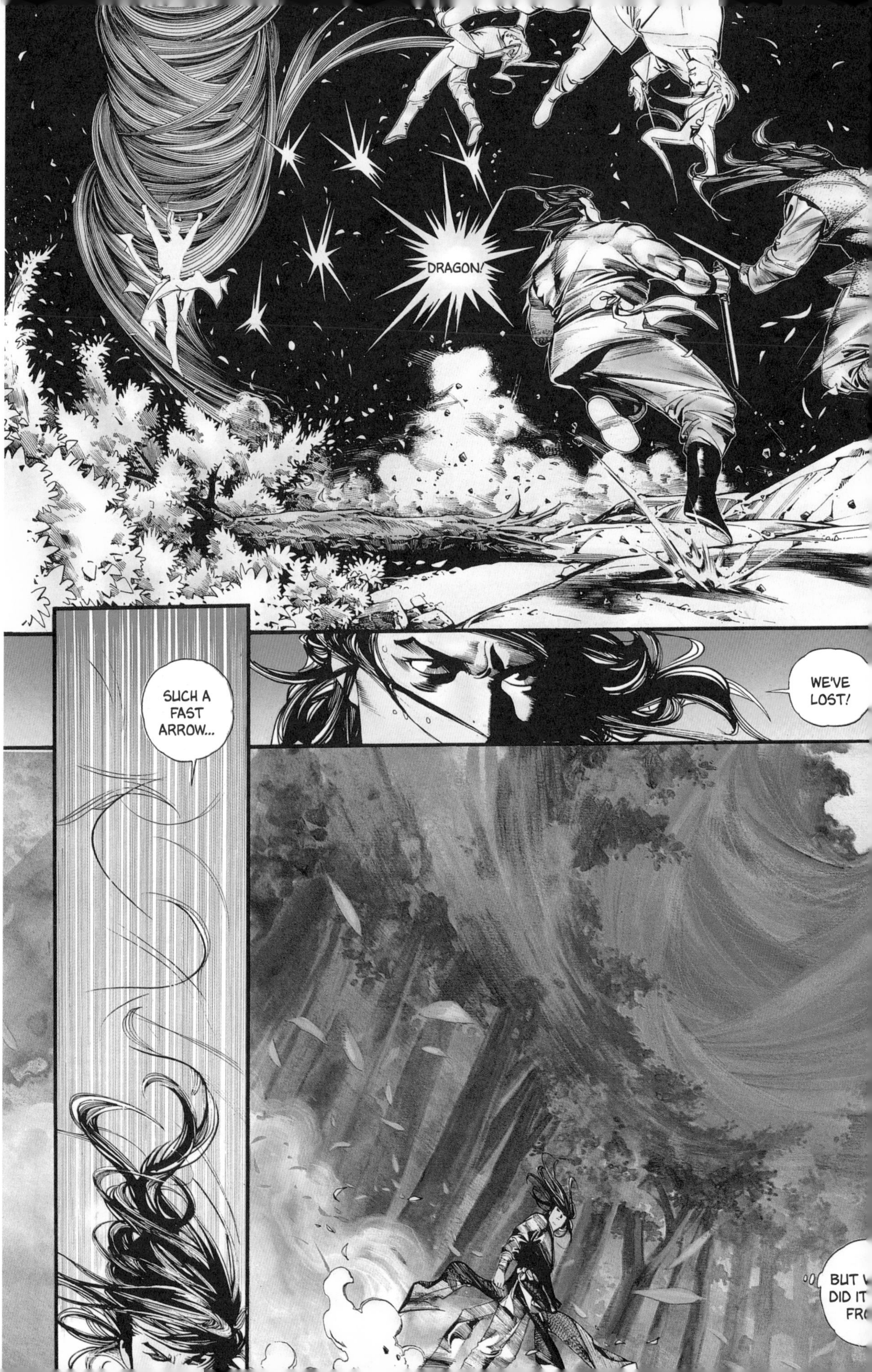

DRAGON!
WE'VE LOST!
SUCH A FAST ARROW...
BUT
DID IT
FR

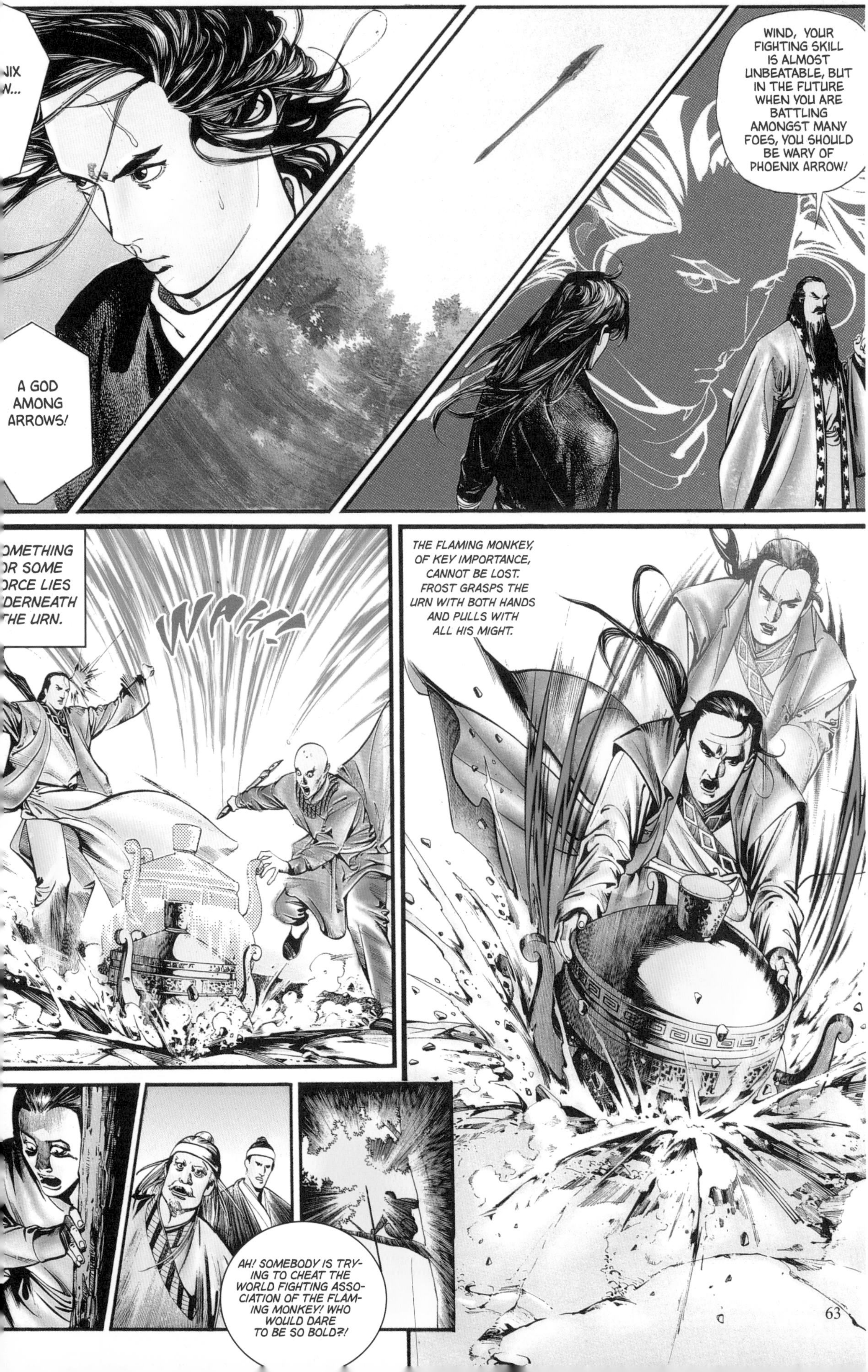

...NIX
...W...
A GOD AMONG ARROWS!
WIND, YOUR FIGHTING SKILL IS ALMOST UNBEATABLE, BUT IN THE FUTURE WHEN YOU ARE BATTLING AMONGST MANY FOES, YOU SHOULD BE WARY OF PHOENIX ARROW!
...OMETHING ...OR SOME ...ORCE LIES ...DERNEATH THE URN.
WAH!
THE FLAMING MONKEY, OF KEY IMPORTANCE, CANNOT BE LOST. FROST GRASPS THE URN WITH BOTH HANDS AND PULLS WITH ALL HIS MIGHT.
AH! SOMEBODY IS TRYING TO CHEAT THE WORLD FIGHTING ASSOCIATION OF THE FLAMING MONKEY! WHO WOULD DARE TO BE SO BOLD?!

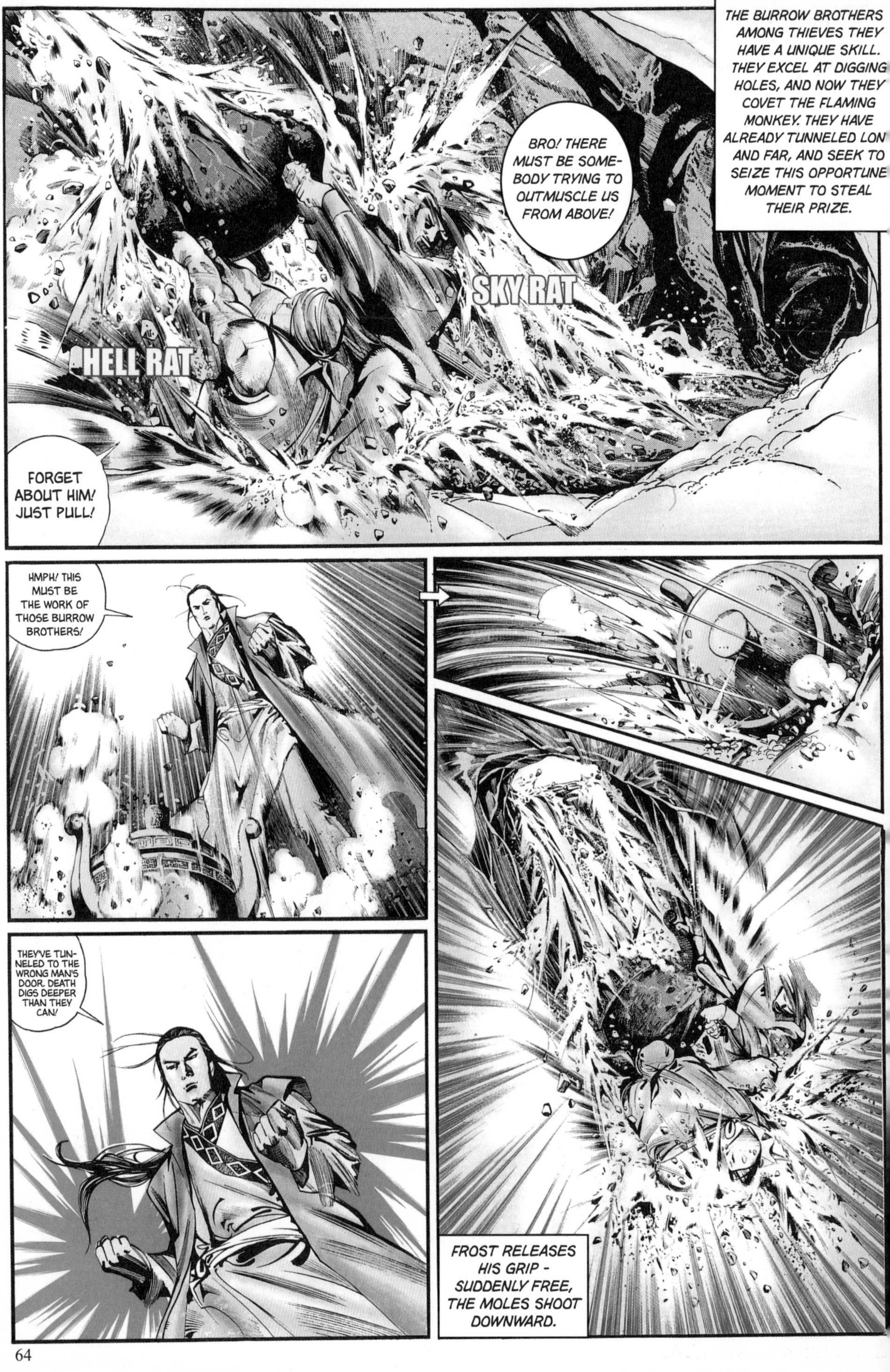
THE BURROW BROTHERS AMONG THIEVES THEY HAVE A UNIQUE SKILL. THEY EXCEL AT DIGGING HOLES, AND NOW THEY COVET THE FLAMING MONKEY. THEY HAVE ALREADY TUNNELED LON AND FAR, AND SEEK TO SEIZE THIS OPPORTUNE MOMENT TO STEAL THEIR PRIZE.
BRO! THERE MUST BE SOMEBODY TRYING TO OUTMUSCLE US FROM ABOVE!
SKY RAT
HELL RAT
FORGET ABOUT HIM! JUST PULL!
HMPH! THIS MUST BE THE WORK OF THOSE BURROW BROTHERS!
THEY'VE TUNNELED TO THE WRONG MAN'S DOOR. DEATH DIGS DEEPER THAN THEY CAN!
FROST RELEASES HIS GRIP - SUDDENLY FREE, THE MOLES SHOOT DOWNWARD.

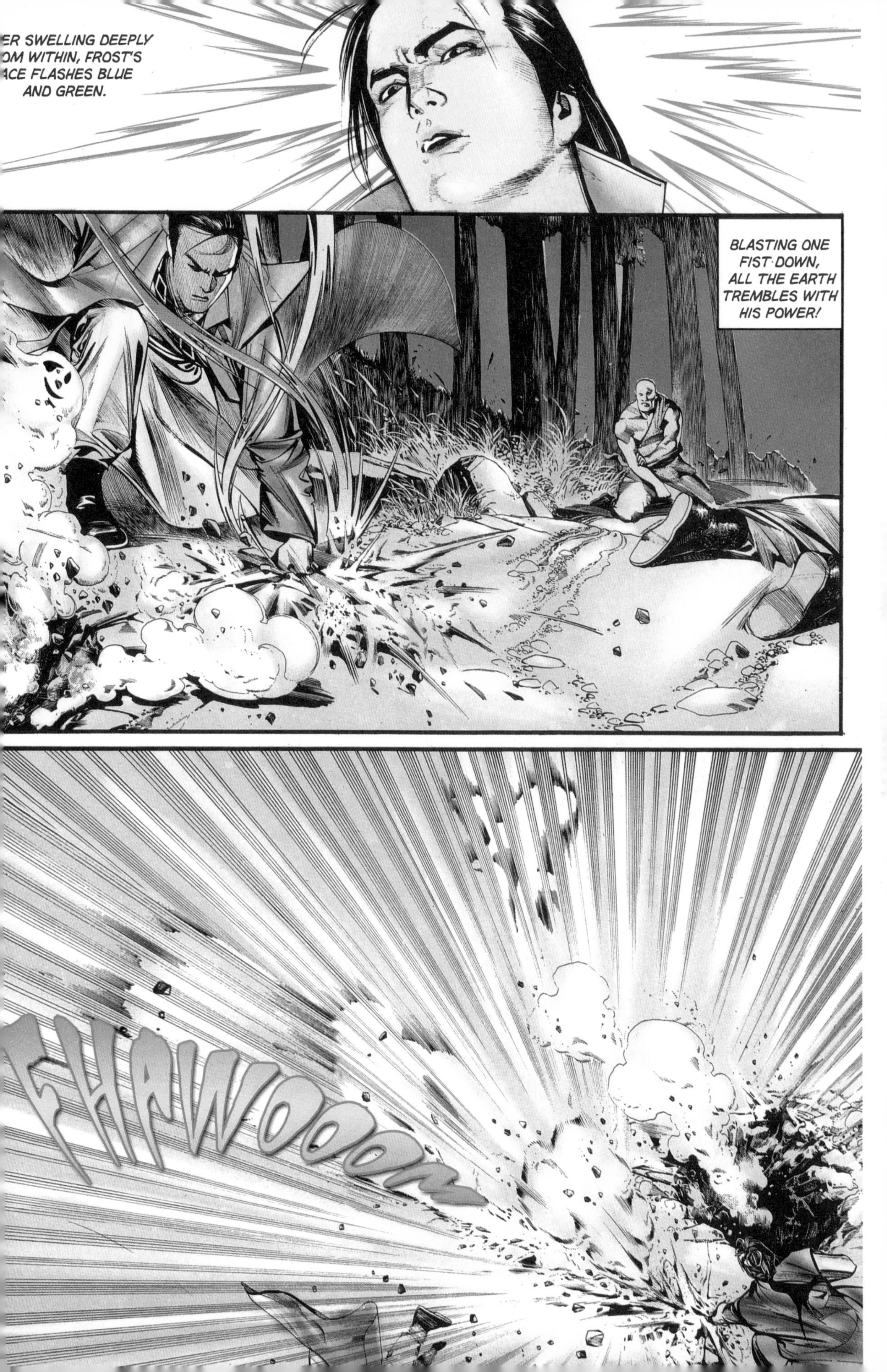
ER SWELLING DEEPLY
OM WITHIN, FROST'S
ACE FLASHES BLUE
AND GREEN.
BLASTING ONE FIST DOWN, ALL THE EARTH TREMBLES WITH HIS POWER!
CHAWOOOM

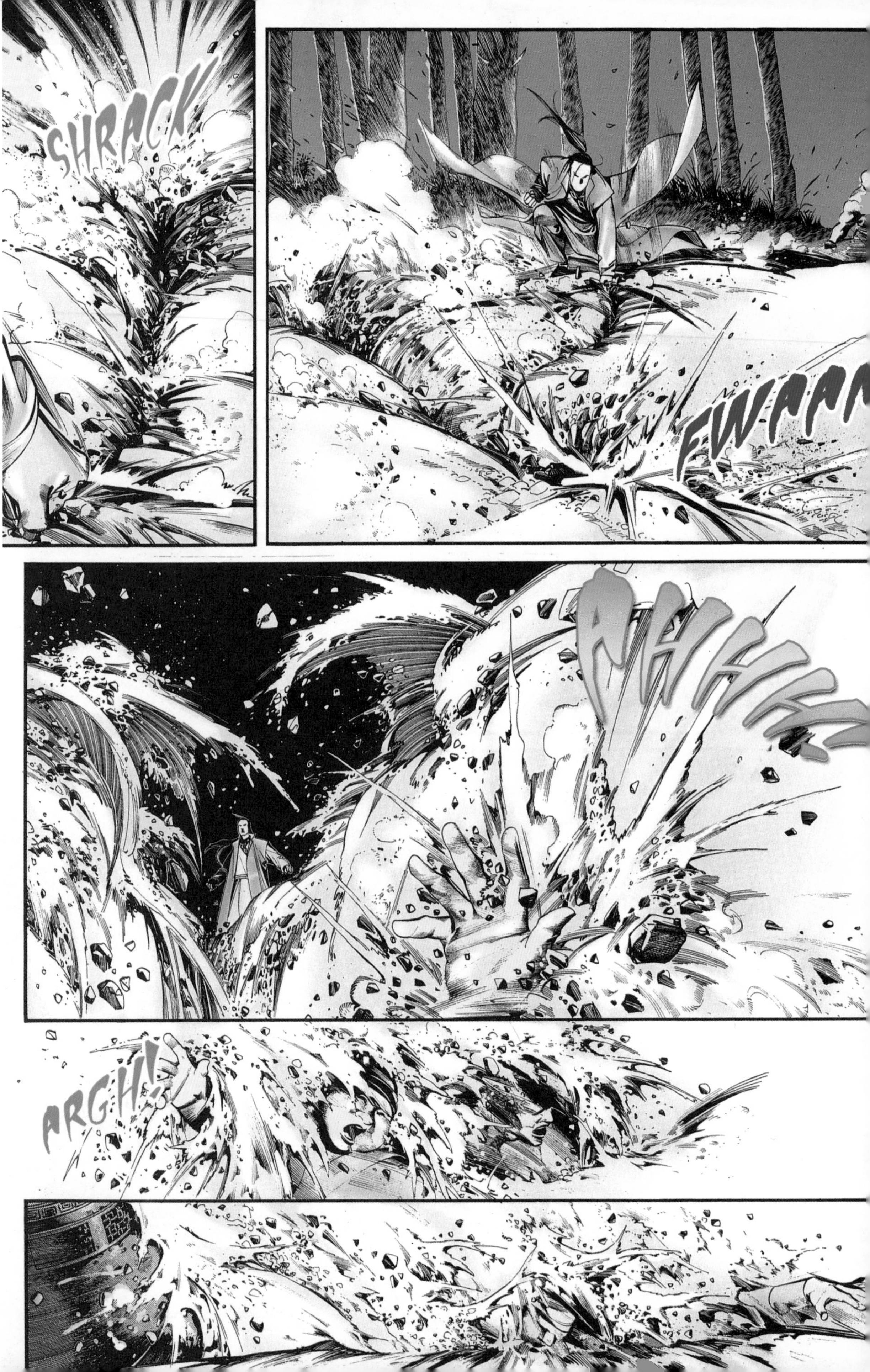
SHRACK
FWAAA
AHHHH
ARGH!

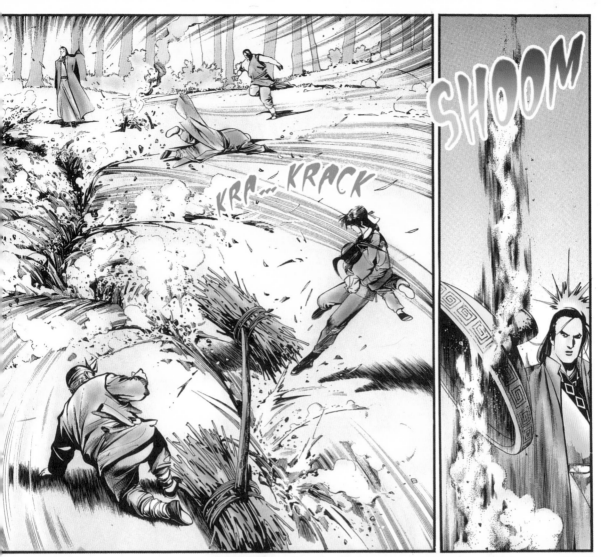

SHOOM

KRA... KRACK

LONG A CAPTIVE, THE FLAMING MONKEY CAN NO LONGER BE HELD. HE BLASTS OUT OF THE URN, BURNING RED, HIS FUR ALL ABLAZE, BLINDING ALL PRESENT!

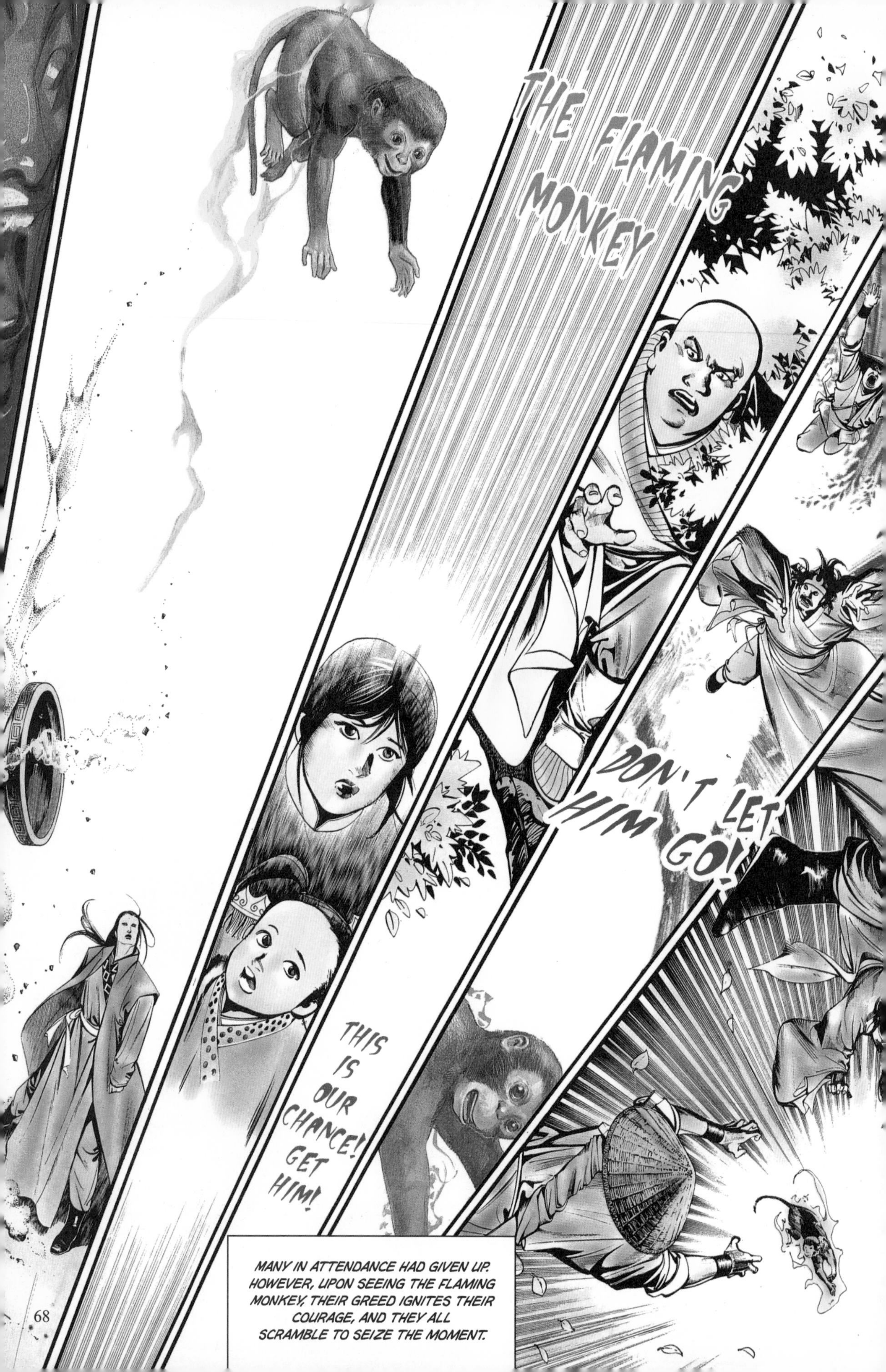
THE FLAMING MONKEY
DON'T LET HIM GO!
THIS IS OUR CHANCE! GET HIM!
MANY IN ATTENDANCE HAD GIVEN UP. HOWEVER, UPON SEEING THE FLAMING MONKEY, THEIR GREED IGNITES THEIR COURAGE, AND THEY ALL SCRAMBLE TO SEIZE THE MOMENT.

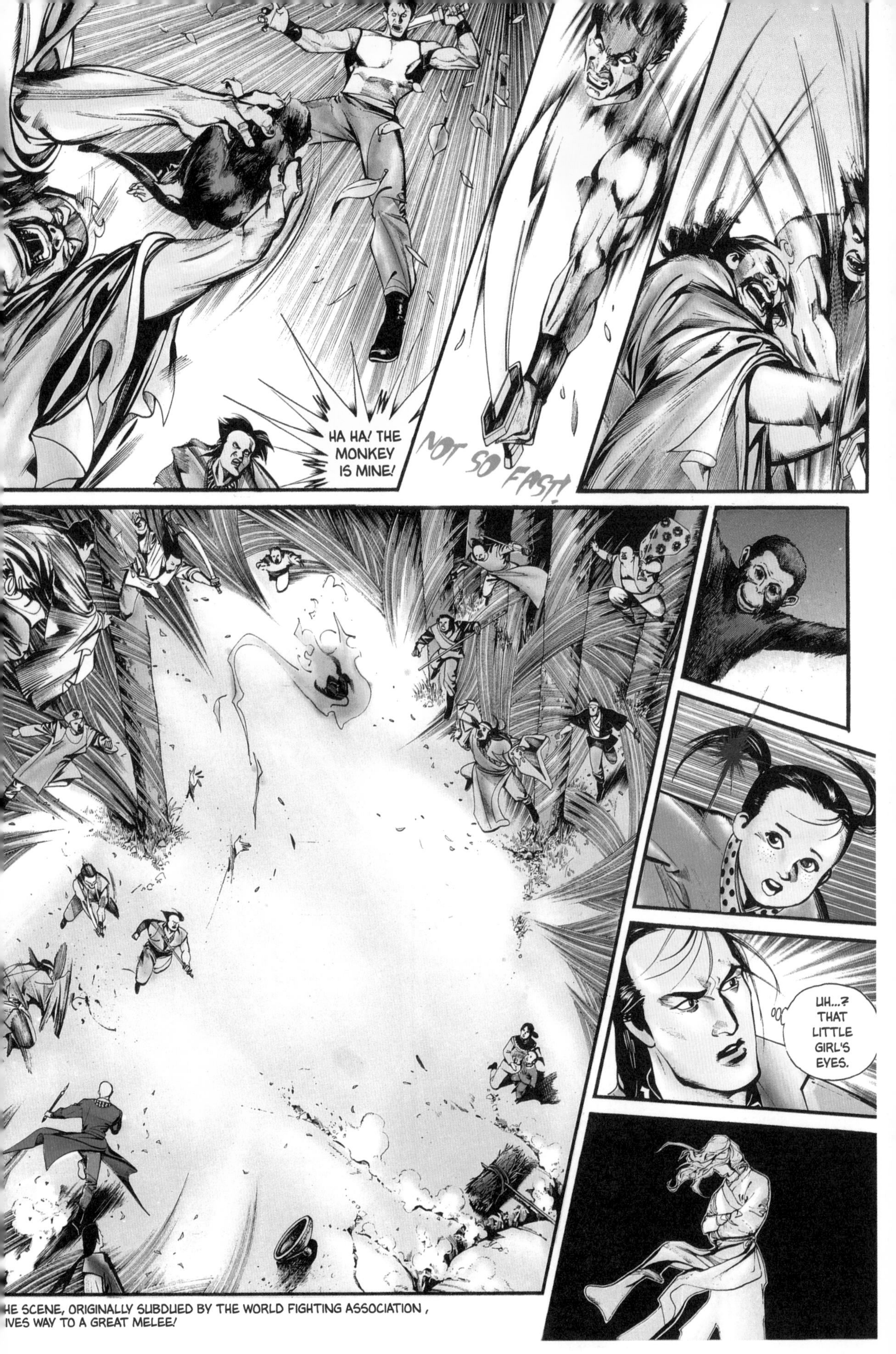
HA HA! THE MONKEY IS MINE!
NOT SO FAST!
UH...? THAT LITTLE GIRL'S EYES.
HE SCENE, ORIGINALLY SUBDUED BY THE WORLD FIGHTING ASSOCIATION ,
IVES WAY TO A GREAT MELEE!

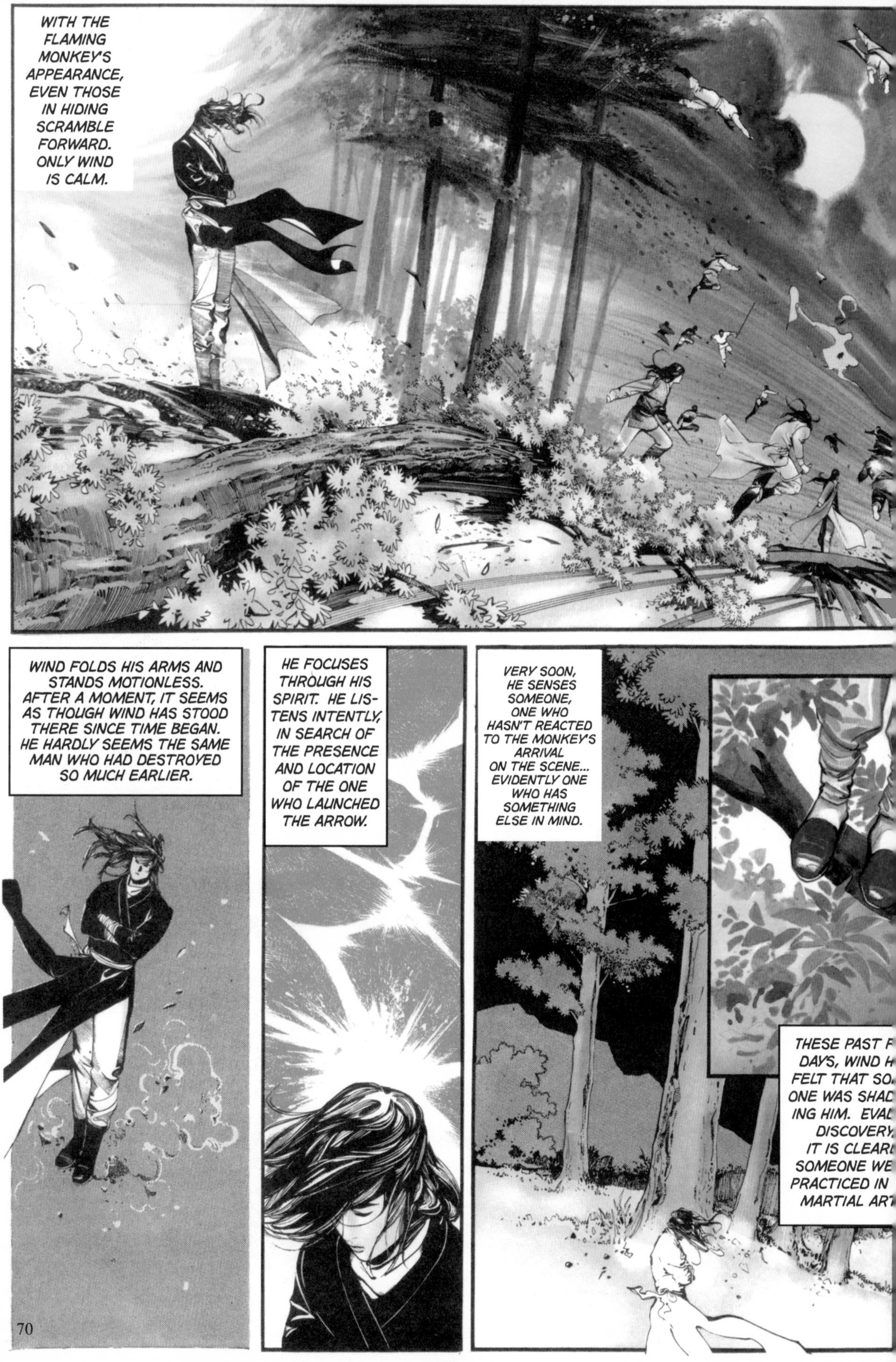

WITH THE FLAMING MONKEY'S APPEARANCE, EVEN THOSE IN HIDING SCRAMBLE FORWARD. ONLY WIND IS CALM.
WIND FOLDS HIS ARMS AND STANDS MOTIONLESS. AFTER A MOMENT, IT SEEMS AS THOUGH WIND HAS STOOD THERE SINCE TIME BEGAN. HE HARDLY SEEMS THE SAME MAN WHO HAD DESTROYED SO MUCH EARLIER.
HE FOCUSES THROUGH HIS SPIRIT. HE LISTENS INTENTLY, IN SEARCH OF THE PRESENCE AND LOCATION OF THE ONE WHO LAUNCHED THE ARROW.
VERY SOON, HE SENSES SOMEONE, ONE WHO HASN'T REACTED TO THE MONKEY'S ARRIVAL ON THE SCENE... EVIDENTLY ONE WHO HAS SOMETHING ELSE IN MIND.
THESE PAST F DAYS, WIND H FELT THAT SO ONE WAS SHAD ING HIM. EVAL DISCOVERY, IT IS CLEAR SOMEONE WE PRACTICED IN MARTIAL AR

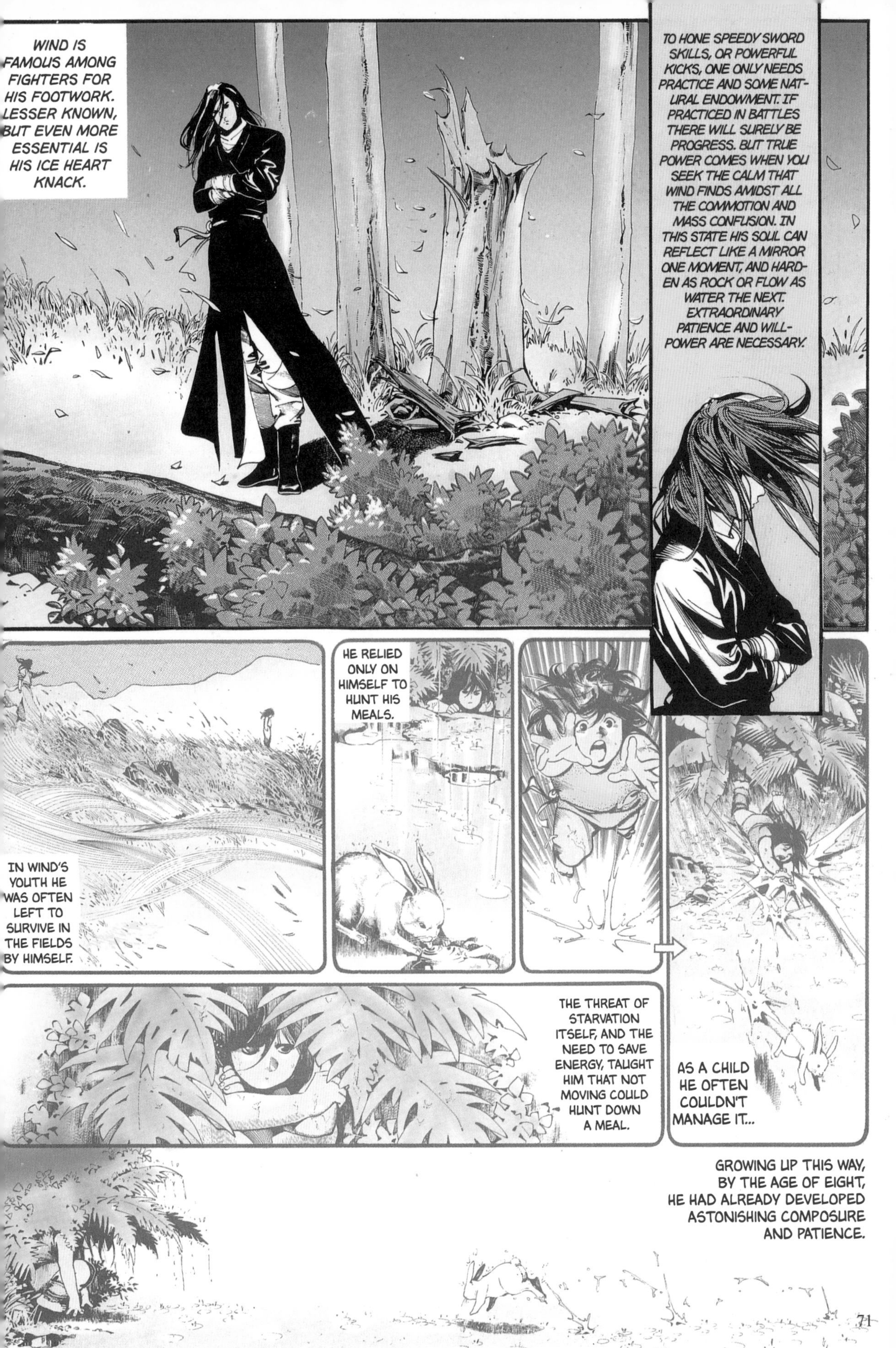
WIND IS FAMOUS AMONG FIGHTERS FOR HIS FOOTWORK. LESSER KNOWN, BUT EVEN MORE ESSENTIAL IS HIS ICE HEART KNACK.
TO HONE SPEEDY SWORD SKILLS, OR POWERFUL KICKS, ONE ONLY NEEDS PRACTICE AND SOME NATURAL ENDOWMENT. IF PRACTICED IN BATTLES THERE WILL SURELY BE PROGRESS. BUT TRUE POWER COMES WHEN YOU SEEK THE CALM THAT WIND FINDS AMIDST ALL THE COMMOTION AND MASS CONFUSION. IN THIS STATE HIS SOUL CAN REFLECT LIKE A MIRROR ONE MOMENT, AND HARDEN AS ROCK OR FLOW AS WATER THE NEXT. EXTRAORDINARY PATIENCE AND WILLPOWER ARE NECESSARY.
IN WIND'S YOUTH HE WAS OFTEN LEFT TO SURVIVE IN THE FIELDS BY HIMSELF.
HE RELIED ONLY ON HIMSELF TO HUNT HIS MEALS.
AS A CHILD HE OFTEN COULDN'T MANAGE IT...
THE THREAT OF STARVATION ITSELF, AND THE NEED TO SAVE ENERGY, TAUGHT HIM THAT NOT MOVING COULD HUNT DOWN A MEAL.
GROWING UP THIS WAY, BY THE AGE OF EIGHT, HE HAD ALREADY DEVELOPED ASTONISHING COMPOSURE AND PATIENCE.

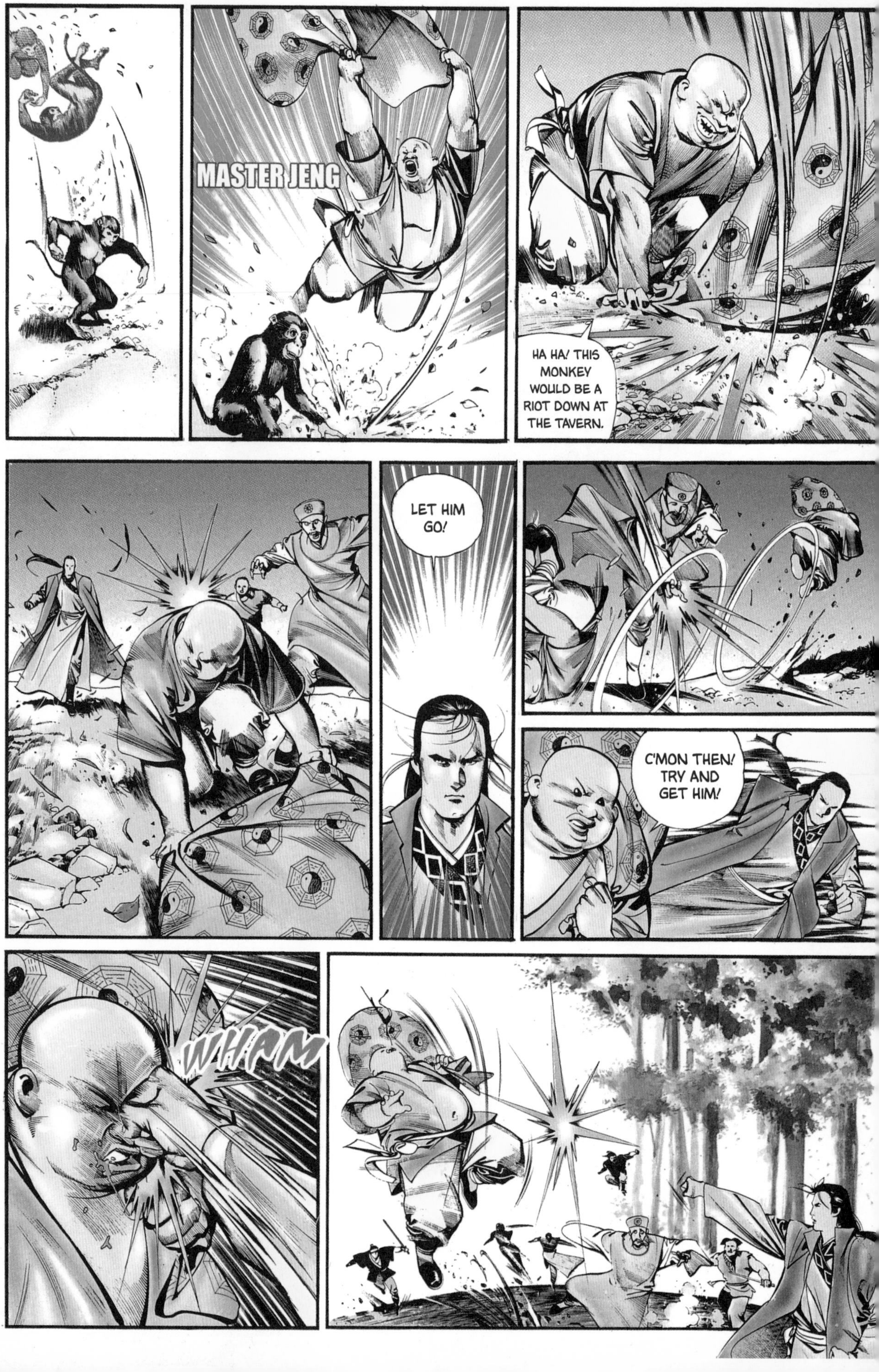
MASTER JENG
HA HA! THIS MONKEY WOULD BE A RIOT DOWN AT THE TAVERN.
LET HIM GO!
C'MON THEN! TRY AND GET HIM!
WHAM

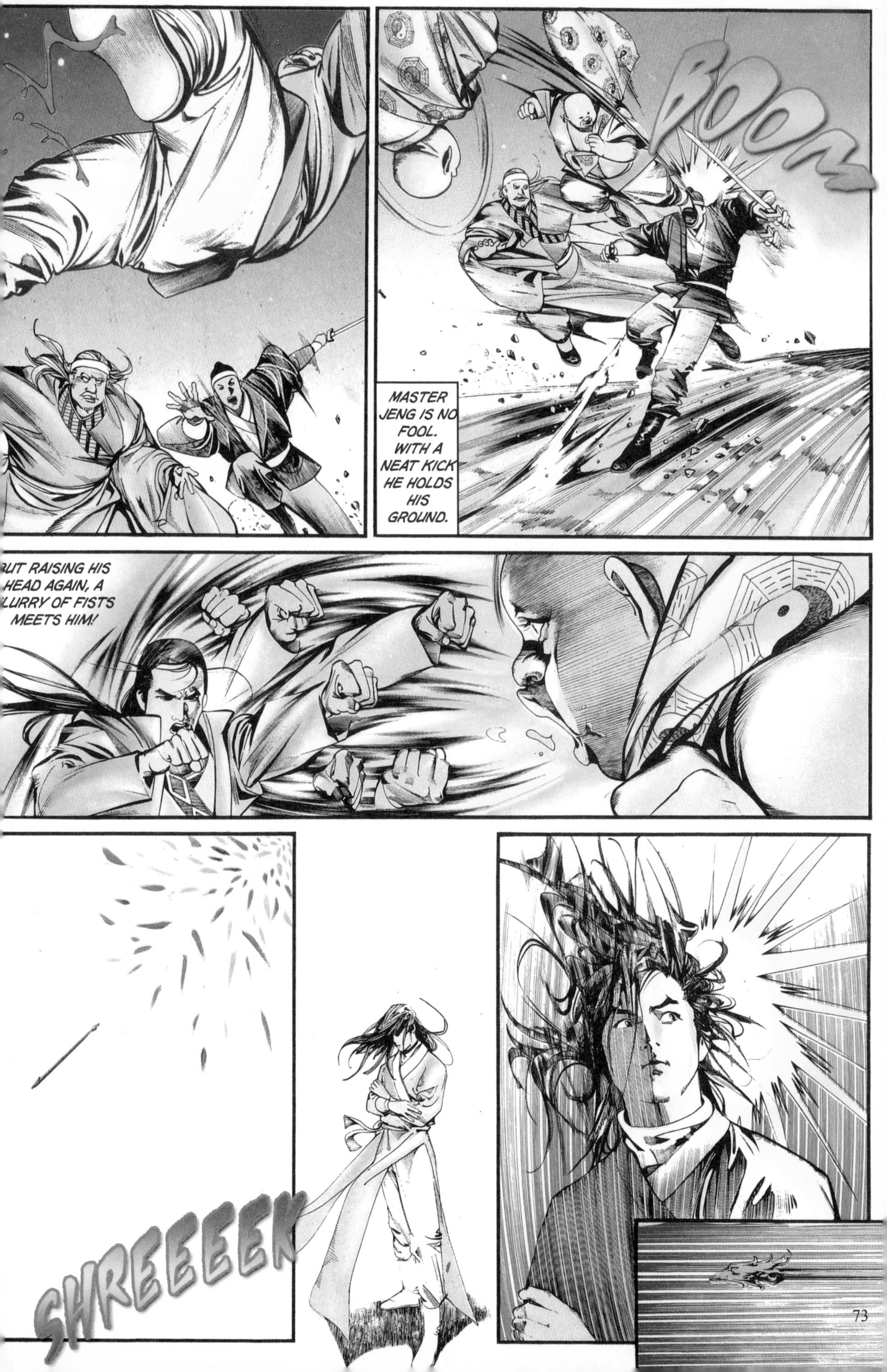
BOOM
MASTER JENG IS NO FOOL. WITH A NEAT KICK HE HOLDS HIS GROUND.
BUT RAISING HIS HEAD AGAIN, A FLURRY OF FISTS MEETS HIM!
SHREEEEK

PHOE
WATCH
FOR W

FWOOSH

WHER
ARE YO

DRAGON SOUNDS
THE ALARM,
AND THEREFORE
IS AIDING
THE ARCHER.
BEFORE
HIS CALL,
WIND HAS
ALREADY STRUCK
OUT FOR THE
BOW'S KEEPER.

NO
FROS

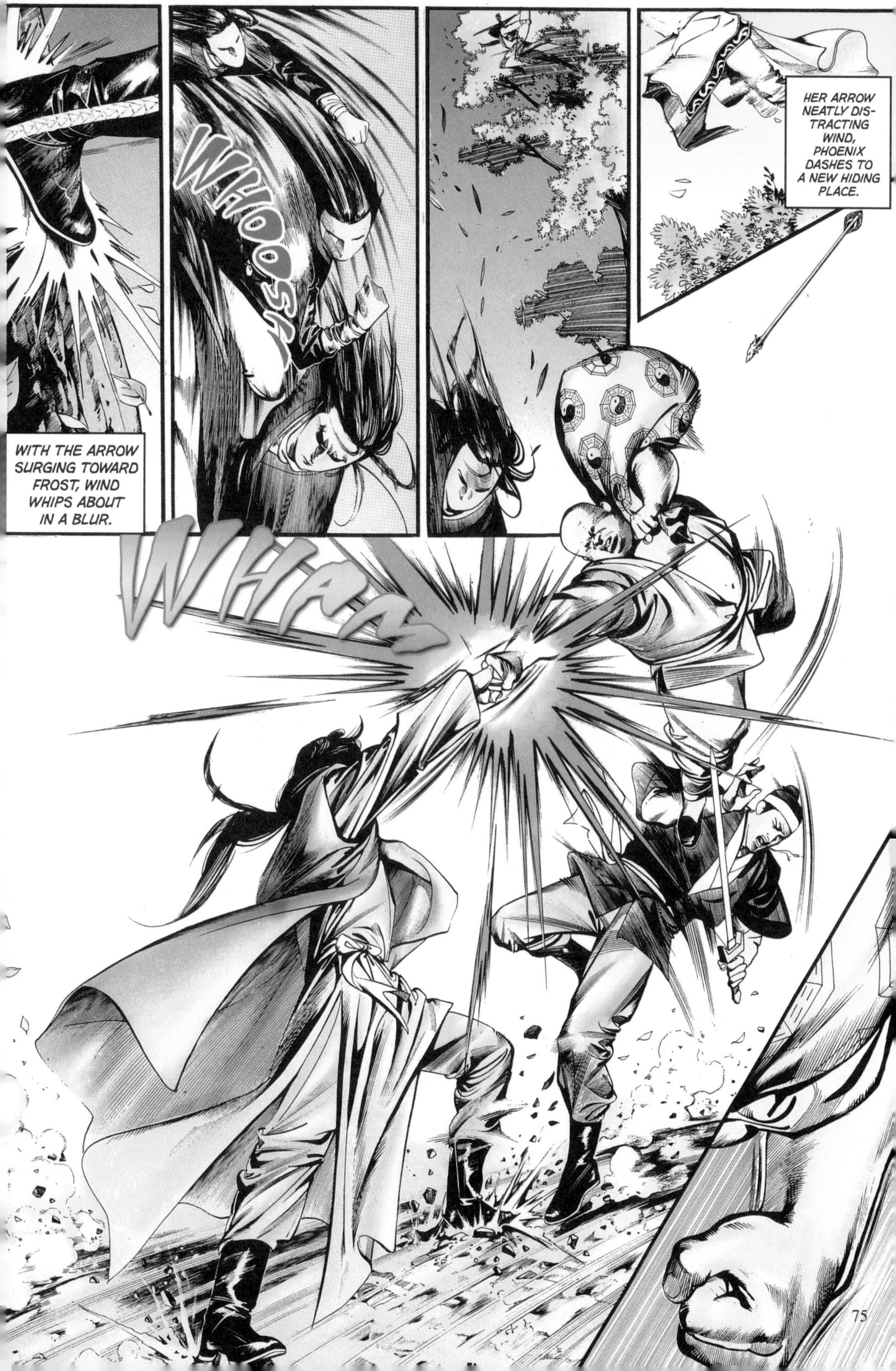
WITH THE ARROW SURGING TOWARD FROST, WIND WHIPS ABOUT IN A BLUR.
WHOOSH
HER ARROW NEATLY DISTRACTING WIND, PHOENIX DASHES TO A NEW HIDING PLACE.
WHAM

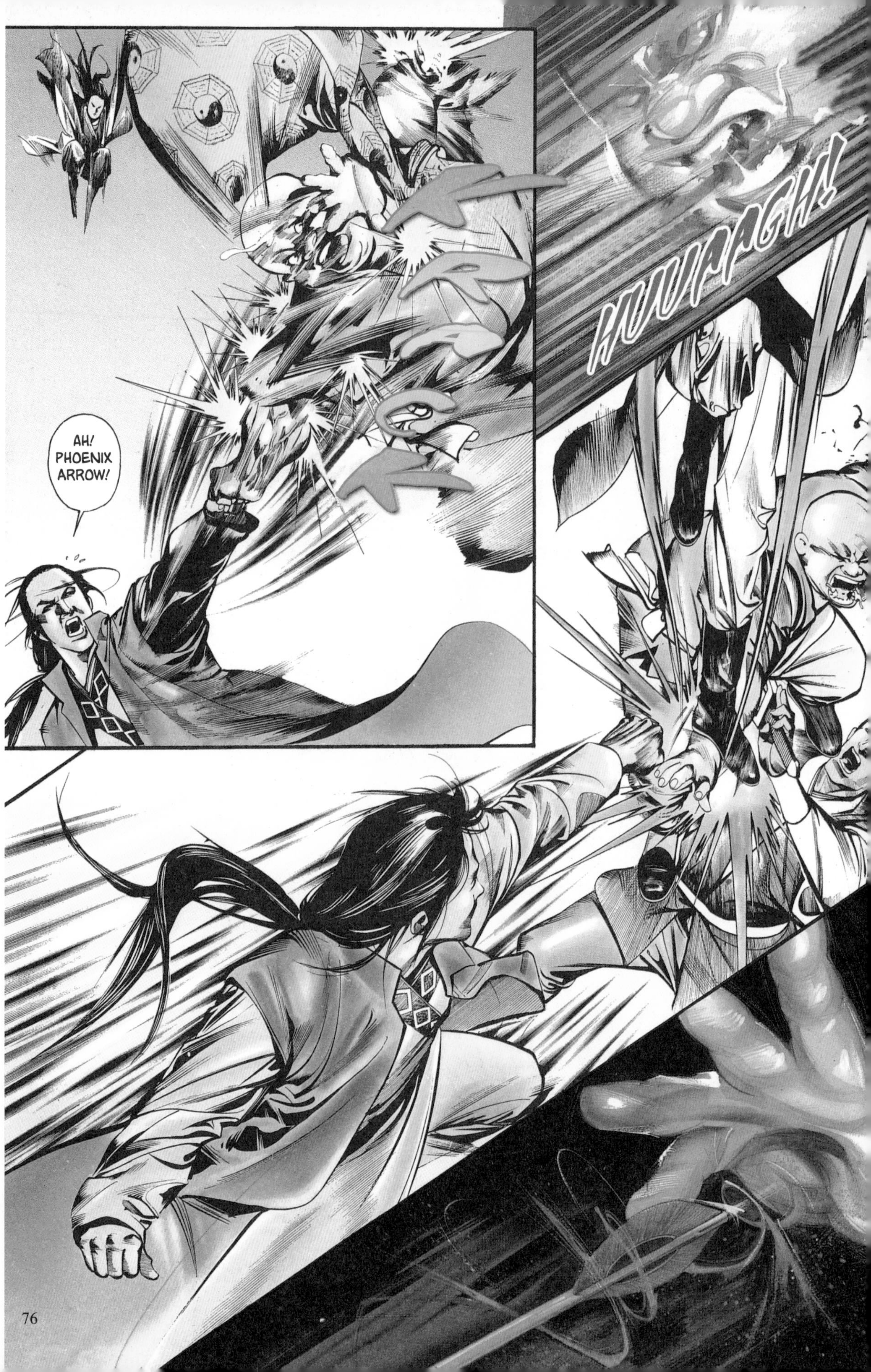
HUUAAGH!
AH! PHOENIX ARROW!

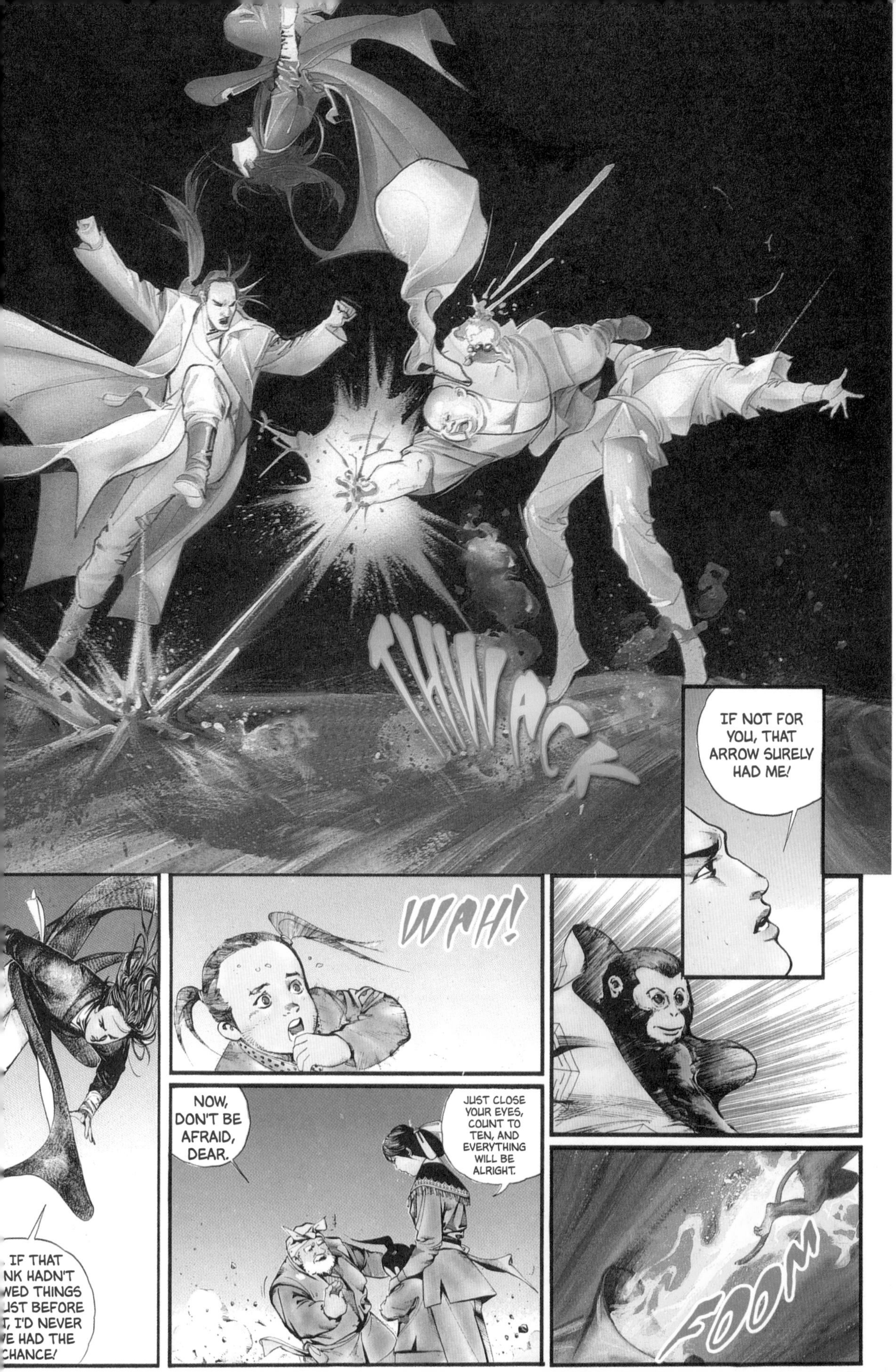
THWACK
IF NOT FOR YOU, THAT ARROW SURELY HAD ME!
IF THAT NK HADN'T WED THINGS UST BEFORE T, I'D NEVER E HAD THE CHANCE!
WAH!
NOW, DON'T BE AFRAID, DEAR.
JUST CLOSE YOUR EYES, COUNT TO TEN, AND EVERYTHING WILL BE ALRIGHT.
FOOM

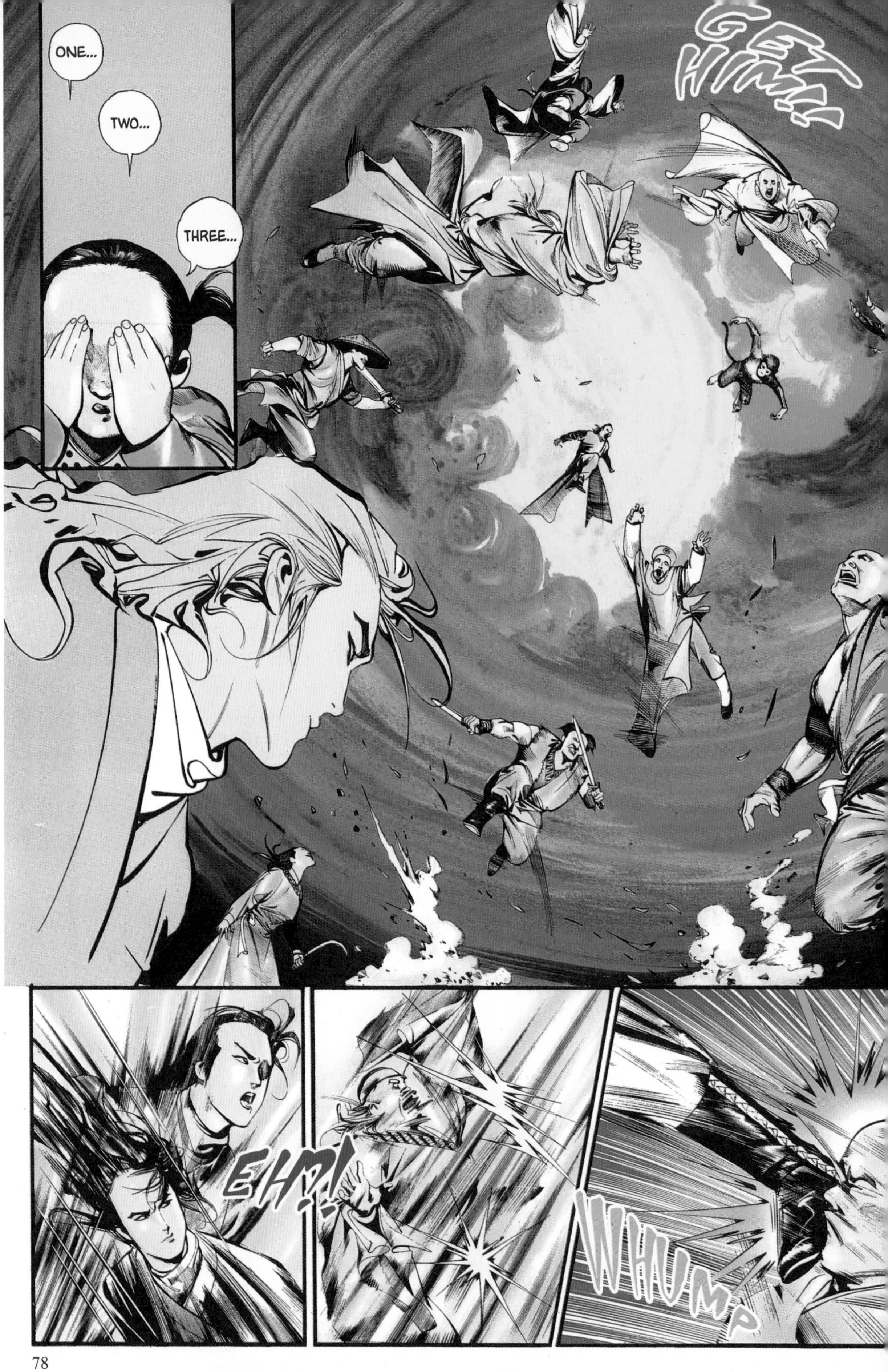
ONE...
TWO...
THREE...
GET HIM!!
EH?!
WHUMP

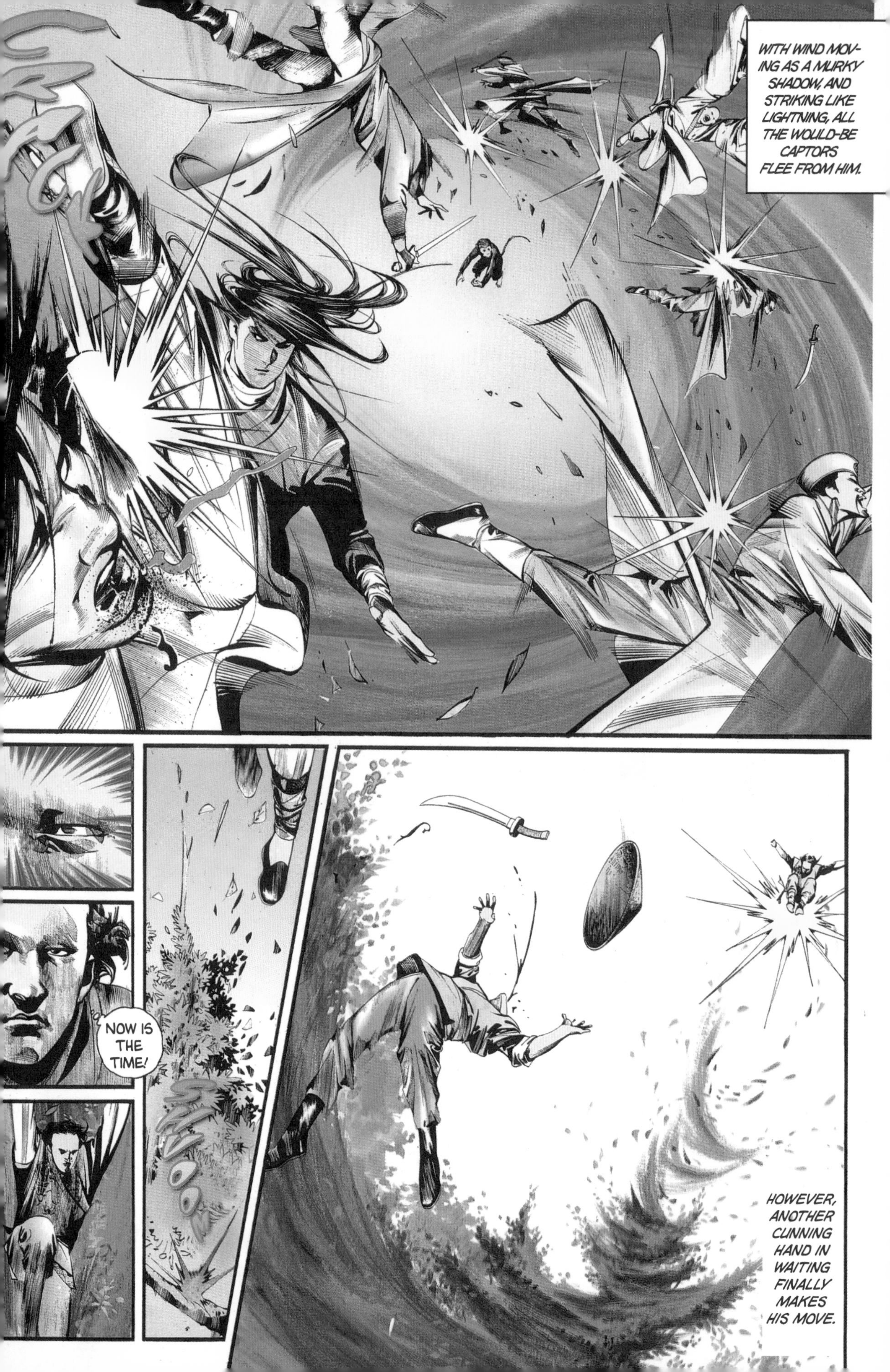
WITH WIND MOVING AS A MURKY SHADOW, AND STRIKING LIKE LIGHTNING, ALL THE WOULD-BE CAPTORS FLEE FROM HIM.
NOW IS THE TIME!
HOWEVER, ANOTHER CUNNING HAND IN WAITING FINALLY MAKES HIS MOVE.

AT THIS POINT, ALL ON THE SCENE FEEL A GREAT, THUNDEROUS FORCE DESCENDING!

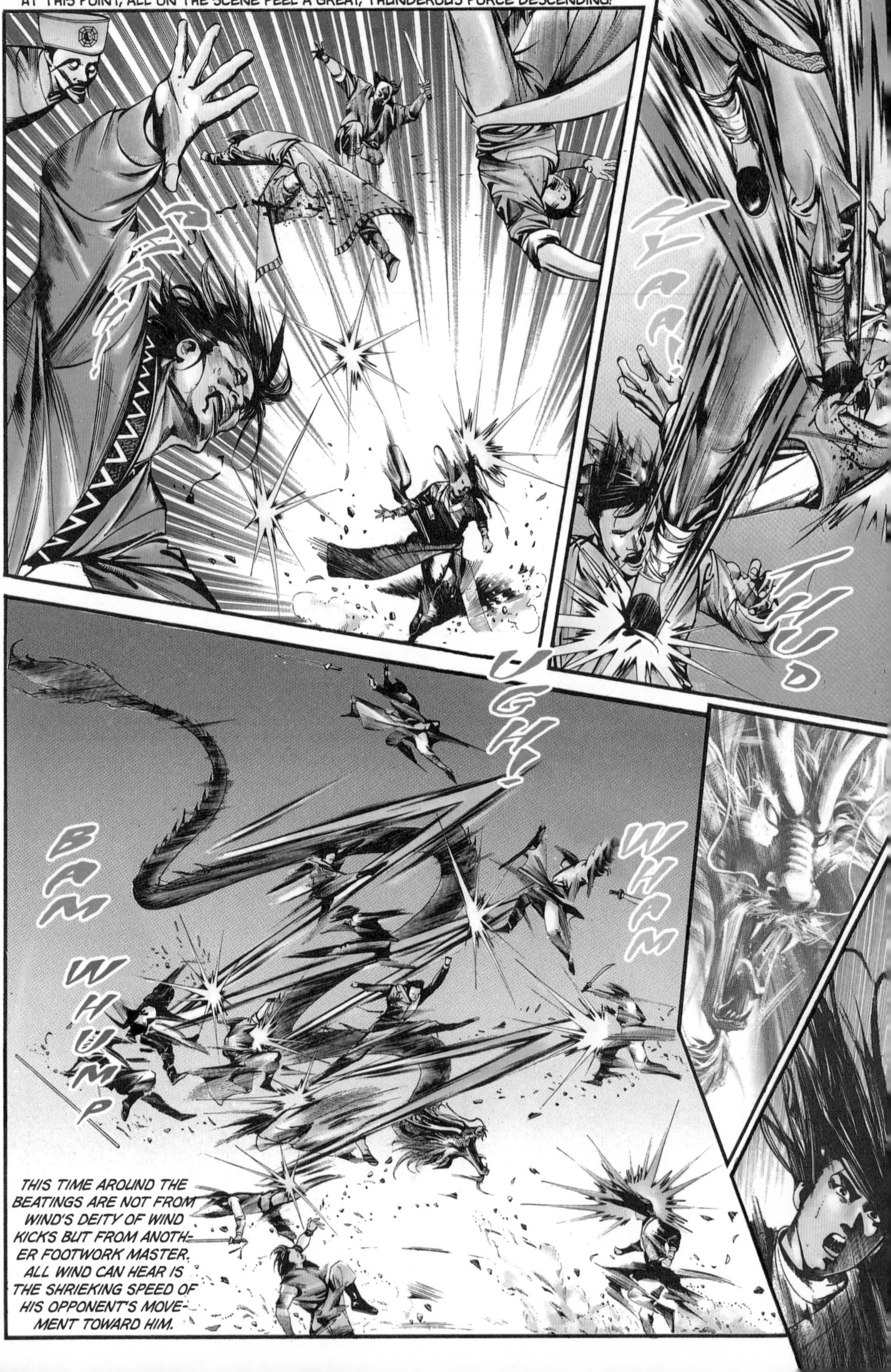

AHHH!
HYAAA!
THUD
UGH!
WHAM
BAM
WHUMP
THIS TIME AROUND THE BEATINGS ARE NOT FROM WIND'S DEITY OF WIND KICKS BUT FROM ANOTHER FOOTWORK MASTER. ALL WIND CAN HEAR IS THE SHRIEKING SPEED OF HIS OPPONENT'S MOVEMENT TOWARD HIM.

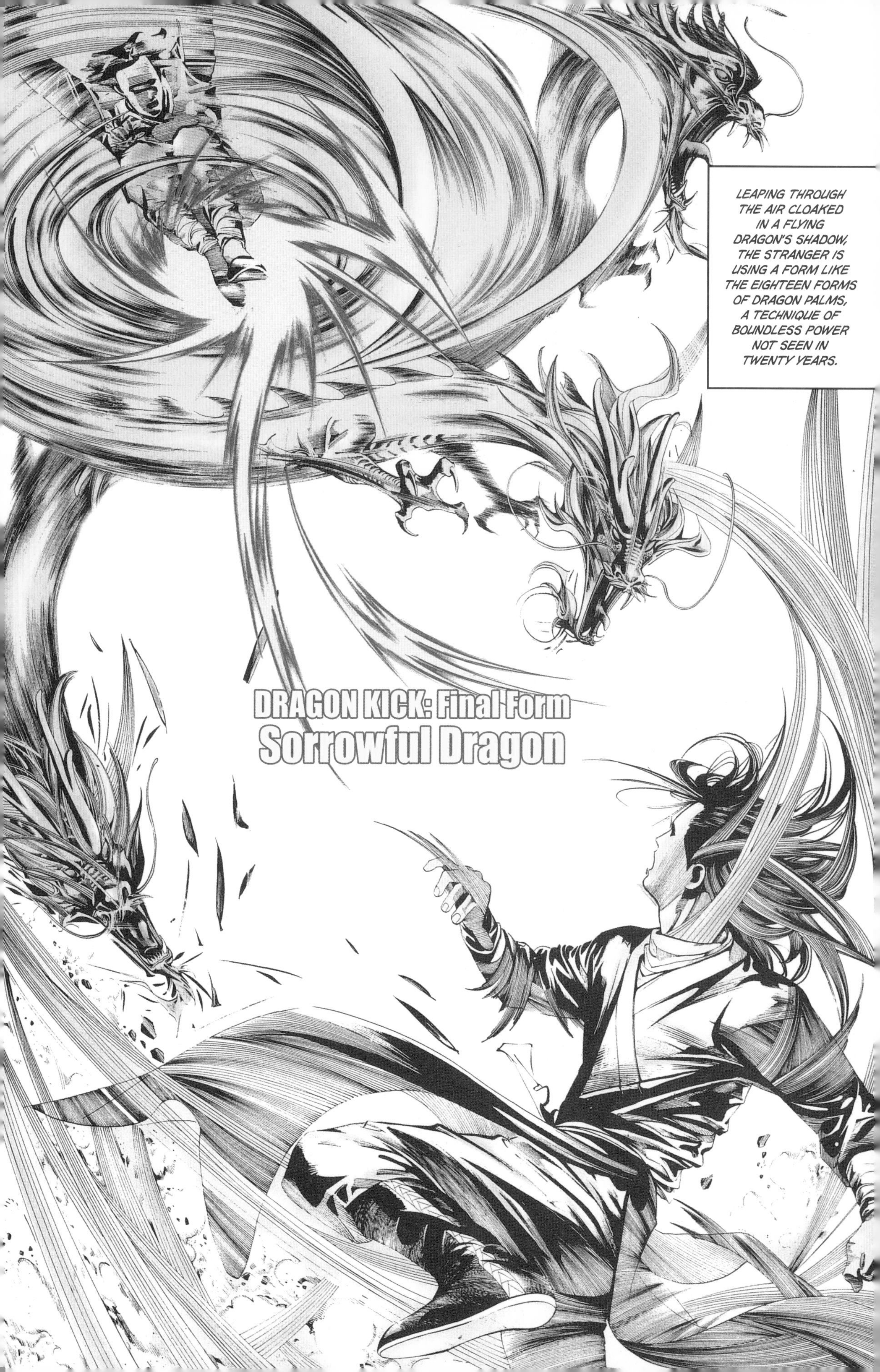
LEAPING THROUGH THE AIR CLOAKED IN A FLYING DRAGON'S SHADOW, THE STRANGER IS USING A FORM LIKE THE EIGHTEEN FORMS OF DRAGON PALMS, A TECHNIQUE OF BOUNDLESS POWER NOT SEEN IN TWENTY YEARS.
DRAGON KICK: Final Form
Sorrowful Dragon

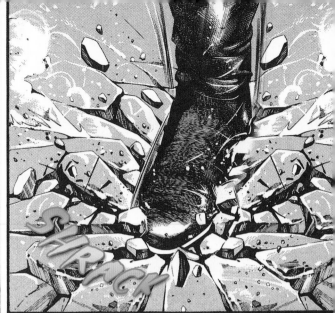

WIND DOESN'T THINK TWICE. HE PLANTS HIS FEET...

THOUGH THE STEP IS ITSELF SLIGHT, THE EARTH FLIES FROM HIS FEET TO FORETELL A MASSIVE ATTACK.

DEITY OF WIND KICK: Fifth Form
Enforcing Thunder

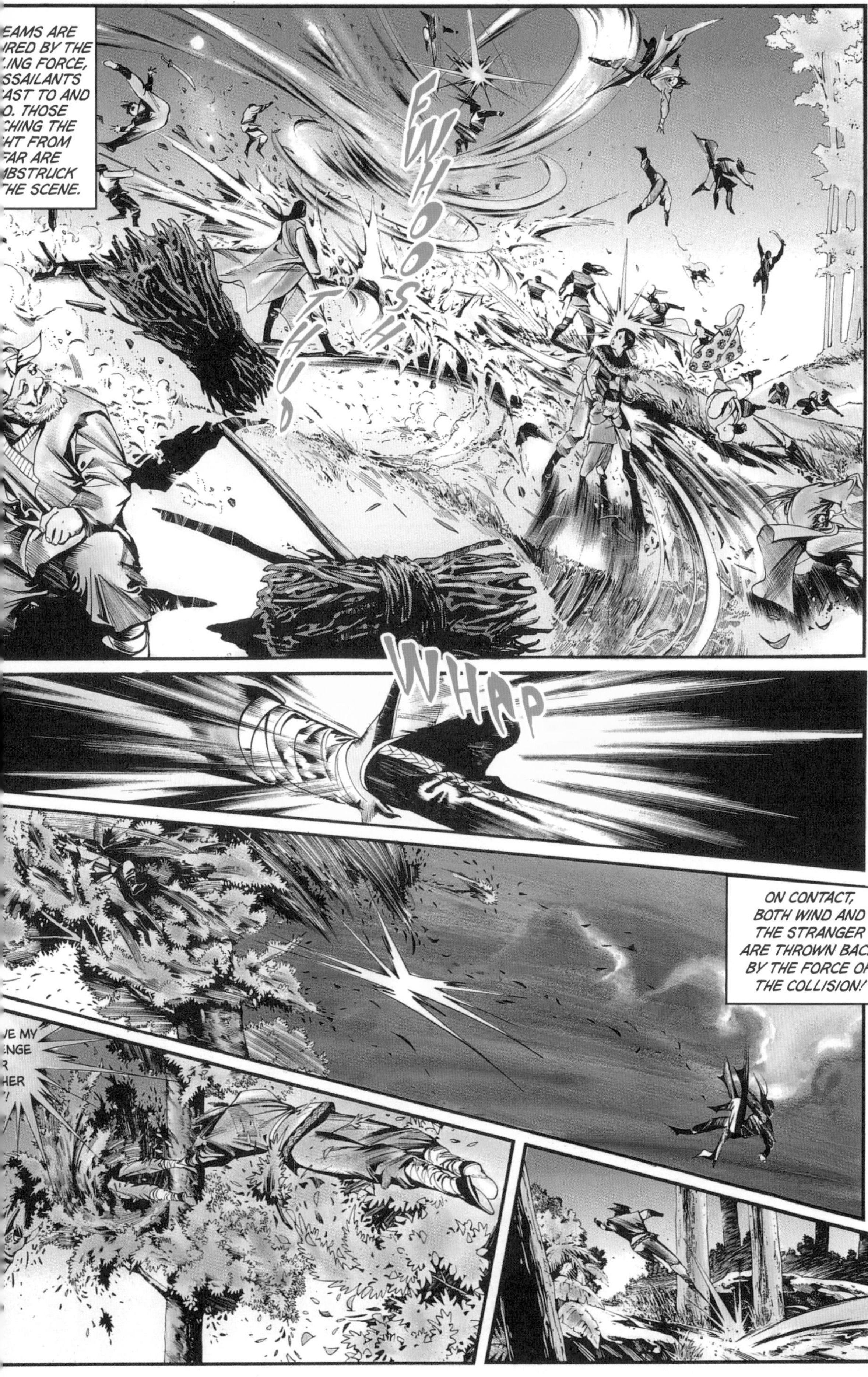
EAMS ARE
URED BY THE
LING FORCE,
SSAILANTS
AST TO AND
O. THOSE
CHING THE
HT FROM
FAR ARE
MBSTRUCK
THE SCENE.
WHOOSH
THUD
WHAP
ON CONTACT, BOTH WIND AND THE STRANGER ARE THROWN BACK BY THE FORCE OF THE COLLISION!
VE MY
NGE
R
HER
!

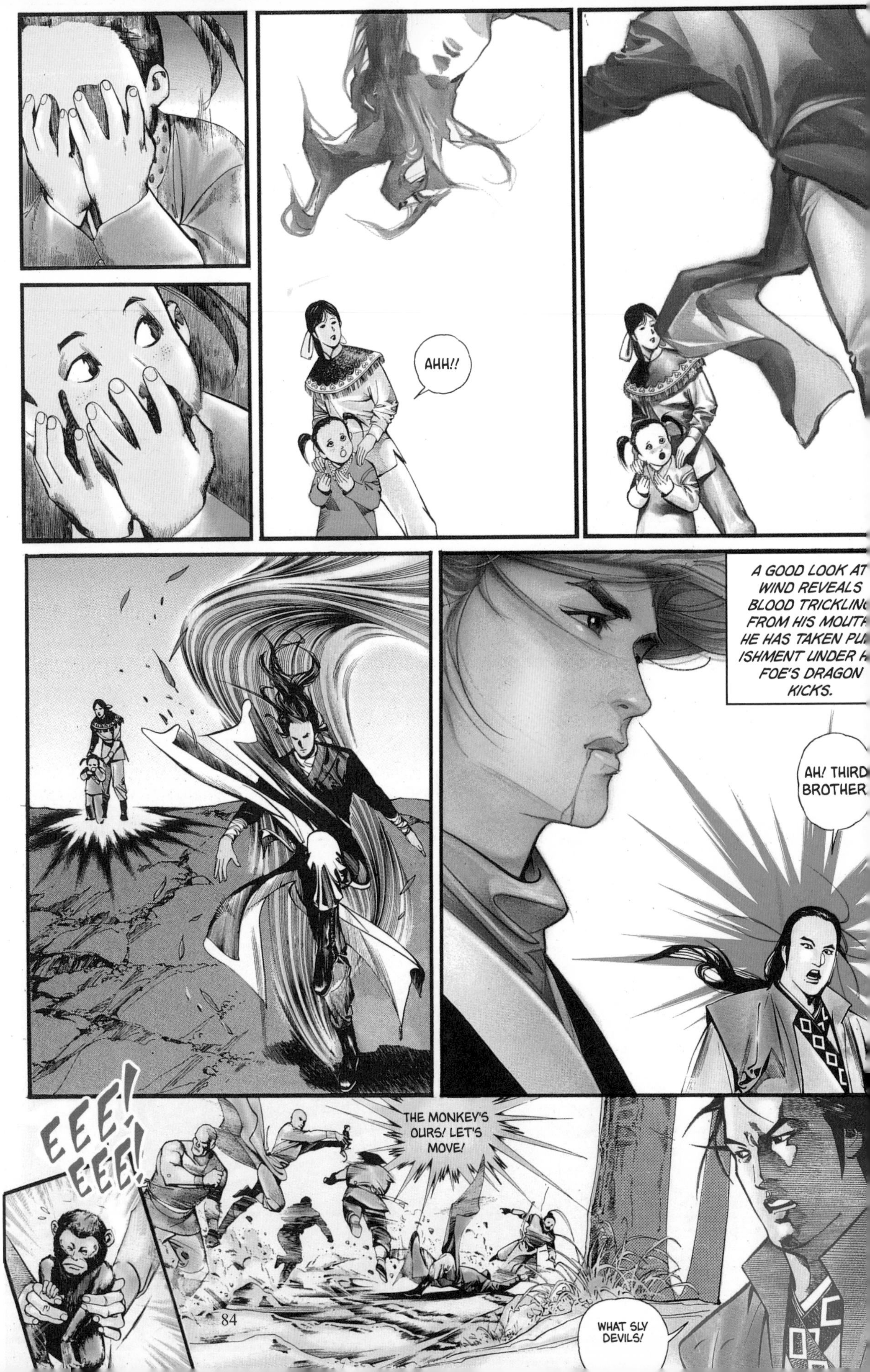

AHH!!
A GOOD LOOK AT
WIND REVEALS
BLOOD TRICKLING
FROM HIS MOUTH
HE HAS TAKEN PU
ISHMENT UNDER H
FOE'S DRAGON
KICKS.
AH! THIRD
BROTHER
EEE! EEE!
THE MONKEY'S OURS! LET'S MOVE!
WHAT SLY DEVILS!

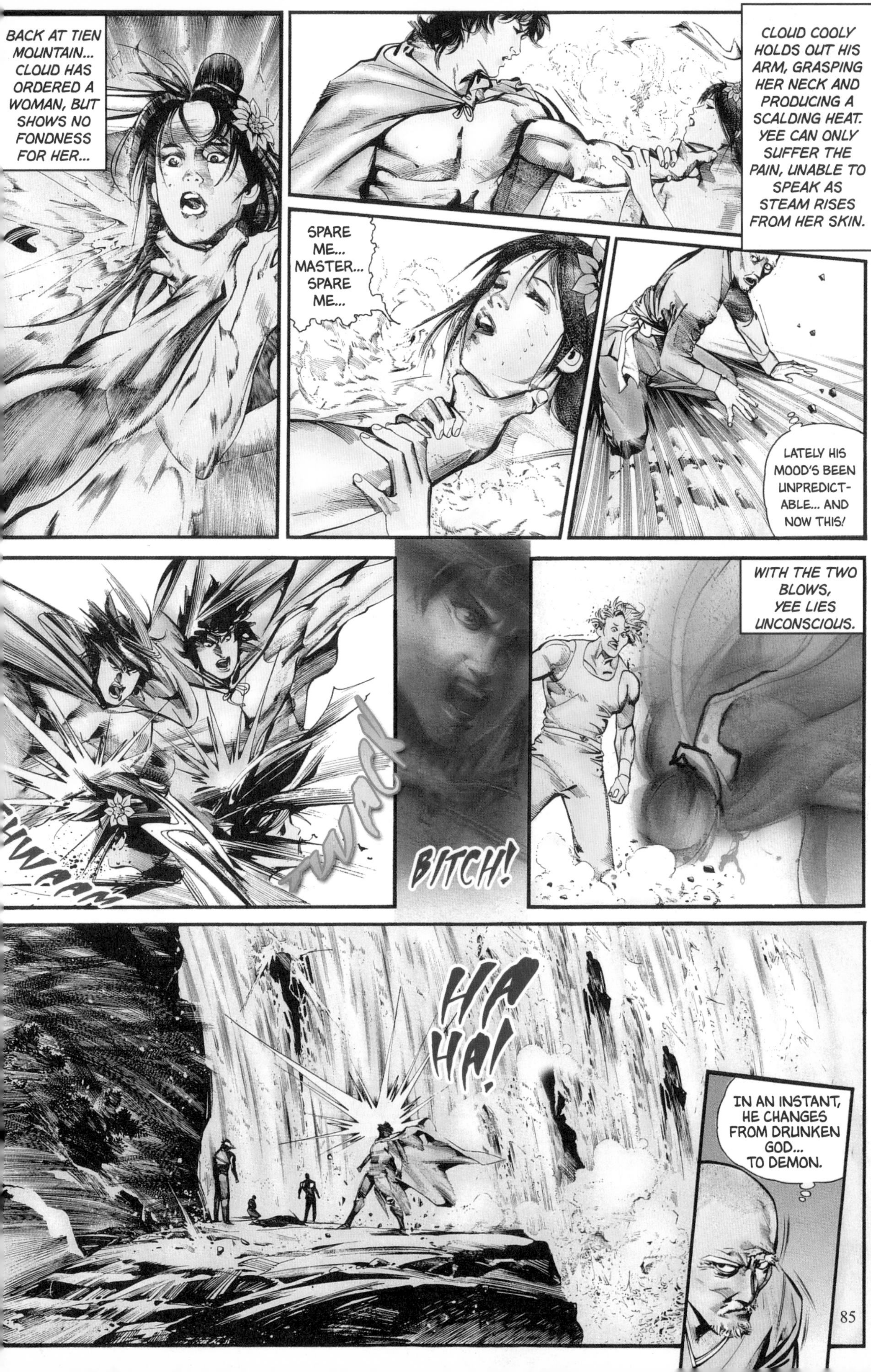
BACK AT TIEN MOUNTAIN... CLOUD HAS ORDERED A WOMAN, BUT SHOWS NO FONDNESS FOR HER...
CLOUD COOLY HOLDS OUT HIS ARM, GRASPING HER NECK AND PRODUCING A SCALDING HEAT. YEE CAN ONLY SUFFER THE PAIN, UNABLE TO SPEAK AS STEAM RISES FROM HER SKIN.
SPARE ME... MASTER... SPARE ME...
LATELY HIS MOOD'S BEEN UNPREDICT-ABLE... AND NOW THIS!
TWACK
BITCH!
WITH THE TWO BLOWS, YEE LIES UNCONSCIOUS.
HA HA!
IN AN INSTANT, HE CHANGES FROM DRUNKEN GOD... TO DEMON.

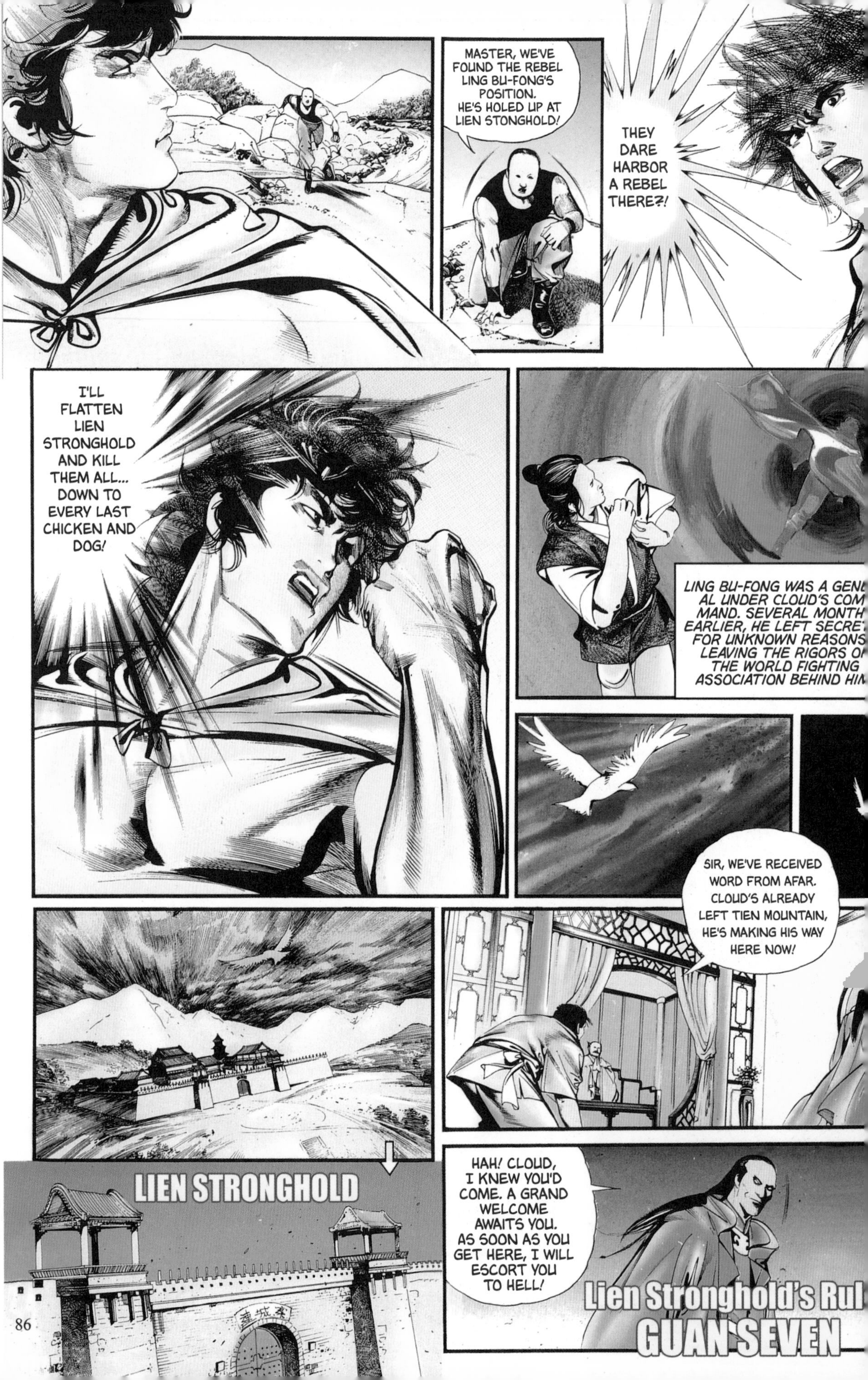

MASTER, WE'VE FOUND THE REBEL LING BU-FONG'S POSITION. HE'S HOLED UP AT LIEN STONGHOLD!
THEY DARE HARBOR A REBEL THERE?!
I'LL FLATTEN LIEN STRONGHOLD AND KILL THEM ALL... DOWN TO EVERY LAST CHICKEN AND DOG!
LING BU-FONG WAS A GENE AL UNDER CLOUD'S COM MAND. SEVERAL MONTH EARLIER, HE LEFT SECRET FOR UNKNOWN REASONS LEAVING THE RIGORS OF THE WORLD FIGHTING ASSOCIATION BEHIND HIM
SIR, WE'VE RECEIVED WORD FROM AFAR. CLOUD'S ALREADY LEFT TIEN MOUNTAIN, HE'S MAKING HIS WAY HERE NOW!
LIEN STRONGHOLD
HAH! CLOUD, I KNEW YOU'D COME. A GRAND WELCOME AWAITS YOU. AS SOON AS YOU GET HERE, I WILL ESCORT YOU TO HELL!
Lien Stronghold's Rul
GUAN SEVEN

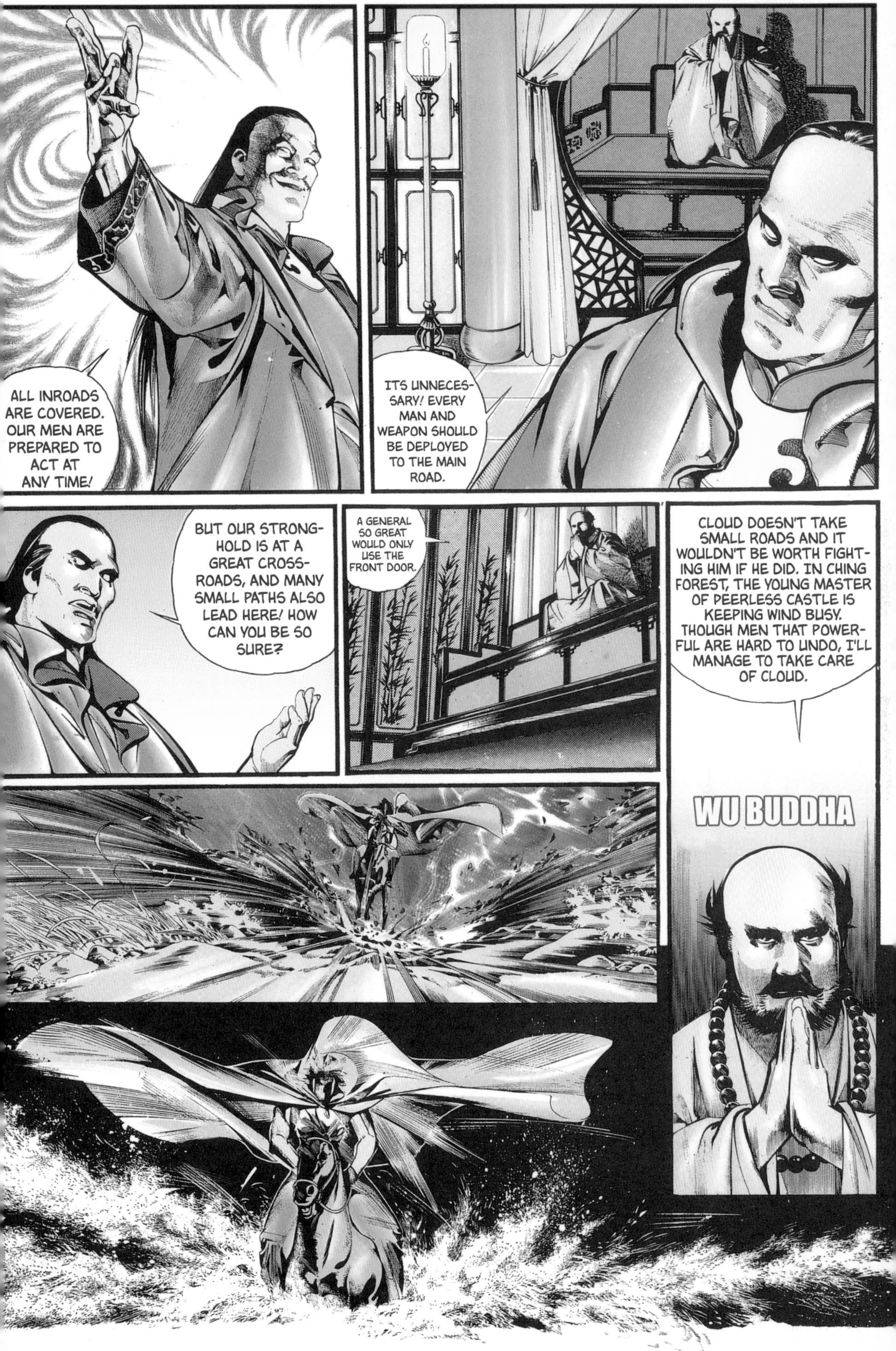
ALL INROADS ARE COVERED. OUR MEN ARE PREPARED TO ACT AT ANY TIME!
ITS UNNECES-SARY! EVERY MAN AND WEAPON SHOULD BE DEPLOYED TO THE MAIN ROAD.
BUT OUR STRONG-HOLD IS AT A GREAT CROSS-ROADS, AND MANY SMALL PATHS ALSO LEAD HERE! HOW CAN YOU BE SO SURE?
A GENERAL SO GREAT WOULD ONLY USE THE FRONT DOOR.
CLOUD DOESN'T TAKE SMALL ROADS AND IT WOULDN'T BE WORTH FIGHT-ING HIM IF HE DID. IN CHING FOREST, THE YOUNG MASTER OF PEERLESS CASTLE IS KEEPING WIND BUSY. THOUGH MEN THAT POWER-FUL ARE HARD TO UNDO, I'LL MANAGE TO TAKE CARE OF CLOUD.
WU BUDDHA

Chapter 8: Phoenix From The Heavens

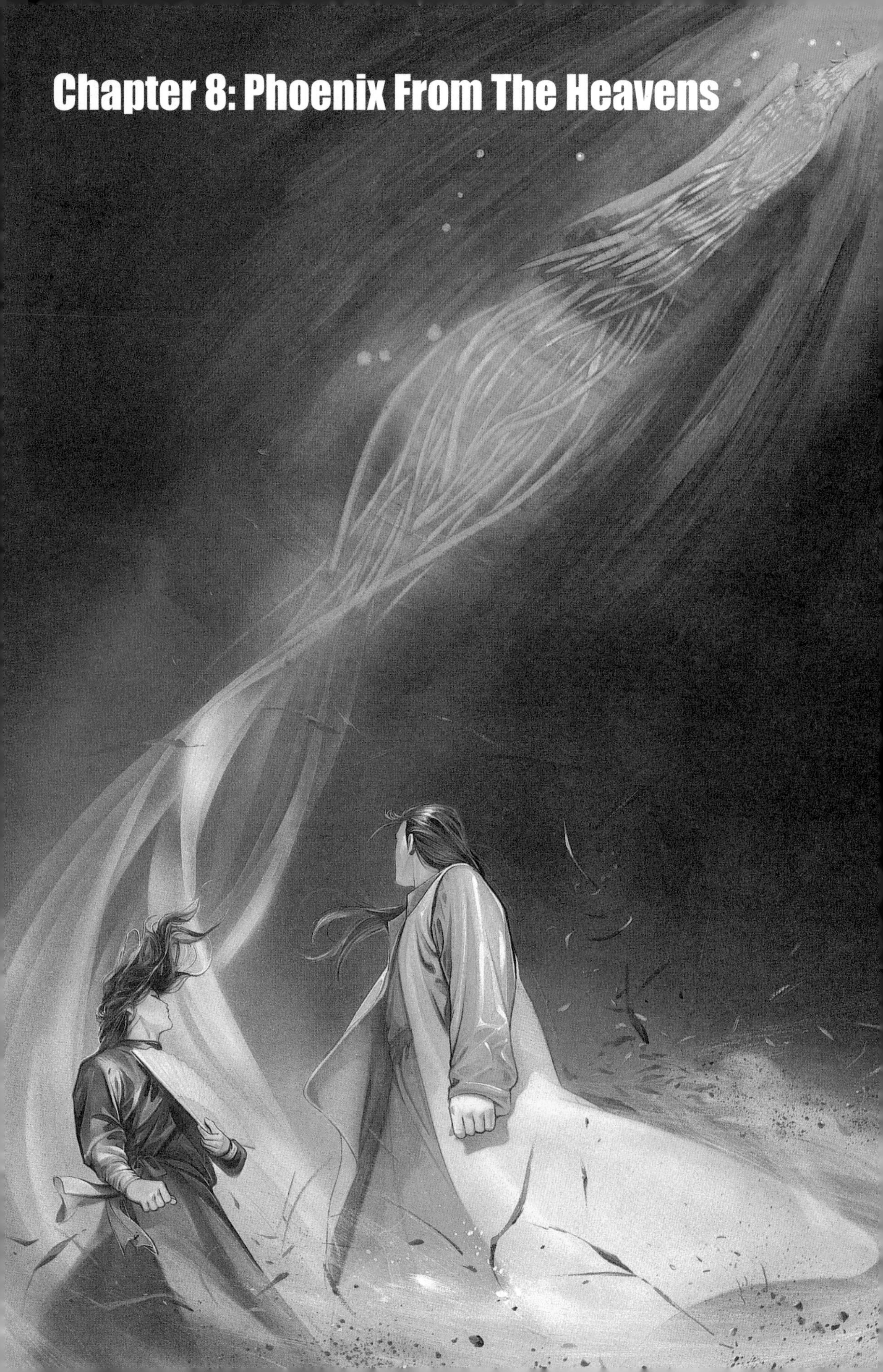

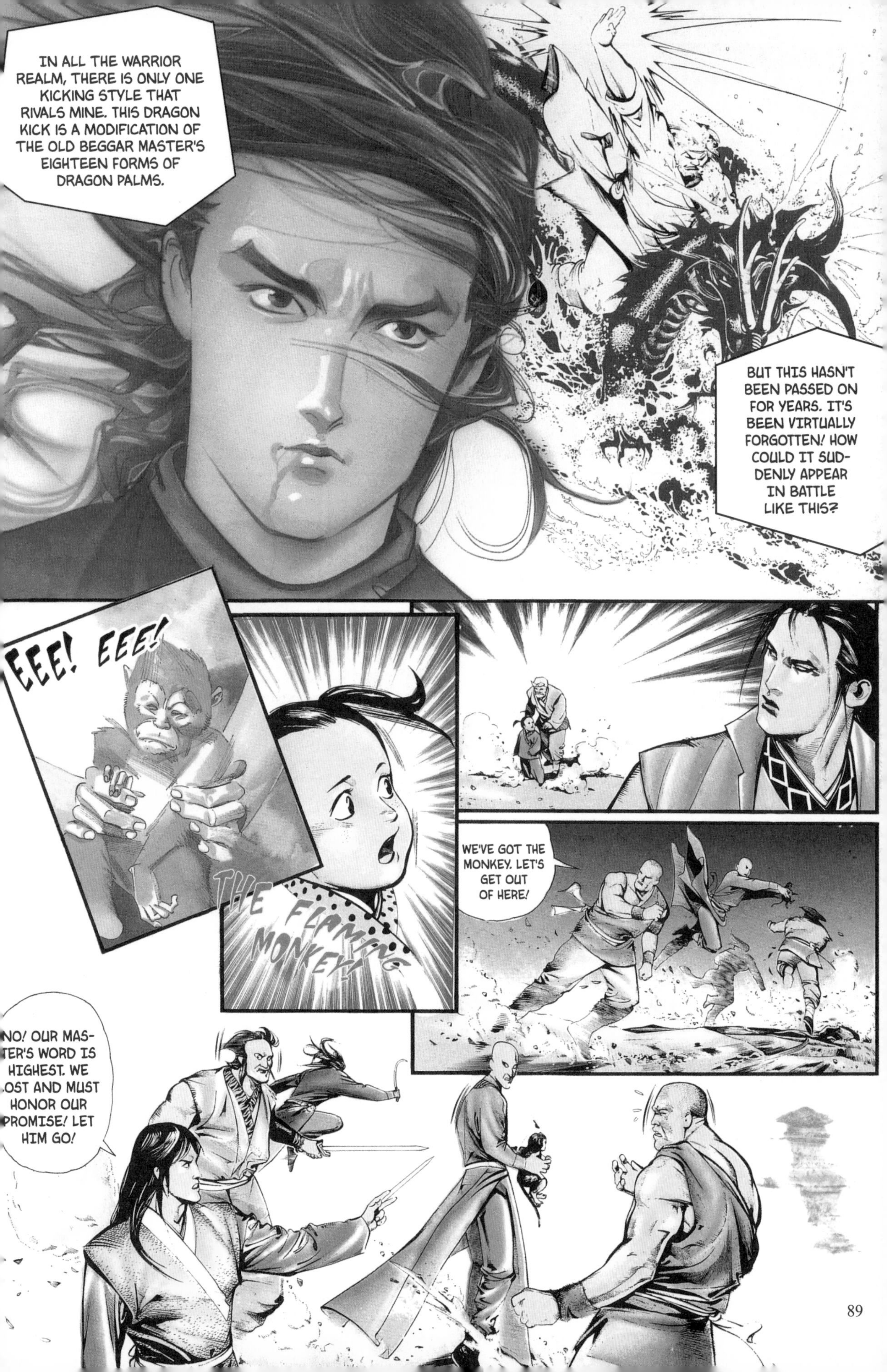
IN ALL THE WARRIOR REALM, THERE IS ONLY ONE KICKING STYLE THAT RIVALS MINE. THIS DRAGON KICK IS A MODIFICATION OF THE OLD BEGGAR MASTER'S EIGHTEEN FORMS OF DRAGON PALMS.
BUT THIS HASN'T BEEN PASSED ON FOR YEARS. IT'S BEEN VIRTUALLY FORGOTTEN! HOW COULD IT SUDDENLY APPEAR IN BATTLE LIKE THIS?
EEE! EEE!
THE FLAMING MONKEY!
WE'VE GOT THE MONKEY. LET'S GET OUT OF HERE!
NO! OUR MASTER'S WORD IS HIGHEST. WE LOST AND MUST HONOR OUR PROMISE! LET HIM GO!

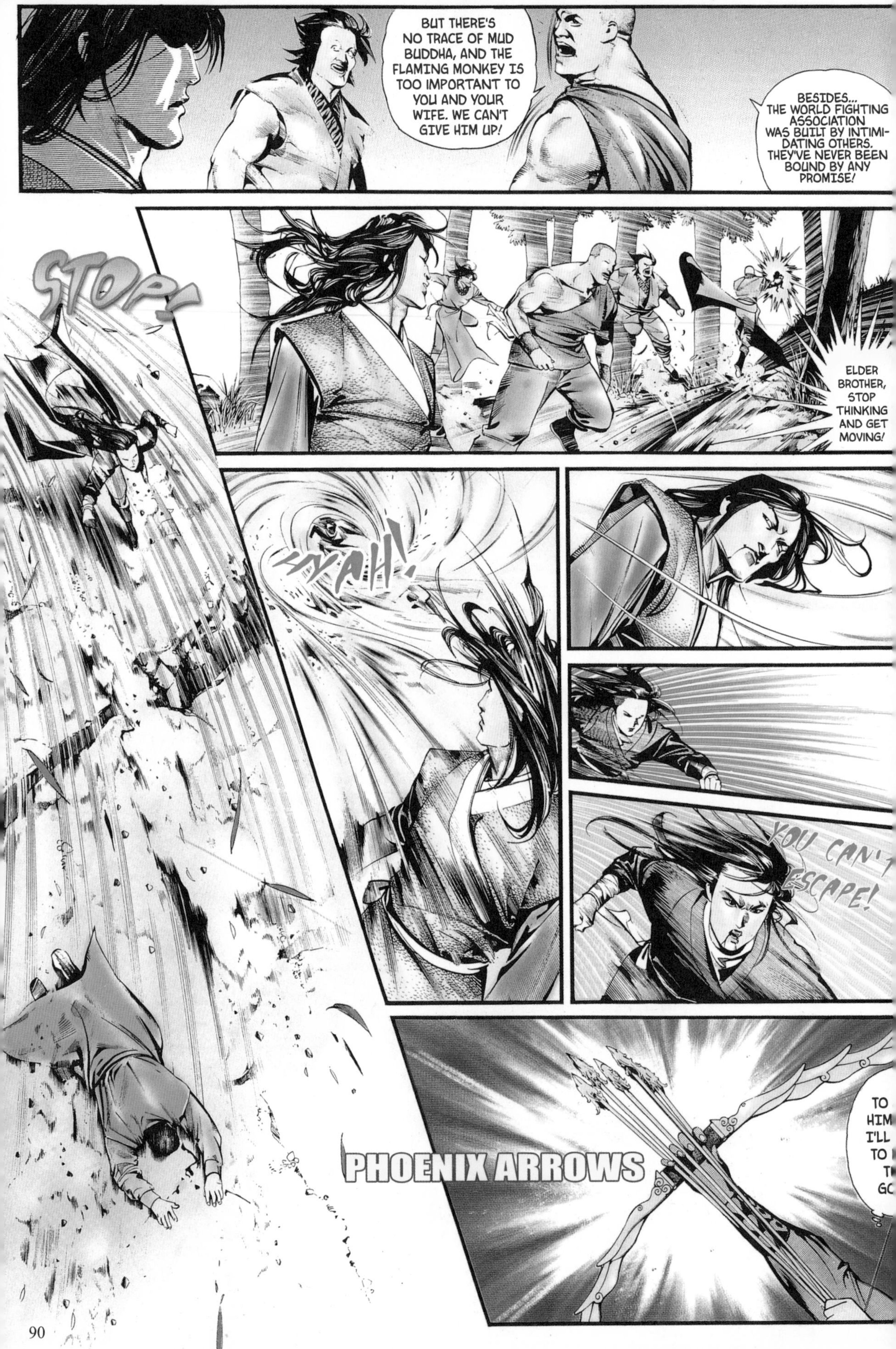
BUT THERE'S NO TRACE OF MUD BUDDHA, AND THE FLAMING MONKEY IS TOO IMPORTANT TO YOU AND YOUR WIFE. WE CAN'T GIVE HIM UP!
BESIDES... THE WORLD FIGHTING ASSOCIATION WAS BUILT BY INTIMIDATING OTHERS. THEY'VE NEVER BEEN BOUND BY ANY PROMISE!
STOP!
ELDER BROTHER, STOP THINKING AND GET MOVING!
HYAH!!
YOU CAN'T ESCAPE!
PHOENIX ARROWS

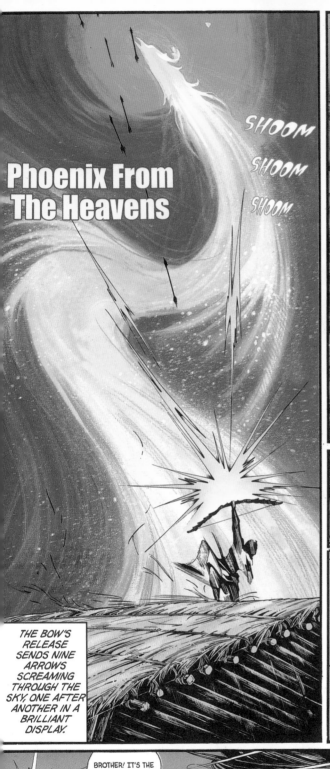

Phoenix From The Heavens

SHOOM

SHOOM

SHOOM

THE BOW'S RELEASE SENDS NINE ARROWS SCREAMING THROUGH THE SKY, ONE AFTER ANOTHER IN A BRILLIANT DISPLAY.

AH! PHOENIX'S MOST CUNNING ATTACK!

BROTHER! IT'S THE PHOENIX FROM THE HEAVENS! WATCH OUT!

AS HE HEARS FROST'S WARNING, THE FLYING ARROWS BEGIN THEIR DESCENT TOWARD WIND.

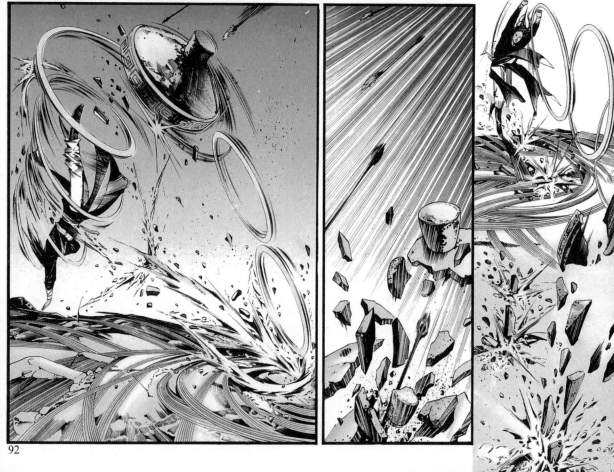

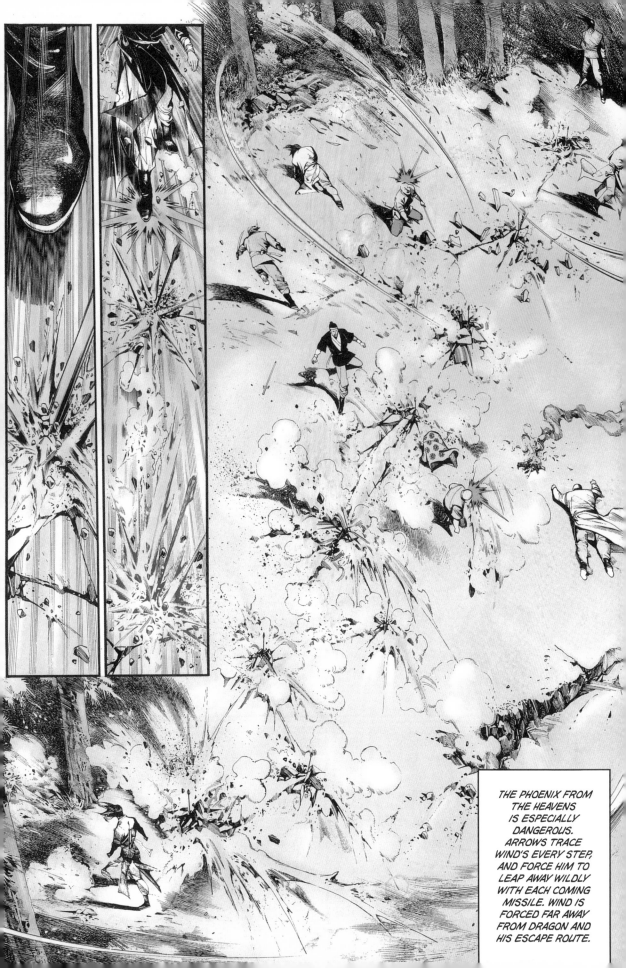

THE PHOENIX FROM
THE HEAVENS
IS ESPECIALLY
DANGEROUS.
ARROWS TRACE
WIND'S EVERY STEP,
AND FORCE HIM TO
LEAP AWAY WILDLY
WITH EACH COMING
MISSILE. WIND IS
FORCED FAR AWAY
FROM DRAGON AND
HIS ESCAPE ROUTE.

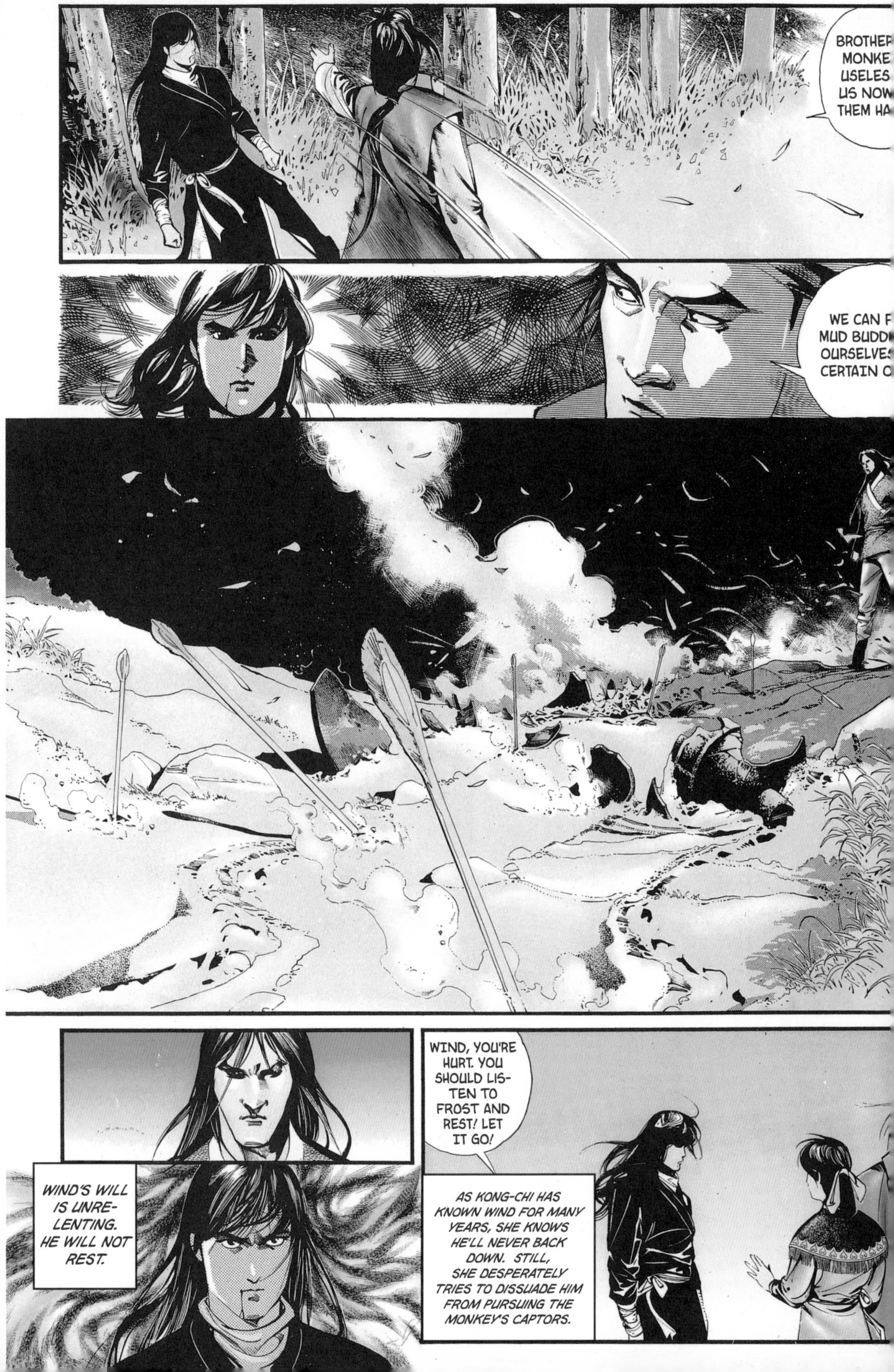

BROTHER MONKE USELES US NOW THEM HA
WE CAN F MUD BUDD OURSELVES CERTAIN C
WIND'S WILL IS UNRE-LENTING. HE WILL NOT REST.
WIND, YOU'RE HURT. YOU SHOULD LIS-TEN TO FROST AND REST! LET IT GO!
AS KONG-CHI HAS KNOWN WIND FOR MANY YEARS, SHE KNOWS HE'LL NEVER BACK DOWN. STILL, SHE DESPERATELY TRIES TO DISSUADE HIM FROM PURSUING THE MONKEY'S CAPTORS.

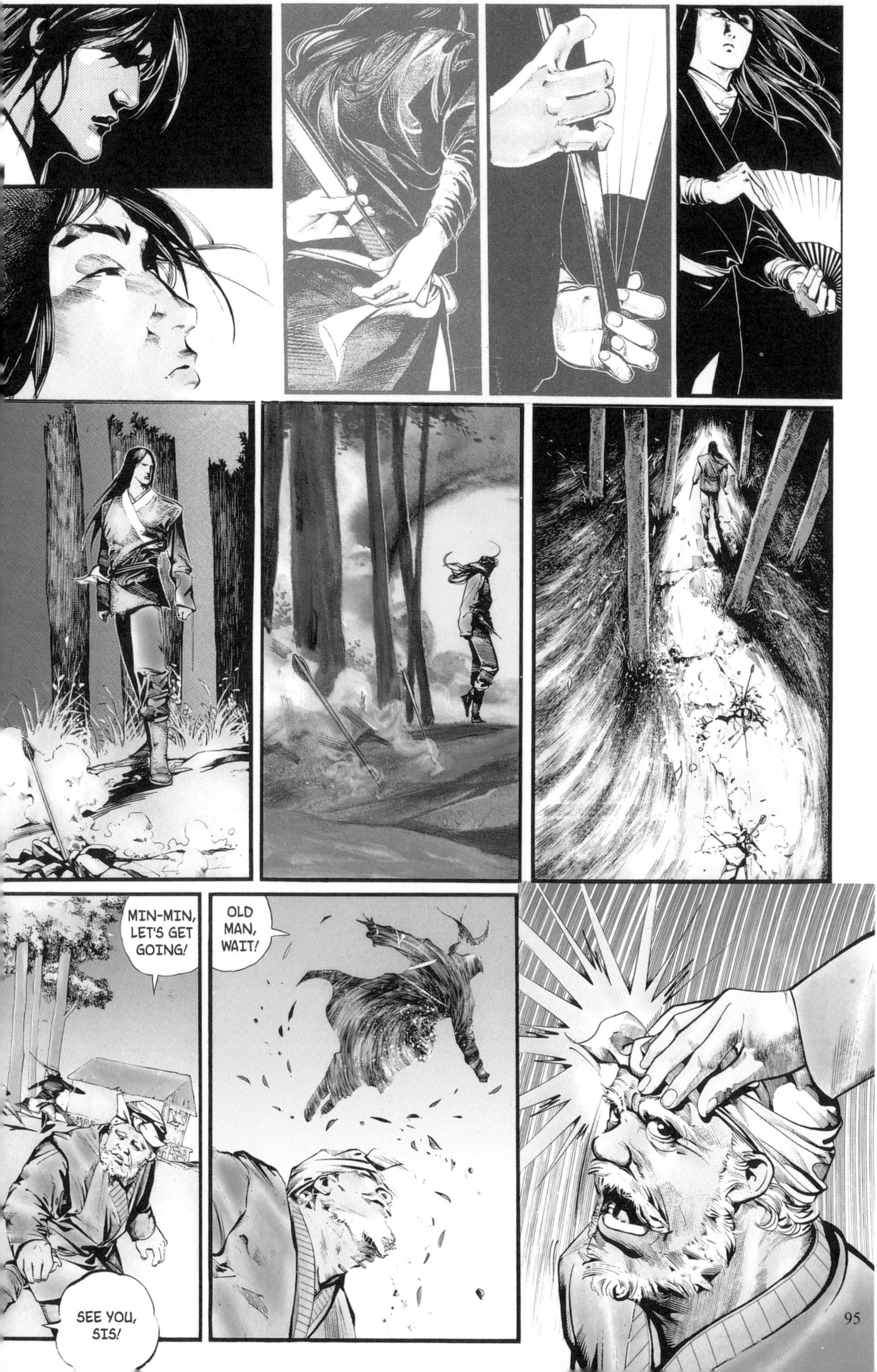
MIN-MIN, LET'S GET GOING!
SEE YOU, SIS!
OLD MAN, WAIT!

MY GOD, MUD BUDDHA WAS HERE WITH US ALL ALONG!

PLEASE FORGIVE US, SIR... BUT FATE COMMANDS THAT I ASK YOU TO ACCOMPANY US TO CONQUER'S COURT.

TEA... OF MAS... FL... AND... FR... REV... THE... MA... T... IDEN...

I HAD HEARD THAT FROST'S MIND IS KEEN... THAT HE SEES THROUGH OTHERS' SCHEMING, AND SURE ENOUGH...

YOU FLATTER ME, SIR.

MUD BUDDHA

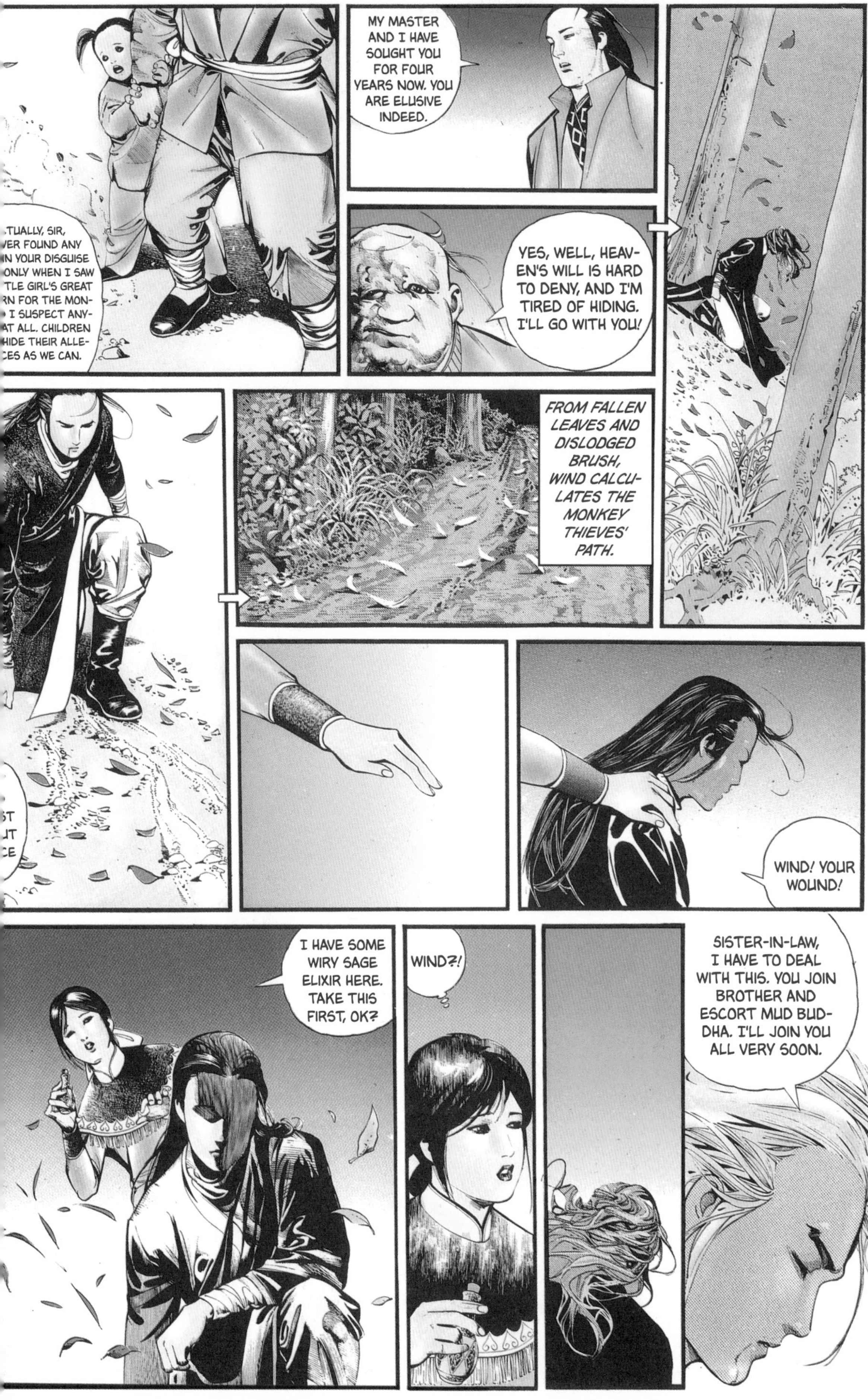
TUALLY, SIR,
VER FOUND ANY
N YOUR DISGUISE
ONLY WHEN I SAW
TLE GIRL'S GREAT
RN FOR THE MON-
I SUSPECT ANY-
AT ALL. CHILDREN
HIDE THEIR ALLE-
CES AS WE CAN.
MY MASTER AND I HAVE SOUGHT YOU FOR FOUR YEARS NOW. YOU ARE ELUSIVE INDEED.
YES, WELL, HEAVEN'S WILL IS HARD TO DENY, AND I'M TIRED OF HIDING. I'LL GO WITH YOU!
FROM FALLEN LEAVES AND DISLODGED BRUSH, WIND CALCULATES THE MONKEY THIEVES' PATH.
ST
IT
CE
WIND! YOUR WOUND!
I HAVE SOME WIRY SAGE ELIXIR HERE. TAKE THIS FIRST, OK?
WIND?!
SISTER-IN-LAW, I HAVE TO DEAL WITH THIS. YOU JOIN BROTHER AND ESCORT MUD BUDDHA. I'LL JOIN YOU ALL VERY SOON.

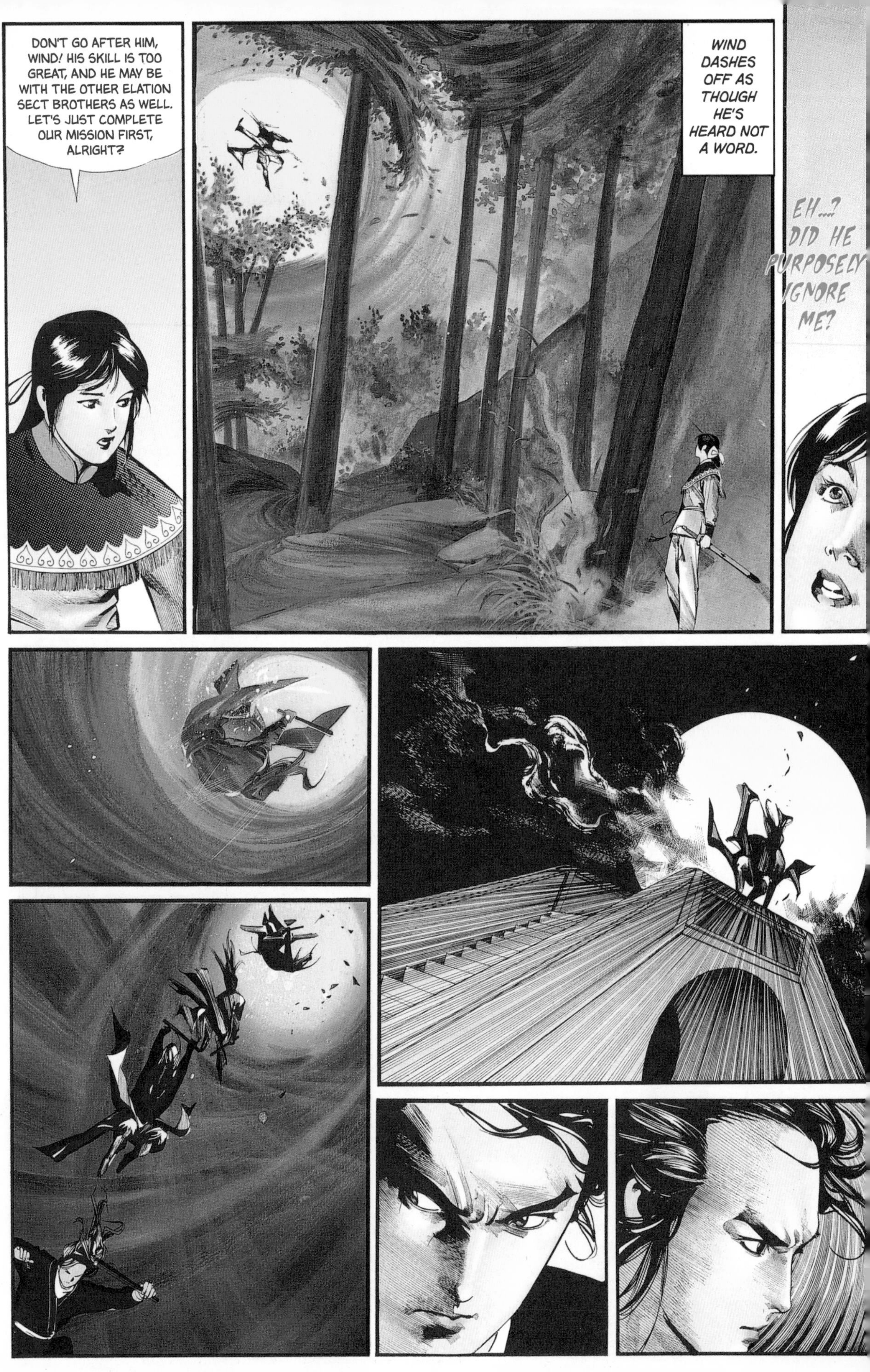
DON'T GO AFTER HIM, WIND! HIS SKILL IS TOO GREAT, AND HE MAY BE WITH THE OTHER ELATION SECT BROTHERS AS WELL. LET'S JUST COMPLETE OUR MISSION FIRST, ALRIGHT?
WIND DASHES OFF AS THOUGH HE'S HEARD NOT A WORD.
EH...? DID HE PURPOSELY IGNORE ME?

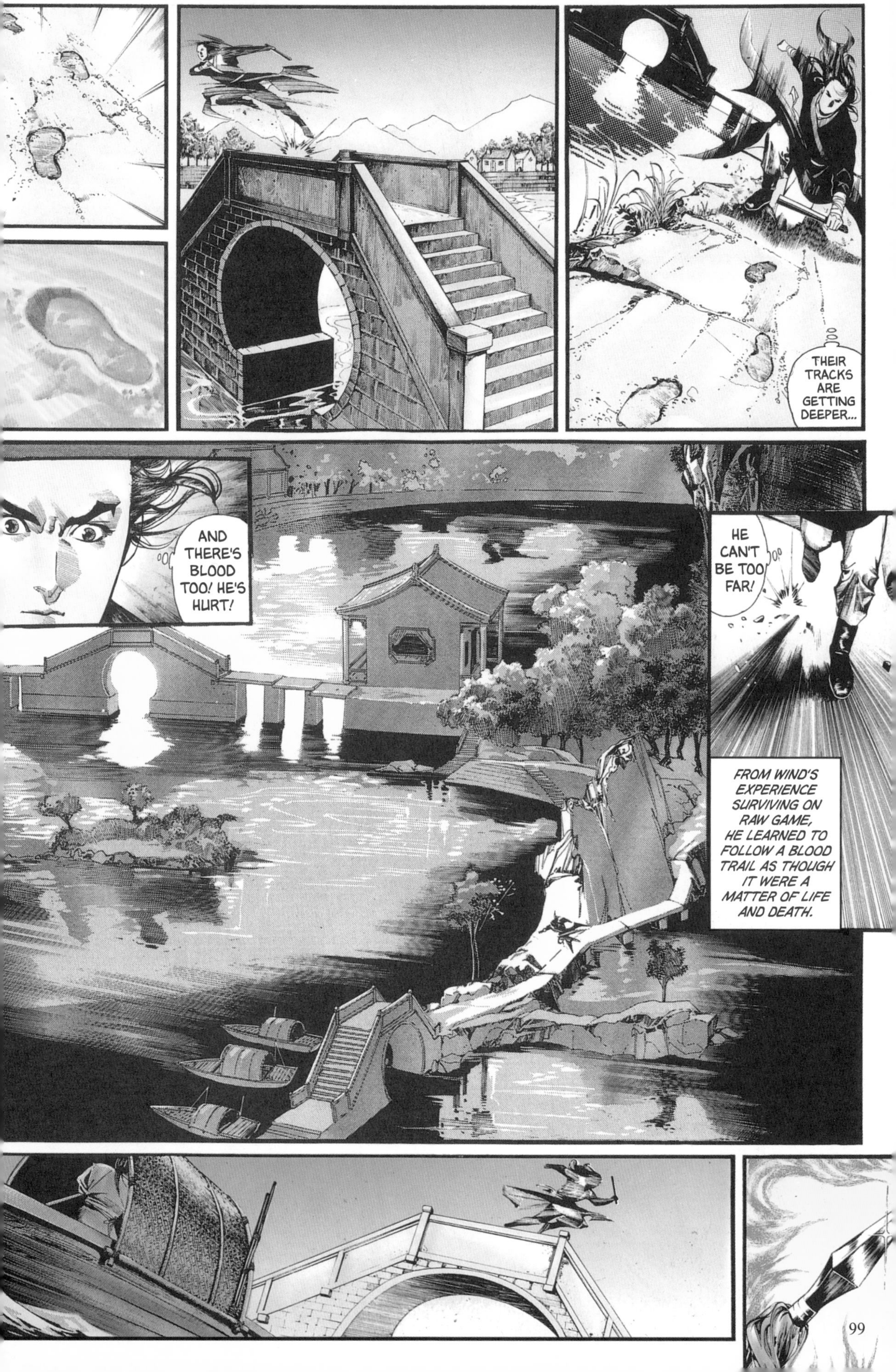
THEIR TRACKS ARE GETTING DEEPER...
AND THERE'S BLOOD TOO! HE'S HURT!
HE CAN'T BE TOO FAR!
FROM WIND'S EXPERIENCE SURVIVING ON RAW GAME, HE LEARNED TO FOLLOW A BLOOD TRAIL AS THOUGH IT WERE A MATTER OF LIFE AND DEATH.

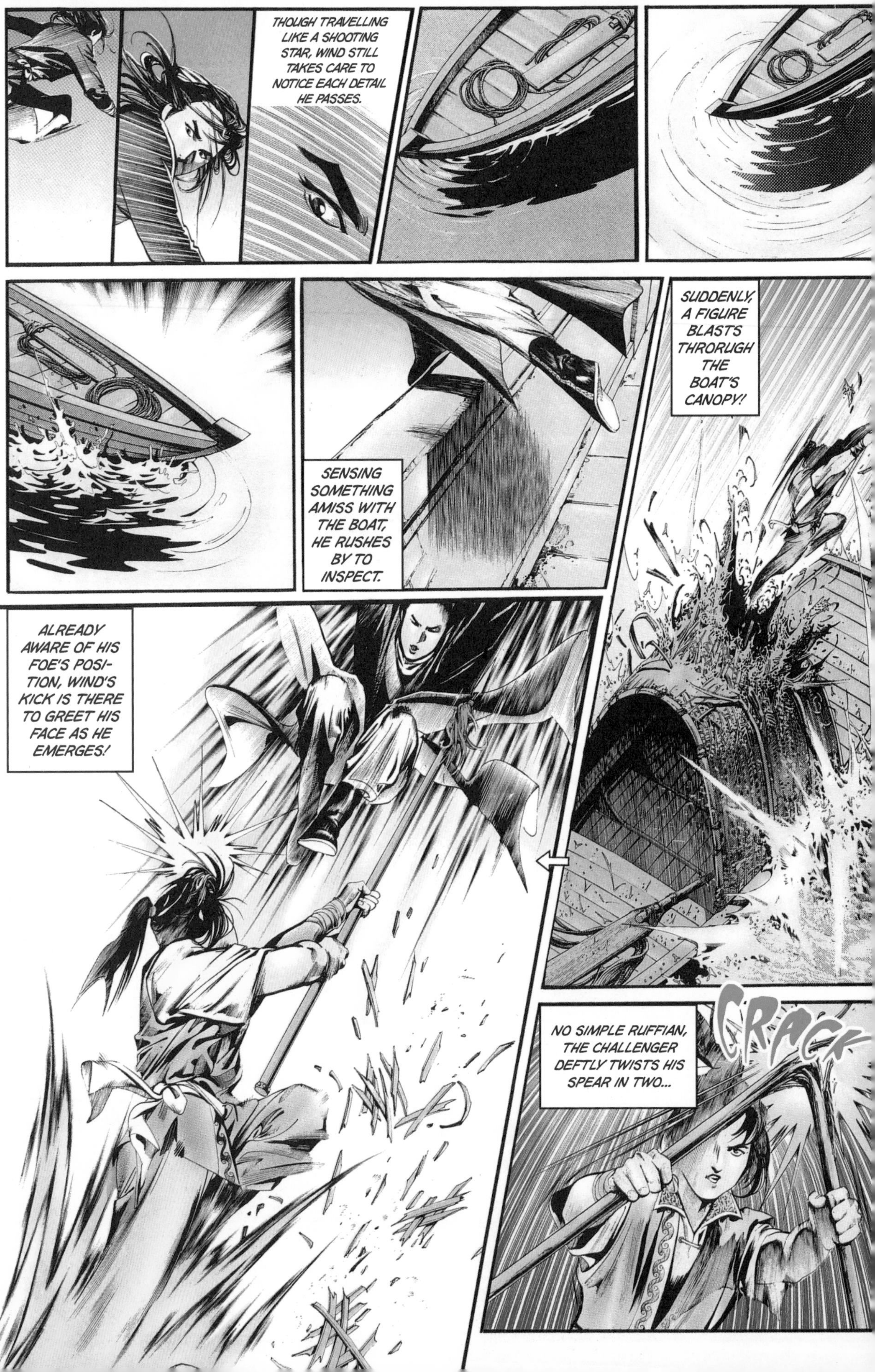
THOUGH TRAVELLING LIKE A SHOOTING STAR, WIND STILL TAKES CARE TO NOTICE EACH DETAIL HE PASSES.
SENSING SOMETHING AMISS WITH THE BOAT, HE RUSHES BY TO INSPECT.
SUDDENLY, A FIGURE BLASTS THRORUGH THE BOAT'S CANOPY!
ALREADY AWARE OF HIS FOE'S POSI-TION, WIND'S KICK IS THERE TO GREET HIS FACE AS HE EMERGES!
NO SIMPLE RUFFIAN, THE CHALLENGER DEFTLY TWISTS HIS SPEAR IN TWO...
CRACK

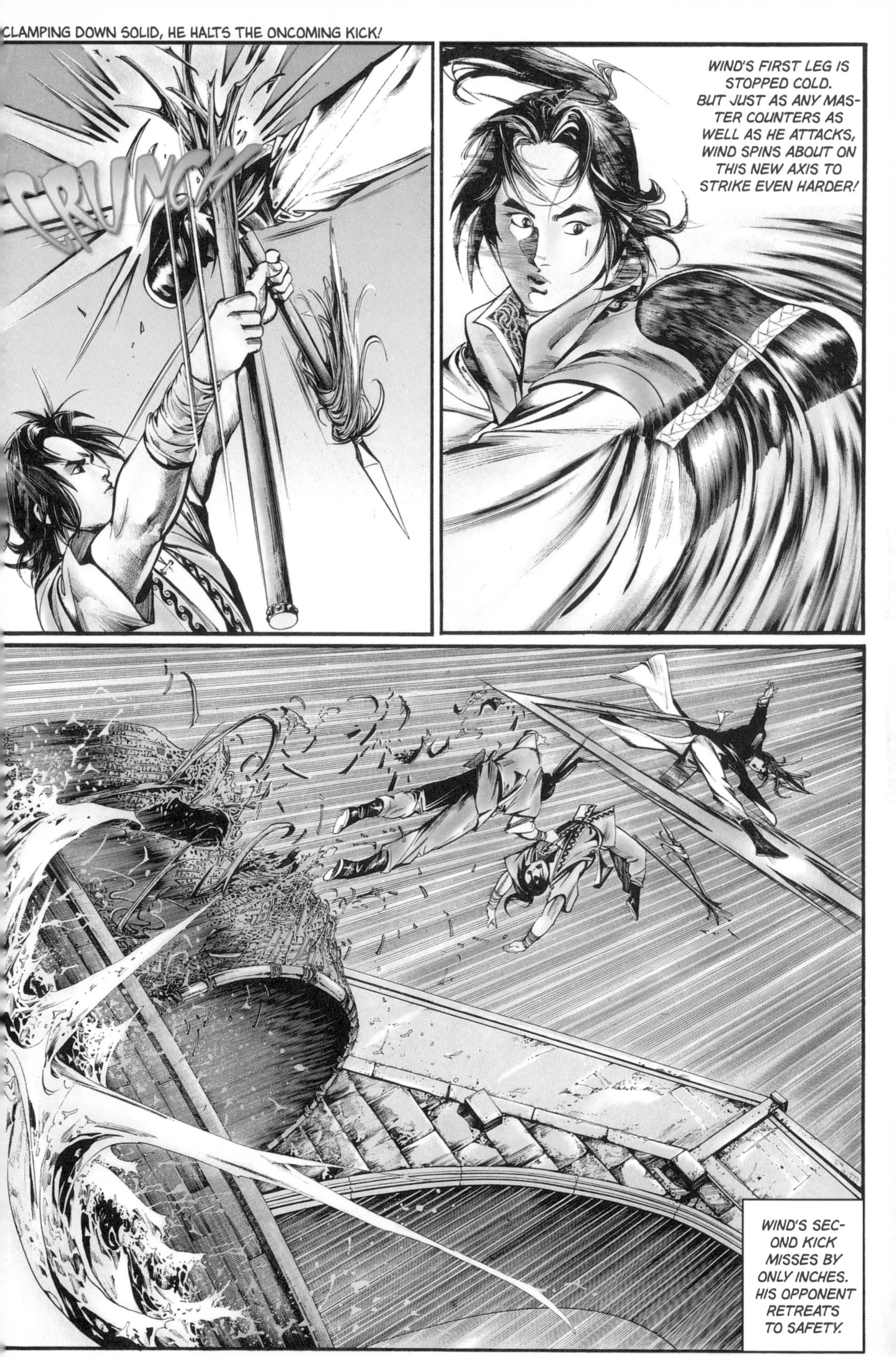
CLAMPING DOWN SOLID, HE HALTS THE ONCOMING KICK!
CRUNCH
WIND'S FIRST LEG IS STOPPED COLD. BUT JUST AS ANY MASTER COUNTERS AS WELL AS HE ATTACKS, WIND SPINS ABOUT ON THIS NEW AXIS TO STRIKE EVEN HARDER!
WIND'S SECOND KICK MISSES BY ONLY INCHES. HIS OPPONENT RETREATS TO SAFETY.

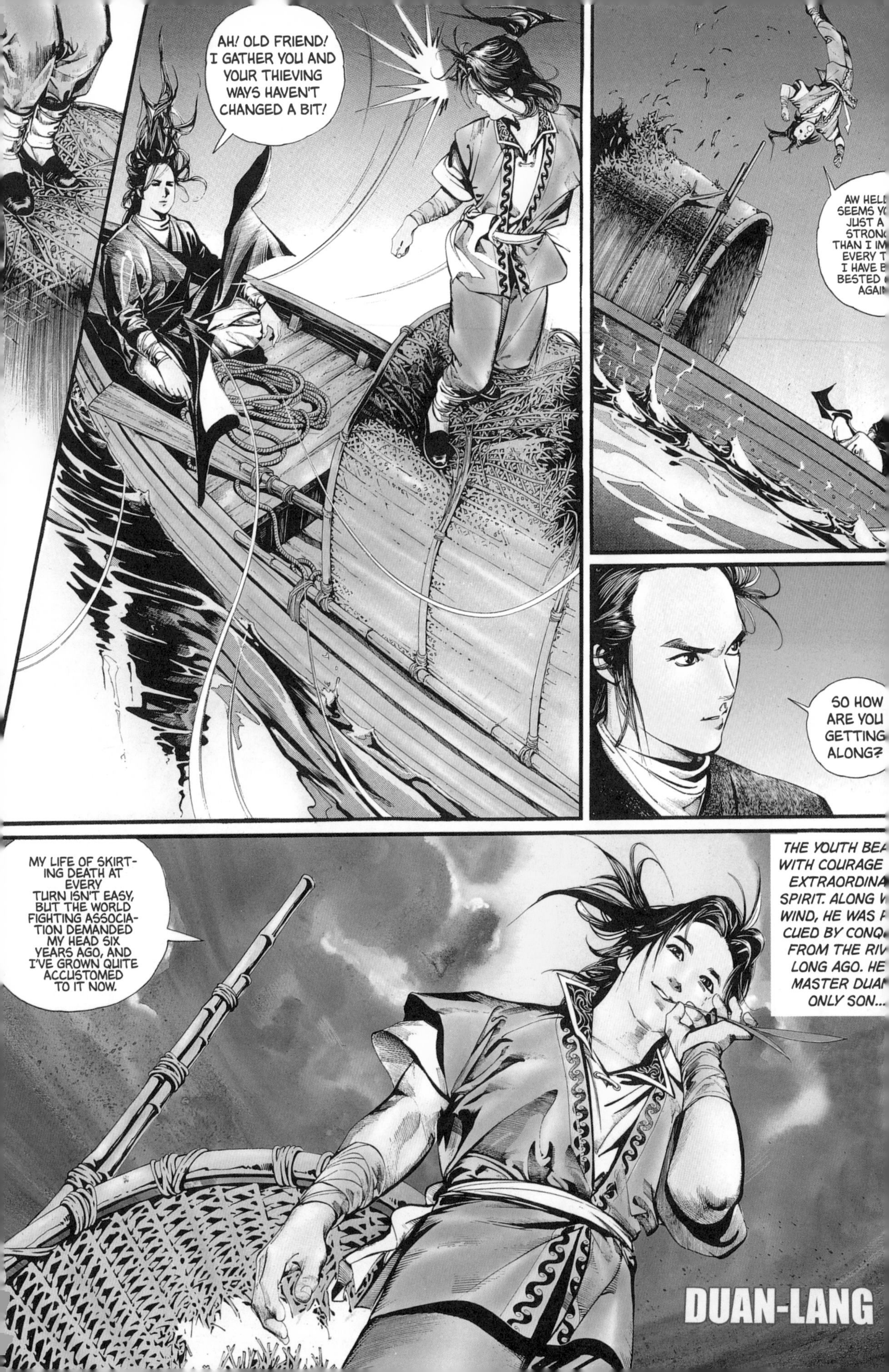

AH! OLD FRIEND! I GATHER YOU AND YOUR THIEVING WAYS HAVEN'T CHANGED A BIT!
AW HELL SEEMS YO JUST A STRONG THAN I IM EVERY T I HAVE B BESTED AGAIN
SO HOW ARE YOU GETTING ALONG?
MY LIFE OF SKIRT-ING DEATH AT EVERY TURN ISN'T EASY, BUT THE WORLD FIGHTING ASSOCIA-TION DEMANDED MY HEAD SIX YEARS AGO, AND I'VE GROWN QUITE ACCUSTOMED TO IT NOW.
THE YOUTH BEA WITH COURAGE EXTRAORDINA SPIRIT. ALONG W WIND, HE WAS R CUED BY CONQ FROM THE RIV LONG AGO. HE MASTER DUAN ONLY SON...
DUAN-LANG

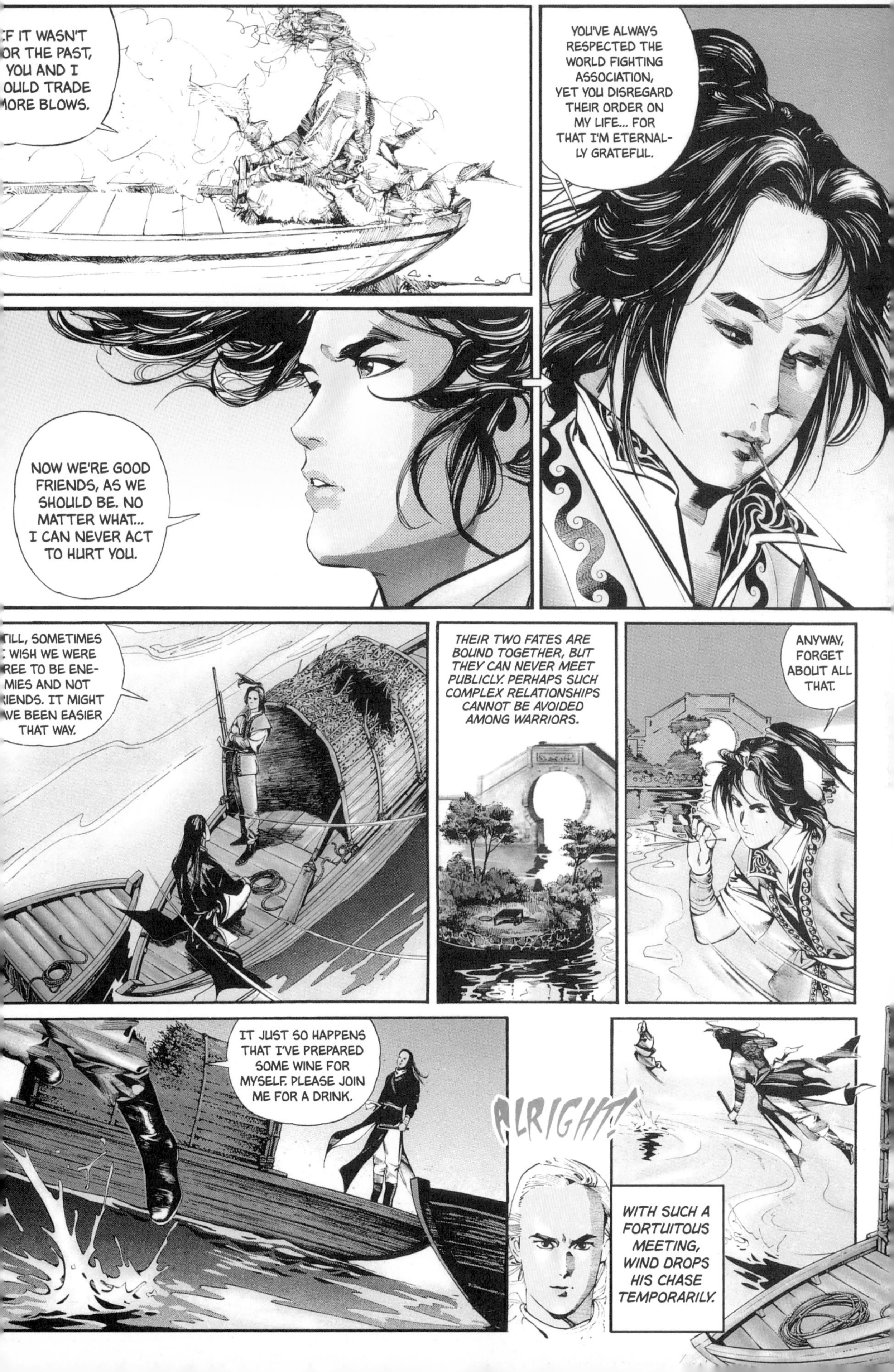

[I]F IT WASN'T [F]OR THE PAST, YOU AND I [W]OULD TRADE MORE BLOWS.
YOU'VE ALWAYS RESPECTED THE WORLD FIGHTING ASSOCIATION, YET YOU DISREGARD THEIR ORDER ON MY LIFE... FOR THAT I'M ETERNALLY GRATEFUL.
NOW WE'RE GOOD FRIENDS, AS WE SHOULD BE. NO MATTER WHAT... I CAN NEVER ACT TO HURT YOU.
[S]TILL, SOMETIMES [I] WISH WE WERE [F]REE TO BE ENEMIES AND NOT [F]RIENDS. IT MIGHT [H]AVE BEEN EASIER THAT WAY.
THEIR TWO FATES ARE BOUND TOGETHER, BUT THEY CAN NEVER MEET PUBLICLY. PERHAPS SUCH COMPLEX RELATIONSHIPS CANNOT BE AVOIDED AMONG WARRIORS.
ANYWAY, FORGET ABOUT ALL THAT.
IT JUST SO HAPPENS THAT I'VE PREPARED SOME WINE FOR MYSELF. PLEASE JOIN ME FOR A DRINK.
ALRIGHT!
WITH SUCH A FORTUITOUS MEETING, WIND DROPS HIS CHASE TEMPORARILY.

IT IS CLEAR THAT DUAN-LANG HAS COME INTO HIS OWN. HIS WATER STEPPING IS LIGHT AND GRACEFUL.

OUR MATCH, THREE YEARS IN WAITING, IS NOW ONLY TWO MONTHS AWAY.

YES, I KNOW!

WHEN THE TIME COMES, IT SHOULD BE DECIDED AT LIN-YIN CAVE

THIS TIME, I BELIEVE I'LL BEAT YOU!

ALL RIGHT, THEN I LOOK FORWARD TO IT. IF YOU'VE GOT IT IN YOU, COME TRY ME! BUT I MUST WARN YOU, I DO STILL TRAIN THESE DAYS.

DUAN-LANG
MATCHED A
FALLEN BEF
WIND THROUG
HIS YOUTH. T
DAYS HELD N
MATCHES, AN
COMPETITION
GROWN INT
FRIENDLY RIVA

REMEMBER, LIN-YIN CAVE, AND GOOD LUCK!

THE REUNION HAS BEEN AN AWKWARD ONE. DUAN-LANG KNEW THIS AS HE LEFT, AND WIND IS ALSO DEEPLY AWARE OF THEIR DIFFERENCES.

DUAN-LANG HAD SURVIVED THAT YEAR AS HE SAID. AT ONE POINT, HE TOO HAD TAKEN REFUGE WITH THE WORLD FIGHTING ASSOCIATION. HOW, THEN, DID IT COME TO CONQUER PUTTING A PRICE ON HIS HEAD... LEAVING HIM FACING DEATH AT EVERY TURN? THIS TOO HAS ITS STORY...

SIR, I HAVE ALREADY CARE-FULLY OBSERVED AND STUDIED WIND'S KICKING FORM IN ACTION, AND EVEN TESTED HIM IN A MATCH!

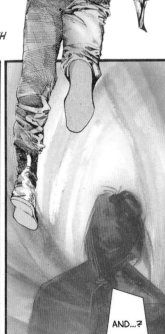

AND...?

HE'S MUCH STRONGER THAN I IMAGINED!

YET WITH THIS SH EXCHANG WORKED C WEAKNES CERTAIN DEFEAT NEXT T

HUH?

DUAN-

SWORD SAINT, YOU ORDERED ME TO WAY-LAY WIND, AND IT IS DONE!

WH TH WIND TAIL ME ALO

HOW YOU LET FOLL HE I C ALR HA AVE FAT DE IN K

DON'T OVER-ESTI-MATE YOUR-SELF!

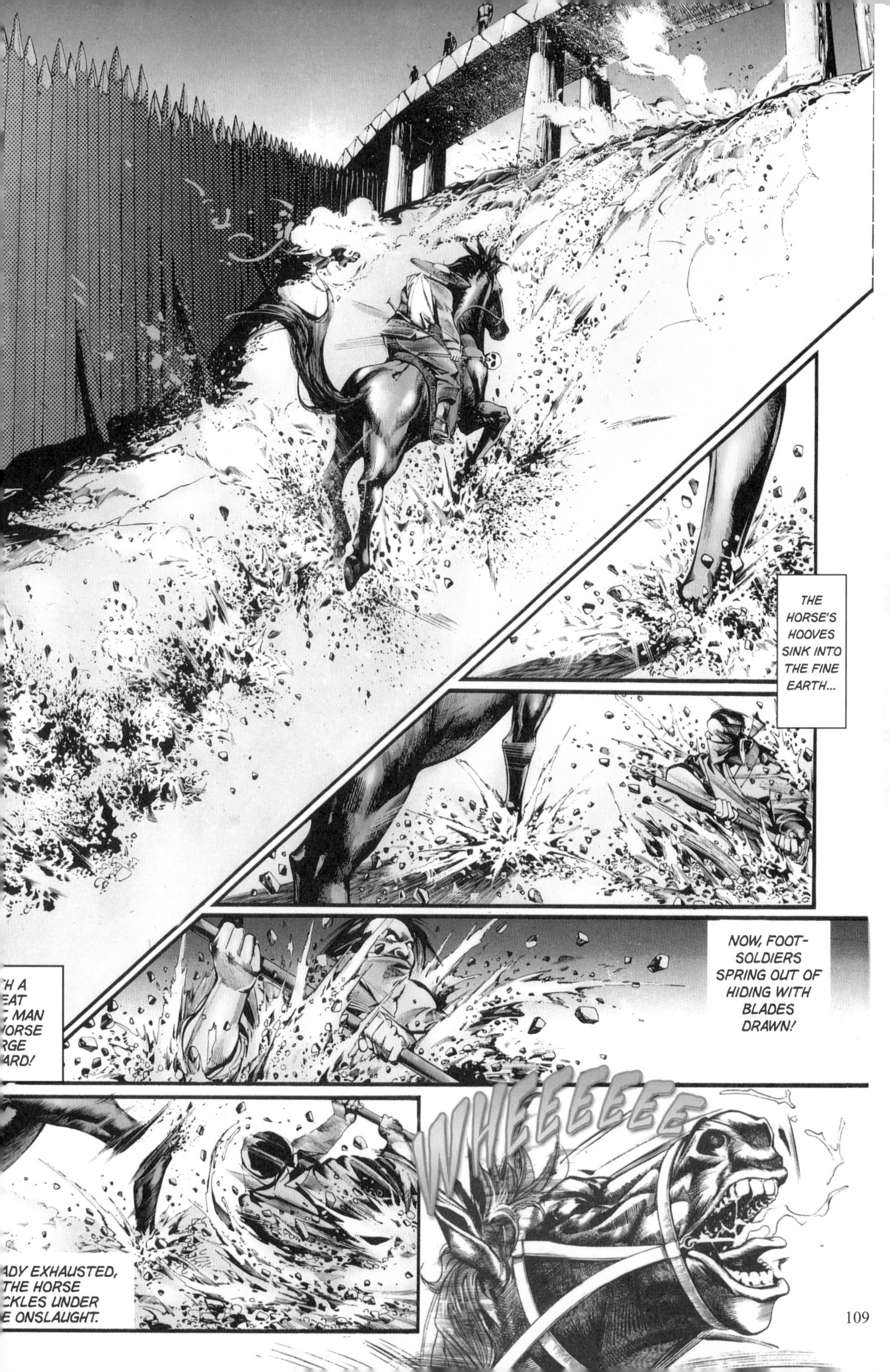
THE HORSE'S HOOVES SINK INTO THE FINE EARTH...
NOW, FOOT-SOLDIERS SPRING OUT OF HIDING WITH BLADES DRAWN!
TH A EAT MAN ORSE RGE ARD!
WHEEEEEE
ADY EXHAUSTED, THE HORSE CKLES UNDER E ONSLAUGHT.

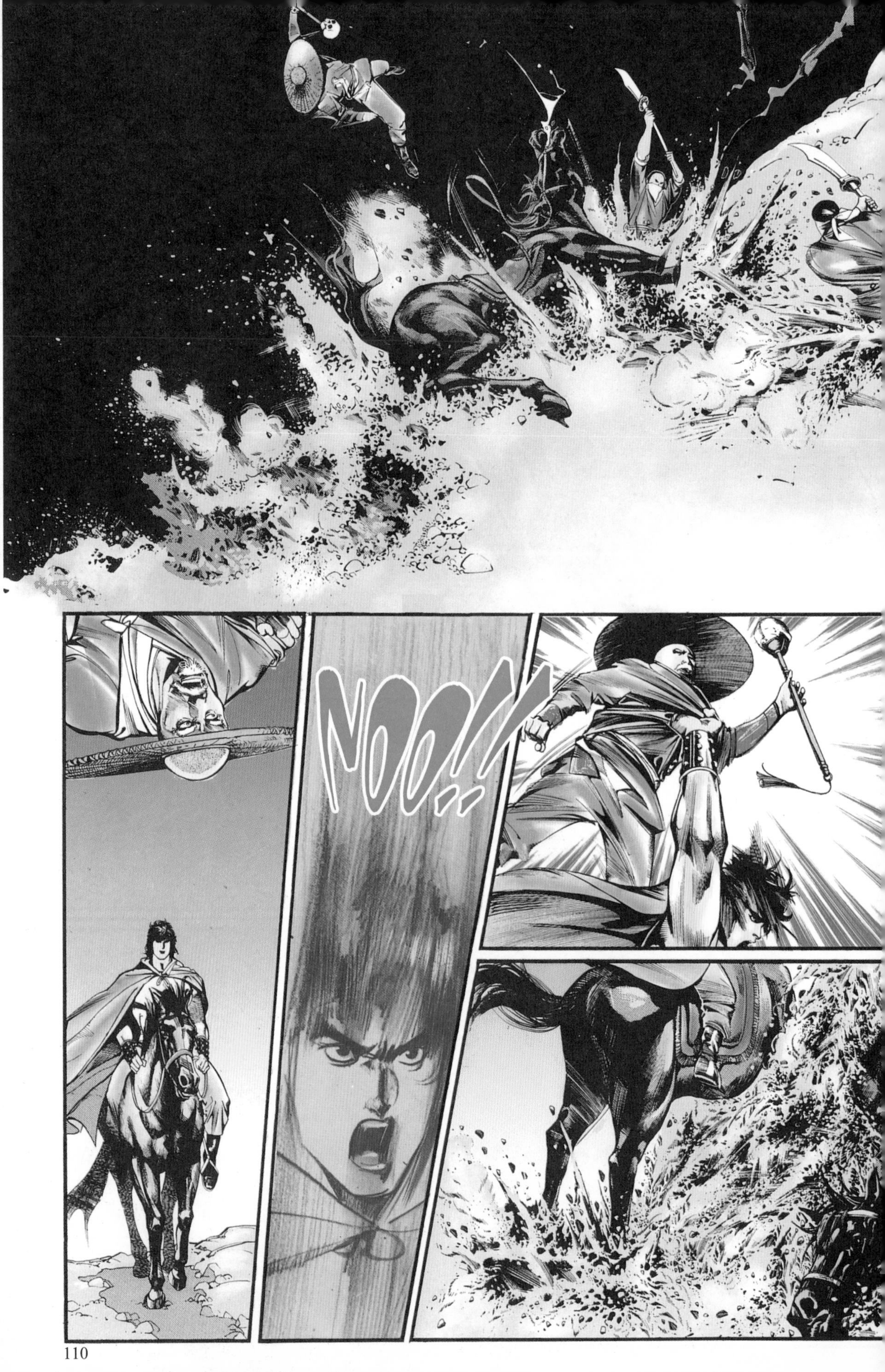
NOO!!

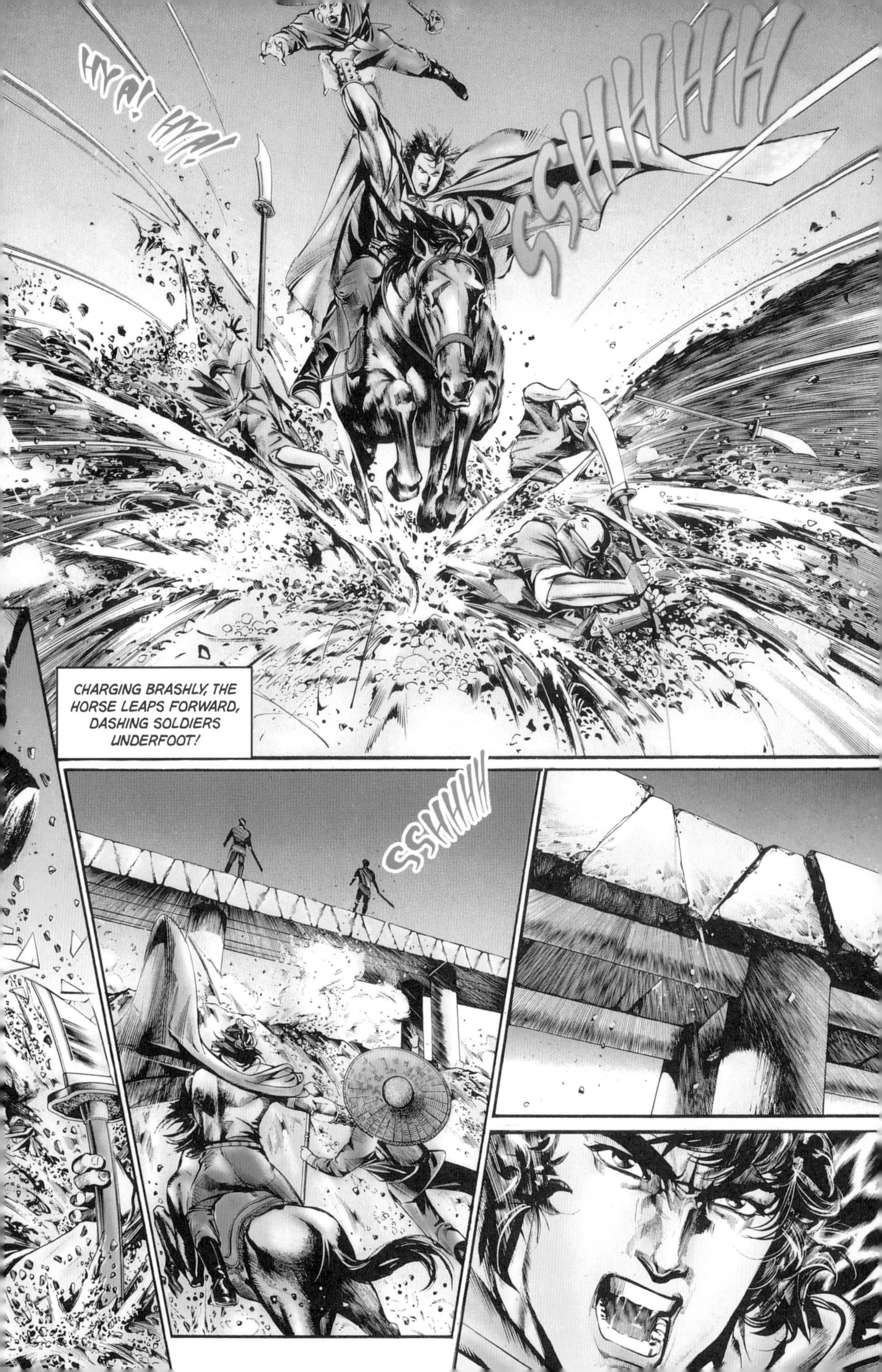
HYA! HYA!
SSHHHHH
CHARGING BRASHLY, THE HORSE LEAPS FORWARD, DASHING SOLDIERS UNDERFOOT!
SSHHHHH

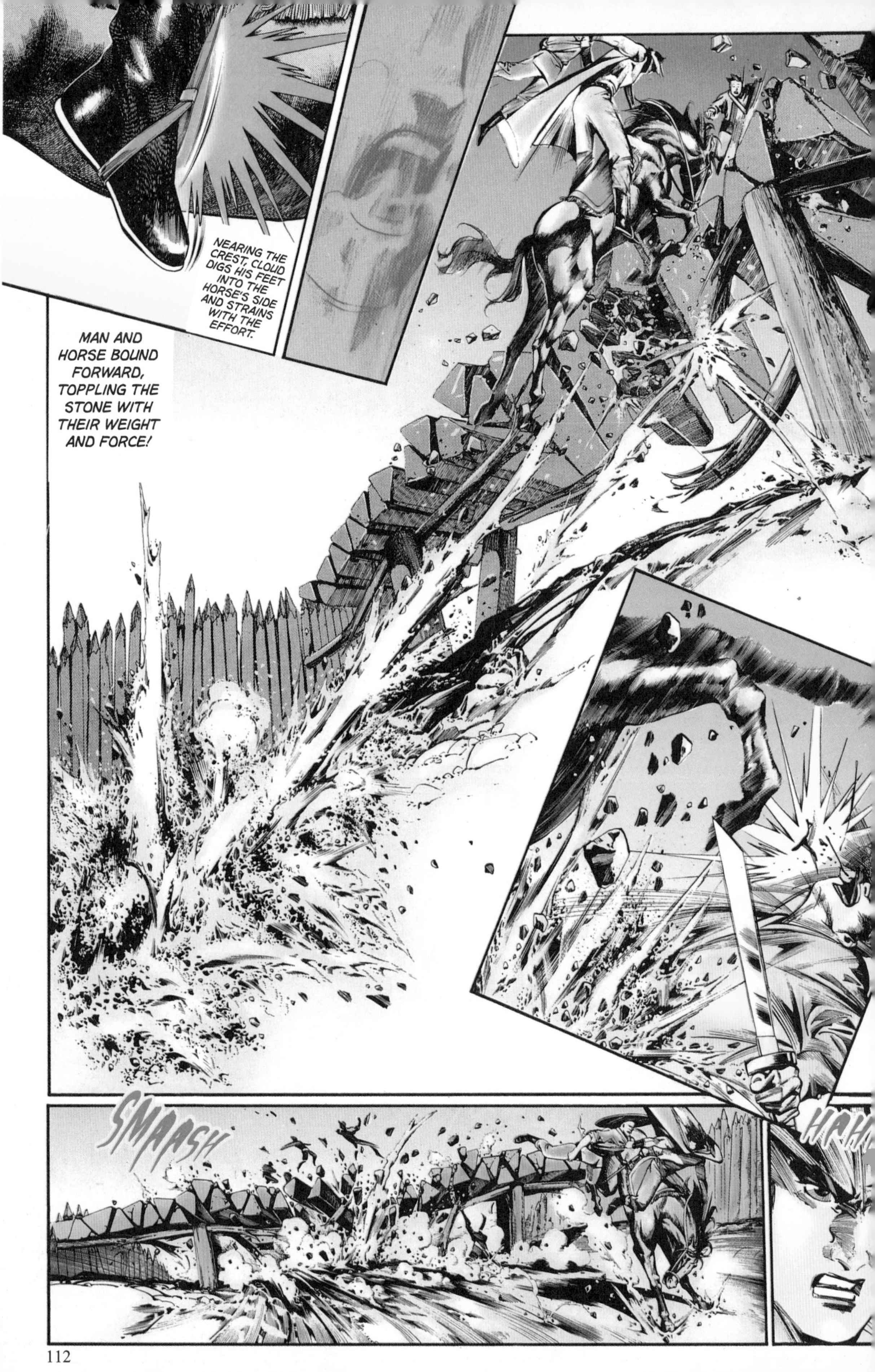
NEARING THE CREST, CLOUD DIGS HIS FEET INTO THE HORSE'S SIDE AND STRAINS WITH THE EFFORT.
MAN AND HORSE BOUND FORWARD, TOPPLING THE STONE WITH THEIR WEIGHT AND FORCE!
SMAASH

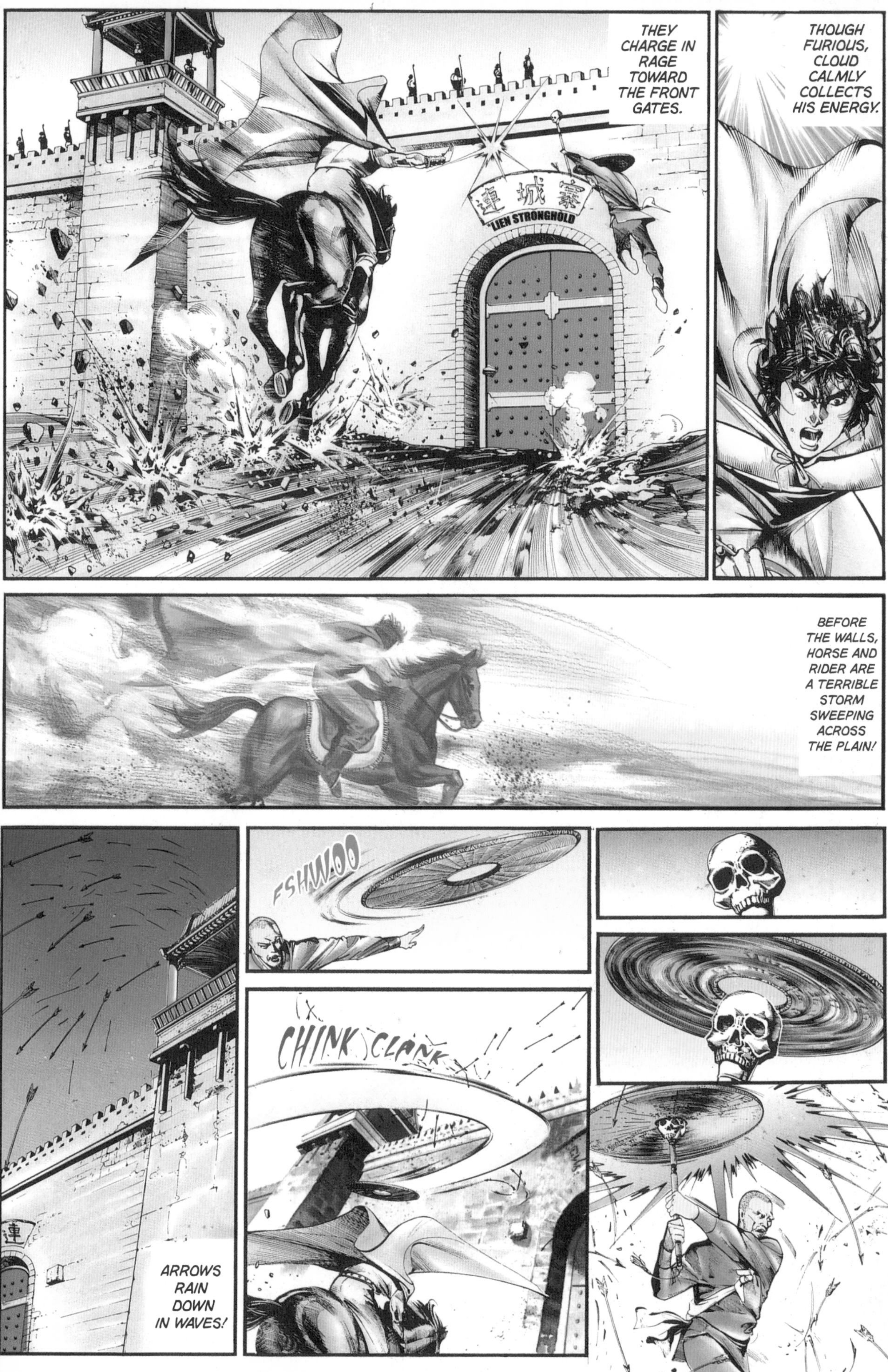
THEY CHARGE IN RAGE TOWARD THE FRONT GATES.
連城寨
LIEN STRONGHOLD
THOUGH FURIOUS, CLOUD CALMLY COLLECTS HIS ENERGY.
BEFORE THE WALLS, HORSE AND RIDER ARE A TERRIBLE STORM SWEEPING ACROSS THE PLAIN!
ARROWS RAIN DOWN IN WAVES!
FSHWOO
CHINK CLANK

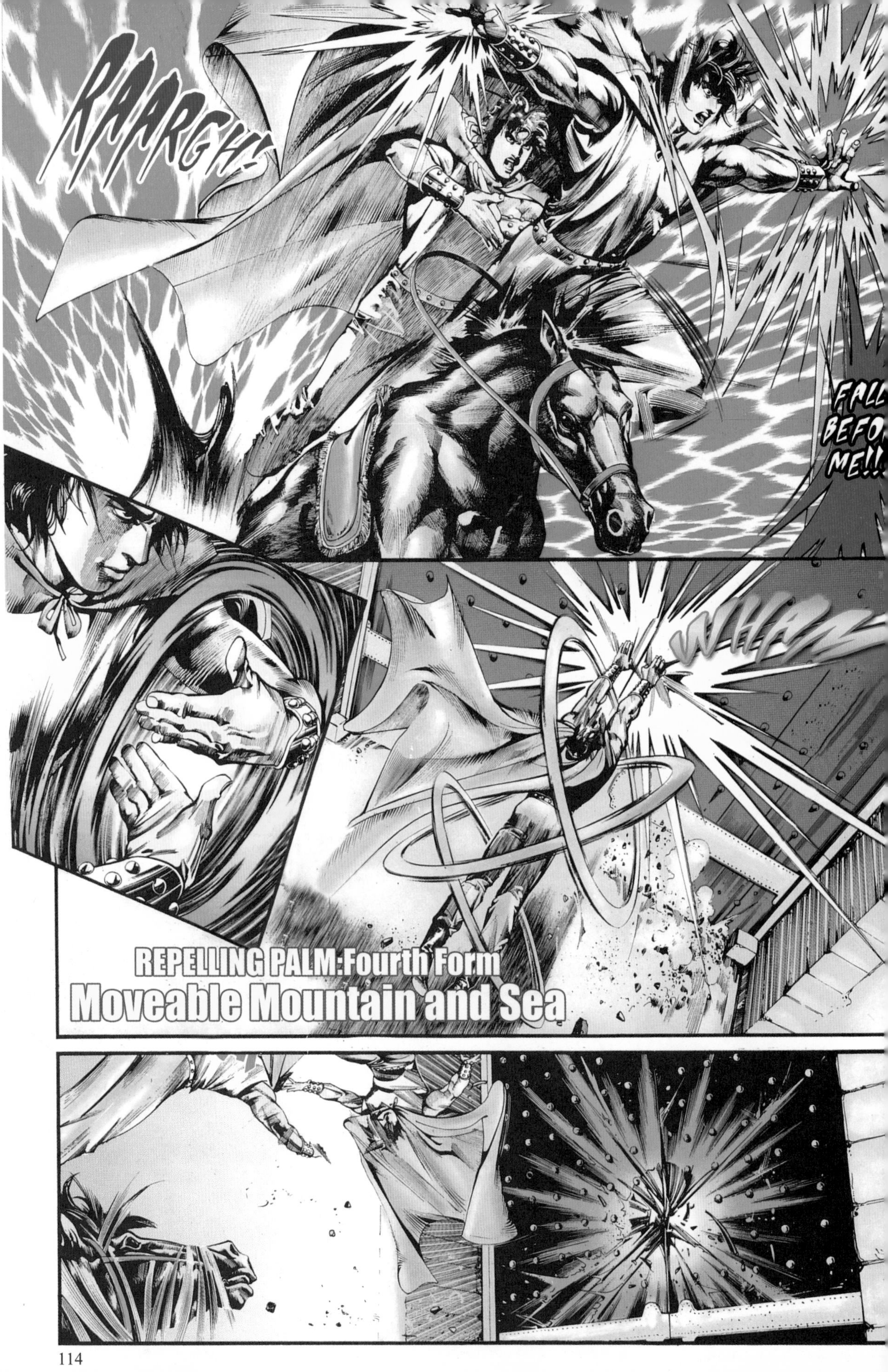
RAARGH!!
FALL BEFO ME!!
WHAM
REPELLING PALM: Fourth Form
Moveable Mountain and Sea

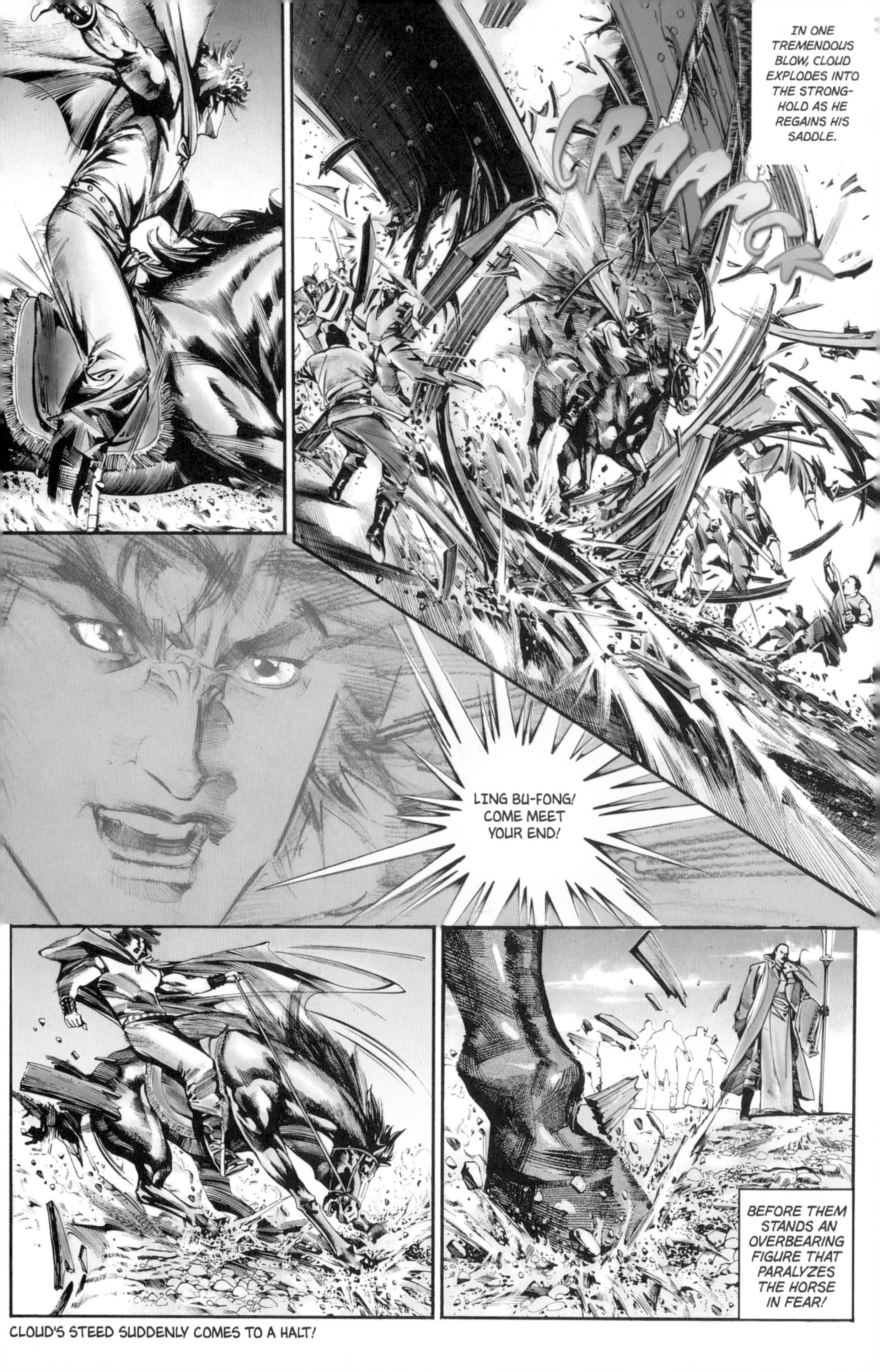
IN ONE TREMENDOUS BLOW, CLOUD EXPLODES INTO THE STRONGHOLD AS HE REGAINS HIS SADDLE.
CRAAACK
LING BU-FONG! COME MEET YOUR END!
BEFORE THEM STANDS AN OVERBEARING FIGURE THAT PARALYZES THE HORSE IN FEAR!
CLOUD'S STEED SUDDENLY COMES TO A HALT!

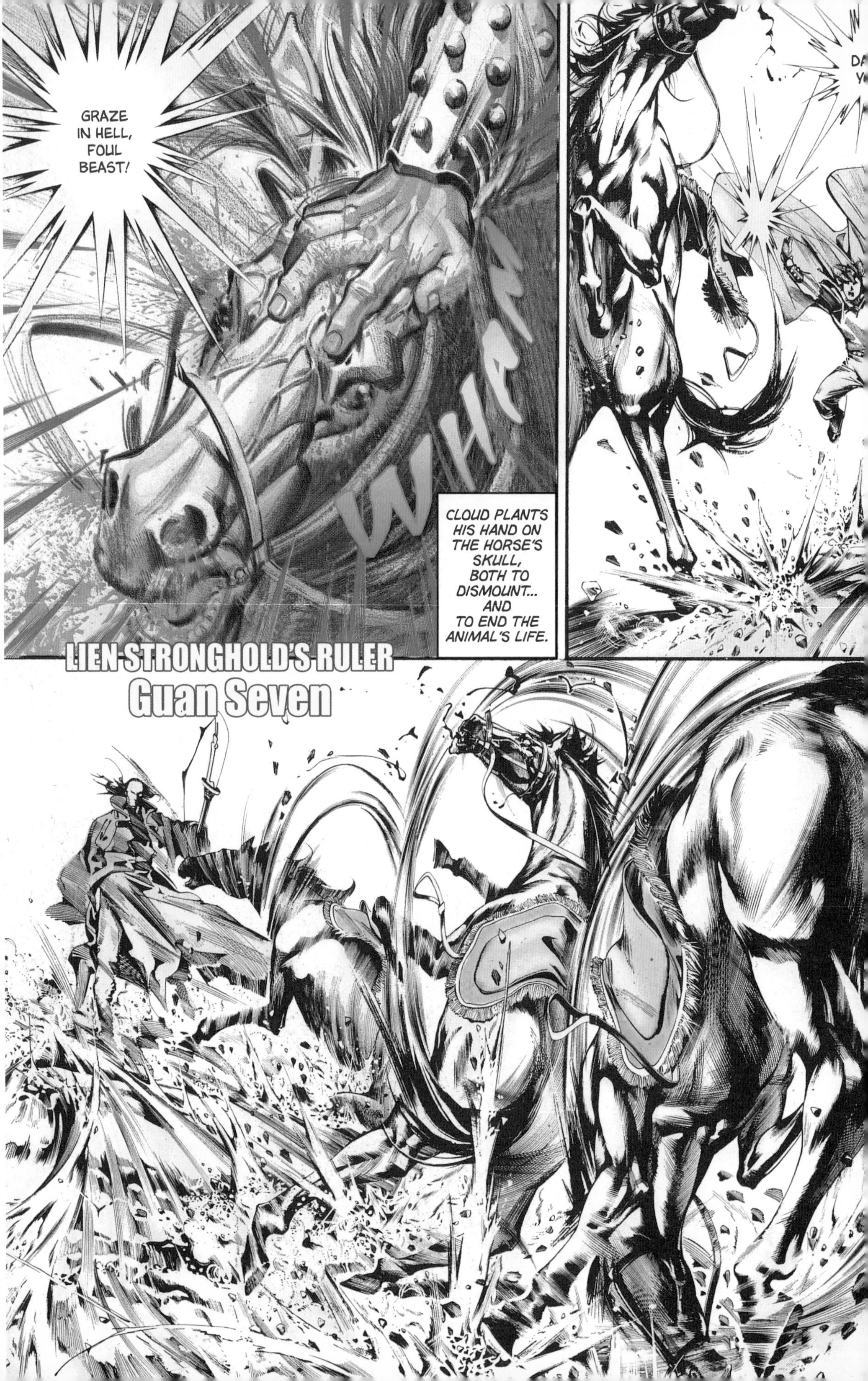
GRAZE IN HELL, FOUL BEAST!
WHAM
CLOUD PLANTS HIS HAND ON THE HORSE'S SKULL, BOTH TO DISMOUNT... AND TO END THE ANIMAL'S LIFE.
LIEN STRONGHOLD'S RULER
Guan Seven

WILD 7

By: Mikiya Mochizuki

Welcome to Wild 7, a wild tale about a group of bandits commissioned by the Japanese government to eradicate any and all potential threats to the status quo. Read as Hiba, an incarcerated felon, gathers a group of outlaws to form and lead the group known as Wild 7. See as this bunch of ruffians try to overthrow a corrupt politician. Using crooks to fight crooks, you say? Fighting fire with fire is a good thing? Finding the good in the bad and the bad in the good is possible? Let's see what happens…

50+ vols - 200+ pages B&W
Hardcopy US $9.95 each

www.comicsone.com

KAZAN

By: Gaku Miyao

Kazan is the last surviving member of a nomad tribe known as The Red Sand, When his village is wiped out by a vicious Water Demon and his best friend Elsie is kidnapped, Kazan begins a journey of discovery that will span 10 years! Befriending a water woman, a cranky old lady, and a bizarre white Eagle, Kazan sets out for the legendary land of Goldene. Get ready for an action-packed ride through the desert as nomads, assassins, slave traders, thieves, and even giant centipedes cross paths with the young hero and his sharp-edged knife…

7 vols - 200+ pages B&W
Hardcopy US $9.95 each
eBook US $2.95 each

www.comicsone.com